DIGITAL CULTURE AND SOCIETY

DIGITAL CULTURE AND SOCIETY

KATE ORTON-JOHNSON

§ Sage

S Sage

1 Oliver's Yard
55 City Road
London EC1Y 1SP

2455 Teller Road
Thousand Oaks,
California 91320

Unit No 323-333, Third Floor, F-Block
International Trade Tower Nehru Place
New Delhi – 110 019

8 Marina View Suite 43-053
Asia Square Tower 1
Singapore 018960

Library of Congress Control Number: 2023944497

British Library Cataloguing in Publication data

A catalogue record for this book is available from the British Library

Editor: Natalie Aguilera
Editorial Assistant: Sarah Moorhouse
Production Editor: Gourav Kumar
Copyeditor: Clare Weaver
Proofreader: Sarah Cooke
Indexer: KnowledgeWorks Global Ltd
Marketing Manager: Elena Asplen
Cover Design: Jennifer Crisp
Typeset by KnowledgeWorks Global Ltd
Printed and bound by CPI Group (UK) Ltd, Croydon, CR0 4YY

ISBN 978-1-5264-3175-2
ISBN 978-1-5264-3176-9 (pbk)

For Mum – with my thanks and love.

Contents

List of Figures and Tables

About the Author

Kate Orton-Johnson is a Senior Lecturer in Sociology at the University of Edinburgh. Her research interests relate to intersections between technology, culture and everyday life. She has conducted research and published work on student use of digital technologies and social media in HE, decentralised social media, digital leisure, and social media and parenting. She is a convenor of the British Sociological Association Digital Sociology study group and is currently Director of Education at the Edinburgh Futures Institute.

Acknowledgements

This book is based on lectures I have delivered as part of undergraduate and post-graduate courses in Digital Sociology over the last 18 years at the University of Edinburgh: my unit on *Digital Societies* in the undergraduate introductory Sociology course, my Honours course *Digital Culture* and postgraduate courses as part of the offering for students on our MSc program *Digital Sociology*. I'm very grateful to the students who have taken these courses over the years. They have helped me refine my ideas, have challenged and questioned me and have taught me about all sort of corners of the Internet and digital culture. I'm also extremely grateful to my colleagues in Edinburgh and beyond that have shaped my understandings of Digital Sociology in myriad ways as we collaborate across research and teaching, particularly Nick Prior, Karen Gregory and Nina Morris who always help me find the humour in it all. Thanks also to Harry Dyer for his invaluable comments and feedback on an earlier draft of this book.

The process of writing this book was a long one with early ideas and plans punctuated by new research projects and work commitments that have taken me in unexpected and time-consuming directions. Perhaps the biggest interruption has caused me the most intellectual reflection. The incompatible demands of the 'pivot' to online teaching and home schooling two children during the pandemic turned digital connectivity into a blessing and a tyranny. Thanks to Michael Ainsley and Natalie Aguilera at Sage for your patience and persistence throughout all of this.

Thanks to my fellow Porty sea swimmers for always helping me find the sanity even in the bitter cold, to dear friends Kev, Rob, Ronnie, Rachel and Vicky for their humour and joy and finally to my family, my Mum, Mike, Oscar and Phoebe for their enduring love and support and for ensuring that I remember what matters most.

1

INTRODUCTION

The rhythm of my day is interwoven with digital technologies. My mobile phone acts as my alarm clock and, as I hit snooze, I use it to browse the news and try to resist the unhealthy temptation to look at my email or social media while still in bed. I check the live bus tracker app before I leave for work to see if there are delays that may necessitate a rethink of my route. While travelling to work I might listen to a podcast, read a book on my Kindle or use one of a number of digital apps to message friends and family. My working day is permeated by use of technologies, from university learning environments and systems to platforms for online meetings and the exchange of files and messages. I bank online, shop online, use my cashless app to pay for goods offline and have an app that reminds me to get up and move from my screen at prescribed intervals. My children's school communicates with parents via a digital platform and my leisure time is, in part, taken up by browsing entertainment choices on Netflix or Amazon Prime, listening to music via Spotify or trying to teach myself how to crochet using YouTube tutorials.

I'm not unusual in these patterns. Figures from April 2023 indicate that there are around 5 billion internet users worldwide, 64 percent of the global population[1]. We have more opportunities to be connected than at any time in human history. Digital media provides us with the tools and channels to explore, produce and share knowledge about the world around us. As I write this at the start of 2023 a prototype artificial intelligence chatbot 'ChatGPT' is garnering media and academic attention following its recent launch. Hailed as a ground-breaking chatbot, ChatGPT is trained to interact with users and generate human-like responses to a wide range of questions. It can write essays, poems, scripts or business plans, summarise text, give advice, answer complex queries and follow up with conversation-like questions:

> 'ChatGPT seems like a human being,' Varun Mayya, CEO of software building company Avalon Labs, told Global News. 'It's just like a human being except it has all the world's knowledge.' (Lavery, 2022)

Social media posts are documenting screenshots of people's strange, compelling and troubling conversations with ChatGPT (Stern, 2022). Despite the limitations of the technology, academics have tested it and generated near perfect responses to exam questions and programmers have used it to rapidly solve obscure coding queries (Lock, 2022). Debates about the potential impacts of this kind of AI on society reflect utopian hopes and dystopian fears about new technologies. I asked ChatGPT what it thought about how digital technologies shape society and the impacts they might have:

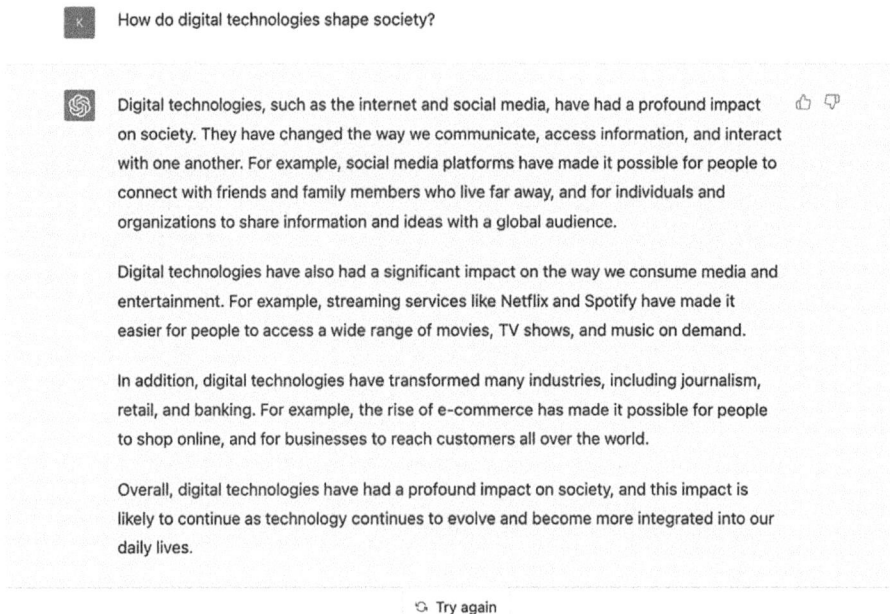

Figure 1.1   Screenshot from ChatGPT interaction December 10th 2022.

This rather balanced response points to the both the changes that new information and communication technologies have facilitated but also to the complex and often contradictory nature of these changes. Technological and social change is not however a uniquely digital phenomenon and the relationship between technology and society has a long history. Social, economic, political, cultural and technological factors have always combined to determine societal change.

The invention of the printing press, the radio, the landline telephone, the television and computers have all shaped how we experience the social world and have been accompanied by moral panics and concern about their potential impacts on us as human beings and on the society we live in. Similarly, the current hype cycle around generative AI will pass, and we will again be reminded

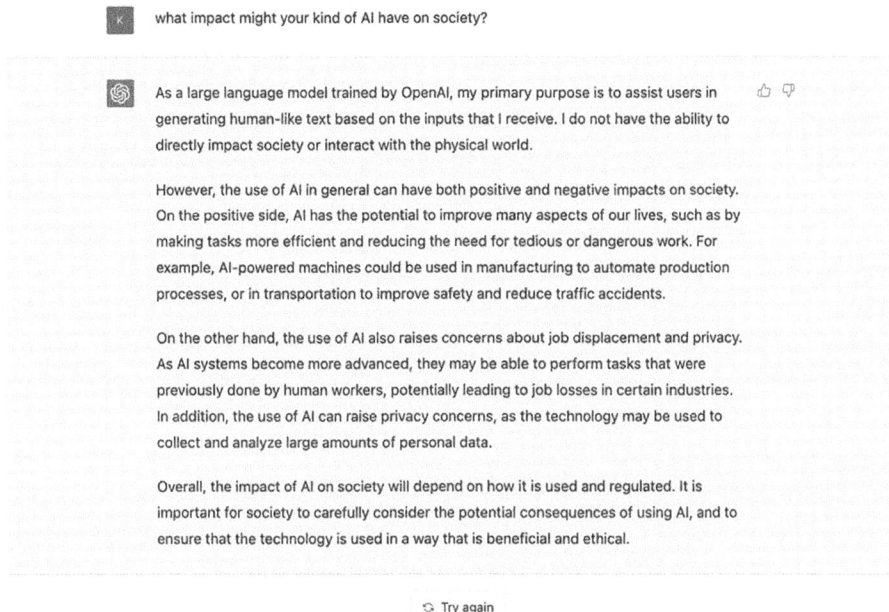

Figure 1.2 Screenshot from ChatGPT interaction December 10th 2022.

that a technology is neither good nor bad but is enacted, performed and reproduced in social contexts and social relations.

Contemporary society is marked apart from all other historical epochs by the rapid development of communication and information resources. Digital technologies have advanced more rapidly than any innovation in our history and in a relatively short period of time they have transformed our lives in myriad ways. The extent of the changes in our present society are reflected in claims about the information 'revolution' (as opposed to 'evolution') that is taking place. The terms 'information society', 'networked society' or 'knowledge society' are often used interchangeably to describe contemporary society and while they do not have precisely defined meanings, their commonality is the implication of *more* information, *more* communication, *more* connectivity.

With our new connectivity comes great convenience, opportunity and scope for innovation. But alongside social, cultural, economic, political and commercial advances are increases in inequality, social division and an acceleration and complication of our overloaded and hyperconnected lives (Hobsbawm, 2018).

The ubiquity of digital technologies can render them almost invisible, but it is vital to remember that our taken-for-granted technologies are designed and implemented in particular social contexts. They are not neutral. They are socially shaped. In other words, we *shape* and are *shaped by* technology, and we need to be critical of narratives that emphasise the effects *of* new technologies *on* society rather than acknowledging a more symbiotic relationship.

Sociology as a discipline has a vital role to play in critically mapping these transformations. The ubiquity of digital and mobile technologies means there are few areas of sociological interest that do not have some kind of digital articulation (Daniels & Gregory, 2016). The emerging field of digital sociology explores how our use of digital technology configures our sense of self and our embodiment of social relations. It looks critically at the role of digital media in the creation or reproduction of social institutions, structures and inequalities (Daniels & Gregory, 2016; Lupton, 2014). Digital sociology is about providing a sociological account of the digital society that we already have, as well as 'constructing plausible alternatives and advocating better futures' (Selwyn, 2019).

In this spirit, the aim of this book is to provide a critical introduction to the ways in which digital technologies have enabled new types of interactions, experiences and collaborations across a range of platforms and media, profoundly shaping our socio-cultural landscapes. These discussions will be grounded in classical sociological concepts; community, the self, gender, consumption, power and exclusion and inequality, to demonstrate the continuities that exist between sociological studies of 'real' world phenomena and their digital counterparts.

Digital sociology is also informed by an understanding that digital technologies make possible new ways of studying social life (Marres, 2017). Debates around methods in digital sociology have posed questions about how we can research digital spaces, structures and interactions. Do they necessitate the digitisation of existing tried and tested methodological techniques, or do these new objects of study demand 'natively digital' methods that take advantage of new technical and computational tools?

These are complex questions rooted in what Savage and Burrows described in 2007 as 'The coming crisis of empirical sociology'. Savage and Burrows argued that sociology uses a series of distinctive methodological tools to generate empirical data and with data science and the prominence of corporations and government agencies generating 'big data', the role of sociologists is now unclear. Big data refers to extremely large datasets that are too complex for traditional data processing and analysis software. Datasets are generated by governments, businesses and a range of other organisations and the term encapsulates a wide range of information, ranging from customer data to data gathered from digital sensors. The term refers to the technologies that generate, store, analyse and process data and speaks to the opportunities and challenges of working with large and complex datasets. For Savage and Burrows, big data means that academic sociology is becoming less of an obligatory point of passage and the traditional methods associated with the discipline appear rather paltry (Savage & Burrows, 2007; Selwyn, 2019).

Methods for studying digital spaces include those that revisit and renew methodologies that have long been employed by social researchers and a range of emergent and novel solutions. These solutions are often borne of innovation and frustration as researchers try to explore and understand new social phenomena in a continually evolving field of study. We face what Marres (2017) describes as a *methodological uncanny* with polarised debates about the appropriate methodologies to employ in studying the digital as both an object and a tool of social research.

Rather than trying to resolve these ambivalences, Marres advocates for a critical and creative engagement with methods and, with that in mind, each chapter of the book concludes with a methodological reflection. The intention here is not to provide a comprehensive coverage of digital methods, a task which would require and is indeed the subject of many entire texts. Rather, I aim to provide examples of some ways in which traditional methods have been reimagined in digital contexts and of some digitally native methods that open new opportunities. These methodological reflections should be seen as prompts for us as sociologists to think creatively about the specificities and contexts of our research questions and to respond in agile, open and collaborative ways as we try and answer the complex and challenging questions that digital sociology poses.

THE STRUCTURE OF THE BOOK

Digital technologies have provided us with new spaces and places in which to work, play and interact. Chapter 2 uses the example of community, a core sociological concept, to consider the impact of a dissolution of temporal and geographical boundaries online. The chapter looks at the ways in which the internet can be seen as a tool and a space that strengthens community and, conversely, as a technology that erodes and weakens traditional forms of connectivity, culture and interaction. The chapter traces a pervasive and dichotomising tendency to focus on either the perils or potentials of a technology as part of a transformation of community.

The chapter moves from ideas about virtual community to the concept of a networked society and uses the example of mobile phones as devices that both connect and atomise us from our networks, offering us powerful ways to connect while also challenging our understandings of place and connectivity.

At the end of Chapter 2 I reflect on the evolution of ethnography as a method and explore how it has enabled researchers to adapt to the fluid nature of online community by using methods that study culture *with* and *through* rather than *on* the internet (Rogers, 2013).

The study of identity, as a social construct enacted through interactions with others and our relationships with them, has been an enduring focus of sociological concern. In the relatively short history of internet research much attention has been paid to the transformative potentials of digital technologies to shape identity processes. Chapter 3 considers the ways in which mediated communications and social networking are shaping our understanding of the self and identity.

Historically, the disembodied and anonymous nature of online settings led many to argue that 'identity' is complicated because traditional identity cues (such as gender or age) are masked, purposefully withheld or misrepresented online. Drawing on symbolic interactionalism the chapter traces early understandings of online identity as they played out in text-based environments before exploring how the highly visual social media landscape we know today offers diverse spaces and tools with which to perform our identities in self-referential narratives and public presentations of self. The chapter does this by introducing the sociology of selfies. Selfies are shown to be a profoundly social phenomena imbued with cultural scripts that help create and construct personal narratives as part of our identity projects. The chapter then concludes with a discussion of how our social media presence is characterised by watching and an awareness of being watched, what Marwick (2012) defines as social surveillance, with our identity work playing out to a range of audiences across a polymedia environment.

The visual in social media demands careful methodological negotiation. The methodical reflection at the end of Chapter 3 focuses on researching the visual online, looking at how we define and sample the visual and the importance of understanding platform vernaculars in research design. The use of scraping and APIs is discussed and the challenges of studying ephemeral visual objects explored.

Web 2.0 environments are increasingly used to socialise and connect. What implications does 'being there together' have for social relationships? Building on the themes in Chapter 3, Chapter 4 considers the ways in which mediated communications are shaping our interpersonal relationships. The chapter highlights a culture of connectivity as digital platforms become social intermediaries, used to communicate with friends and strangers.

Social media use extends intimacy beyond the private sphere of the home, blurring boundaries of public and private life as hyperconnected individuals lead increasingly mobile and individualised lives. Technologies mediate and constitute intimacy by providing tools and platforms through which we can make personal connections and the chapter explores some of the ways in which the concept of intimacy is central to our understanding of social media.

New technologies create new forms of visibility and scalability and the chapter introduces the concept of networked publics and public intimacies (boyd, 2010) exploring the challenges that we face in managing our hyperconnected networks and negotiating emergent practices of digital intimacy. We return to the concept of social surveillance to reflect on how the affordances of the platforms we use shape our relationships in new landscapes of digital capitalism.

Chapter 4 concludes with a methodological reflection on studying the apps and platforms that act as engineers of techno-sociality. I discuss the walkthrough method as a tool for incorporating an understanding of the technological features of an app alongside a critical analysis of the cultural meanings embedded in its design and use.

Digital technologies have changed the ways in which we interact with mainstream media and have changed the ways in which we produce and consume culture. Chapter 5 explores what has been defined as participatory culture and the rise of the digital 'prosumer'. We, as ordinary users of the web, can create and share content in models of communication that are many-to-many rather than between us as single individuals. These new models of consumption and participation take place in a new landscape of media and cultural convergence (Jenkins, 2006).

The chapter introduces debates about a participatory culture of content creation and production as social and collaborative, before outlining critiques that argue that the reality of participatory culture is a digital space in which only a vocal minority are active. Using examples of YouTube humour, TikTok use during the pandemic and Black Twitter (now renamed as X^2), the chapter considers prosumption as a continuum of activities with political prosumption at one end of a scale with acts of leisure and play at the other. Participatory culture is positioned as a communicative act that influences our understanding of how we relate to civil society, creating a new kind of 'personal public' (Asenas & Hubble, 2018).

Reflecting methodologically, Chapter 5 explores small story research as a tool for sensitising us to the structures and affordances of a technology. I use this example to make the point that while digitally native methods have great value, they do not necessarily tell the whole story. 'Traditional' methods, like the qualitative interview, reimagined and rearticulated in digital spaces, may help our understanding of users and their intentions, subjectivities and experiences.

Digital technologies in everyday life have transformed how we experience and understand leisure and Chapter 6 explores the ways in which digital technologies blur the boundaries of work and play and shape how we experience our leisure time. The chapter introduces the idea of leisure as a historical and social construct that has always had a symbiotic relationship with technology. Contemporary leisure practices are entangled with digital culture and the chapter explores the digitisation and mediation of traditional leisure activities as well as leisure practices that have emerged as a result of technological developments.

Using examples of craft and leisure travel, the chapter demonstrates how digitisation has shaped traditional leisure practices as social media enhances and reconfigures how we experience them. The chapter explores new kinds of digitally native leisure practices using examples of wearable devices and apps in a discussion of mediated leisure, gamification, datafication and dataveillance (van Dijck, 2014).

The chapter concludes by reflecting on inequalities in leisure and, drawing on examples of lockdown leisure, marginalised gaming, Black Instagram and travel narratives, explores digital leisure as a site of both resistance and exclusion and inequality.

Methodologically, Chapter 6 focuses on a small data approach to the use of mobile methods that seeks to prioritise meaning making and reflection. Challenging ideas around the generation of big data, the chapter explores mobile methods and the use of digital devices as part of a creative methodological toolkit.

Chapter 7 addresses a theme that runs throughout the earlier chapters of the book in a discussion of privacy and surveillance. As technologies have embedded themselves in our everyday lives they create new possibilities for communicating and accessing information, simultaneously presenting new challenges for managing, negotiating and protecting privacy (Palen & Dourish, 2003). Chapters 3 and 4 discuss the concept of social surveillance and the domestication of surveillance practices as they exist in day-to-day interaction.

Chapter 7 shifts focus from social privacy to institutional privacy in a discussion of the relationship between datafication, privacy and surveillance. The chapter explores definitions of privacy and surveillance and the digital capacities of dataveillance using new and intensified technological possibilities that are unequally distributed in society. Drawing on the concept of surveillance capitalism (Zuboff, 2019), the chapter discusses the relationship between contemporary democracies and large technology companies, emphasising our social dependence on digital technologies that are central to contemporary surveillance practices. The chapter concludes with two examples of institutional privacy and surveillance: learning analytics and the quantification of the student experience and the domestication of surveillance in the home via smart home devices and corporate networks.

The final methodological reflection focuses on ethics and privacy in digital research. There are particular issues around operationalising key ethical concepts like privacy and confidentiality, informed consent and anonymity in networked publics where our data is replicable, searchable, scalable and highly visible (boyd, 2010). These issues are challenging for digital research, but ethical decisions must be grounded in moral principles that maximise the benefits of research, minimise possible harms and protect human dignity.

The concluding chapter draws together the overarching themes of the book and reflects on how the social and cultural opportunities afforded to us by digital technologies are not equally available. Far from early utopian hopes of the internet being a great equaliser, opening accessible networks of communication and opportunity to all, digital technologies create new kinds of inequalities and exacerbate existing socio-economic divisions. The chapter explores the ways in which the concept of the digital divide has evolved from early definitions focused on inequalities in *access* to technology, to more nuanced understandings that emphasise the complexities of access as bound up with issues of infrastructure, digital literacy and social and cultural capital at local and global levels. It then looks at how issues of digital inequality were brought sharply to the fore during the pandemic. Digital amenities became digital necessities providing, for some, a lifeline for work, school and leisure as well as enabling us to maintain social interaction with friends and family outside our isolation bubbles. TikTok thrived as a space of connectivity and participatory culture and digital spaces connected global communities. At the same time, the COVID-19 crisis deepened pre-existing digital inequalities putting the most socially and economically disadvantaged people in society at more risk and compounding the numerous socio-economic consequences of the pandemic on a global scale.

The chapter concludes by turning its attention to new kinds of digital divides based on the infrastructures that increasingly dominate how we interact with digital technologies. Drawing on critical algorithm studies it explores the impacts of algorithms on justice and policing, health and employment practices to illustrate the fundamentally unequal ways in which the technologies that mediate our daily lives shape how we experience the world.

NOTES

1. https://www.statista.com/statistics/617136/digital-population-worldwide/
2. I will refer to Twitter as X for the remainder of this book except where existing research uses "Twitter" to refer to the platform.

2

SPACE, PLACE AND DIGITAL COMMUNITY

Digital technologies have provided us with new spaces in which to interact and participate in online environments. This chapter will use the example of 'community', a core sociological concept, to consider the impact of the dissolution of temporal and geographical boundaries. The chapter will look at the ways in which the internet can be seen as a space that strengthens community or, conversely, as a technology that erodes and weakens traditional forms of connectivity, culture and interaction. We will explore the ways in which the concept of a network might help us understand new digital articulations of community and reflect on how we experience digitally mediated places. The chapter then explores how mobile technologies in particular have impacted on our understandings of physical space in a discussion of digital placemaking. The chapter concludes by thinking about how we might study digital communities and considers the evolution of ethnography as a method.

As you read this chapter I encourage you to think about the following questions:

- In what ways has the sociological study of community underpinned our understanding of what virtual community is?
- How have debates about the decline in community shaped our understandings of virtual community?
- What potentials and drawbacks might virtual communities afford us?
- How are communities different from networks?
- How does the concept of technological individualisation fit with our understandings of communities and networks?
- In what ways do digital technologies mediate our experiences of place?

WHY COMMUNITY?

The concept of community is central to sociology, encompassing many social phenomena and a vital building block of culture and society (O'Connor & Goodwin, 2012). It is important because it gives us a sense of belonging, solidarity and shared meaning. However, community is also one of the discipline's most ill-defined and contested concepts and has been operationalised and researched in myriad ways in a long history of community studies:

> The figurations of people which are investigated today under the name 'community' vary a great deal. The term community can refer to villages with some characteristics of a state...it can be used with reference to a suburban community, a neighbourhood region or an ethnic minority of a large industrial city...one could prolong the list. (Bell & Newby, 2012:IX)

One way in which Bell and Newby's list has been prolonged is by a resurgence of interest in what community means when it is articulated in and through digital spaces. Indeed, one of the first major debates around the social impact of the internet was if the spaces it provided for interaction could constitute and be defined as 'community'.

A (BRIEF) HISTORY OF COMMUNITY

Before we think about what community might mean in digital spaces, we need to understand that debates about community are rooted in classic sociological literature.

German sociologist Tönnies (1963) observed that the development of industrial capitalism was associated with a change in the basis of social cohesion in society. He introduced the concept of *'gemeinschaft'* (translated from German as community) to describe the support and intimacy that small villages, bound together by kinship and geographical proximity, provided for each other. He contrasted this with the concept of *'gesellschaft'* (translated from German as association) which described a social life that was more isolated and individual, characterised by the relative loneliness and isolation of the big city and the nuclear family. Gesellschaft relationships were based on rational and calculated exchange rather than the emotional interdependence of gemeinschaft relationships. These ideal types of *gemeinschaft* and *gesellschaft* reflected a discontent with the processes of modernity, industrialisation and urbanisation (Bell & Newby, 2012). They also reflected concerns that modernity had atomised us as individuals by moving us away from networks based on family, religion and ethnicity that had once offered support, protection and solidarity.

Tönnies' work shaped sociological understandings of community in two important ways. First, a recognition that community represented a particular quality of social relationships among members of a social group; community was about intimacy, trust and emotional attachment. Second, that community was being 'lost' and that a decline in community was an important social change in industrial nations that had developed capitalist market economies (Goe & Noonan, 2007).

As research on communities continued in the twentieth century, definitions of what constituted community proliferated. A review of research undertaken in the mid 1950s (Hillery, 1955) identified 94 different definitions. More usefully, amongst these multiple definitions Hillery found that the literature broadly agreed that community could consist of groups of people who (i) engaged in social interaction, (ii) were within a geographic area, or (iii) had a common tie or ties. This broadened Tönnies' conception of community and enabled an understanding of community as a group of people who do not necessarily have to be geographically close or emotionally bonded. The notion of common ties allowed communities to be conceived of as groups of people who are more loosely attached and connected by shared lifestyles, interests, beliefs, institutions, goals or values. This challenged the emphasis on stable physical proximity and instead focused on the quality or character of human relationships (Gans, 1982; Macionis, 1978; Wellman, 1979).

COMMUNITY IN DECLINE?

Debates about the impact of the internet on community formation were preceded by over a century of sociological work exploring how technological change, alongside industrialisation, urbanisation, modernisation and capitalism, had shaped community (Wellman & Gulia, 1999). This work was often oriented around a concern that community was in decline.

The rise of urban life was widely believed to signal a loss of traditional community, replaced by more rational and utilitarian associations and leaving the modern individual devoid of communal identity and certainty (Macionis, 1978). The notion of community became a symbol of romanticised longing for a return to a time when life appeared to be simpler, an antidote to the vulnerability and uncertainty of modernity. This reflects an ongoing problem with defining community; definitions have primarily focused not on what community *is* but what it *should* be (Bell & Newby, 2012).

Perhaps it should be no surprise then that these tensions in sociological theory and definition are mirrored in debates about the impact of digital technologies on

community. Indeed, one of the early fears surrounding the internet was that traditional forms of community would be undermined and that internet use would
replace or isolate people from their offline communities and relationships (Nie,
2001). But before we consider these fears we need to understand that the argument that technology undermines community long pre-dates the internet. The
next section of this chapter takes a brief look at this history before we go on to
think about digital articulations of community.

OLD TECHNOLOGIES AND ENDURING CONCERNS

From Socrates' critiques of writing and the alphabet as communicative tools that
would erode our memory and undermine wisdom (Griswold, 1980), to fears the
telegraph would impair the social cues that provide the meaning, context and
grounding of our communication, there is a long history of moral panic accompanying technological change (Czitrom, 1982; Hanifan, 1916; Marvin, 1990;
Standage, 1998).

New technologies have historically been met with a presumption that they
are causal, active determinants of social change; transforming communication
and social relations in ways that we as humans have little power to resist (Baym,
2015). We have habitually seen a pervasive and dichotomising tendency to focus
on either the perils or potentials of a technology as part of the social transformation of community. For example, social histories of the telephone (as a radical
new form of communication) point to concerns about its potential to disrupt
established social relations and unsettle traditional divides between the privacy
of the family home and the public setting of the community (Marvin, 1990).
Introduced initially as a broadcast system and then as a tool of business communication, telephone companies were horrified to find that people were using the
telephone for personal communication. Particularly concerning was their use by
women for idle chit chat and gossip (Fischer, 1994). However, the telephone profoundly shaped social relations and was a technology of sociability that played a
crucial role in community life; enabling the organisation of social relationships,
alleviating rural isolation and facilitating social activity (Fischer, 1994; Marvin,
1990).

Bowling alone and social capital

Concern over civic and social life was also the focus of a 1995 article by Robert Putnam, *Bowling alone: America's declining social capital,* in which he traced a
decline in community life in the USA in the late 1960s and early 1970s. He argued

that American communities were withering. They were being replaced by 'edge cities' and 'exurbs' that functioned as anonymous places where people did little more than sleep, eat and watch TV between their commutes to and from work. Little time was left for joining community groups or voluntary organisations or for socialising with neighbours, friends or even family.

Putnam supported his claims by using the illustrative metaphor of bowling. He argued that while more Americans than ever before were participating in the sport, league bowling had seen a dramatic decline. For Putnam, the decline of the community networks and leagues that once led Americans to bowl together represented a loss of social capital. Social capital refers to connections between individuals, our social networks and the reciprocity, trust and shared values that arise from these relationships and networks. The origins of the concept date back to 1916 when Hanifan, a state supervisor of rural schools in West Virginia, invoked the idea of social capital to emphasise the importance of community as a part of successful schooling:

> those tangible substances [that] count for most in the daily lives of people: namely good will, fellowship, sympathy, and social intercourse among the individuals and families who make up a social unit...The individual is helpless socially, if left to himself...If he comes into contact with his neighbor, and they with other neighbours', there will be an accumulation of social capital, which may immediately satisfy his social needs and which may bear a social potentiality sufficient to the substantial improvement of living conditions in the whole community. (Hanifan, 1916: 131)

Social capital has been a salient concept in the sociological imagination for a number of decades (Bourdieu, 1986; Coleman, 1988). While definitions vary across context, common emphasis is placed on the benefits that membership of social networks bring. Social groups share norms, values and a sense of identity and, as such, build up relationships of trust, co-operation and reciprocity. These relationships bring tangible and intangible resources; having someone on hand to feed your cat when you go on holiday or to give you a ride if your car breaks down, as well as fostering a sense of resilience and trust in your social networks.

For Putnam, the most important aspect of social capital was in facilitating co-operation and maintaining supportive relations in communities and, as a result, nations. Putnam identified two types of social capital, *bonding* and *bridging*.

Bonding social capital comes from social networks that are inward looking; groups of people that are largely homogenous and that share similar values and beliefs, for example, relatives, groups of close friends or members of a club or sports team (Nichols et al., 2013). Bonding capital creates horizontal ties (in contrast to vertical social ties *between* groups) and serves to knit groups more tightly together, reinforcing their homogeneity and providing social and psychological support.

Bridging capital provides what Putnam describes as 'sociological WD-40' (2000: 23), the vertical social ties between groups. Bridging capital comes from social networks that are outward looking and that link members from different networks and social circles. Bridging capital brings together people from diverse socio-economic and socio-demographic groups enabling members to access information and resources from outside of their immediate networks. These have weaker ties and are characterised by 'thin trust' in ever-changing networks (Widn-Wulff et al., 2008).

Bridging and bonding social capital are not mutually exclusive and exist in both forms simultaneously. For example, being a member of a sport team (or indeed being a student at a university studying sociology) may bond individuals based on shared interest and activities and also bridge individuals together along lines of class, gender, age or ethnicity.

In *Bowling alone,* Putnam charts a sharp decline of social capital in America, in part related to what he describes as technological individualising. He argued that our leisure time is increasingly dominated by technologically mediated *individual* activities, like watching TV, that remove us from the sphere of public life and from civil and public engagement. *Bowling Alone* was written at a time when the internet was not the ubiquitous presence in our lives that it is today and while Putnam alluded to the potential future impacts of the internet on social capital, he argued that it is premature to predict what those impacts might be. But it is not difficult to see how his arguments about individualised leisure can be applied to digital technologies. Almost a decade and half later, Putnam and colleague Sander noted that while adult Americans have shown varying levels of civic and social engagement, their use of social media as a form of 'civic technology' suggests different kinds of engagement (Putnam & Sander, 2010) and we will consider this later in the chapter.

Community in late modernity

'Loss of community' has been a pervasive narrative in popular and academic debate. While research has documented the persistence of community (Wellman & Gulia, 1999; Young & Willmott, 1957), the idea of community in crisis in late modernity has dominated. Sociological literature focusing on late modernity has emphasised the impact on community of globalisation and the separation of time, space and social relationships (Giddens, 1991).

For Giddens, late modernity is characterised by a disembedding of time and space. We no longer have to spend time and travel great distances to communicate with friends or family who don't happen to live in our immediate vicinity. As such, our social interactions have become disembedded from their local contexts. Trans global systems of transport, culture and economics, alongside new forms of electronic communication, have dissolved geographic boundaries. This is accompanied by a shift away from tradition and an emphasis on individual choice (Giddens, 1991; Mellor, 1993).

Unlike pre-modern society where tradition dictated social structures, in late modernity the individual becomes the new centre of agency and responsibility. Together, global networks, individualism and mobility have altered contemporary social life and changed our understandings of the local and the global (Bauman, 2001; Urry, 2000). Given this context it is perhaps not surprising that articulations of community that started to incorporate digital technologies defined new forms of community as 'virtual'.

The internet provides new spaces and opportunities for community formation. One obvious way in which it does this is by removing the barriers of geography and enabling people who are not in close proximity to one another to connect and bond. The possibilities of community in cyberspace excited early internet researchers who argued that computer-mediated communication had created spaces in which, 'passions are inflamed, problems are solved, social bonds are formed, tyranny is exercised, love and death are braved, legacies are born' (Fernback, 1999: 217). However, as with traditional definitions of community, there has been a lack of consensus on what constitutes a virtual community (Komito, 1998) and opinion has been divided on what the possibilities afforded by these spaces might be.

VIRTUAL COMMUNITY

The term 'virtual community' is associated with the work of Howard Rheingold (1993). Rheingold argued that in the early days of the internet, email, bulletin board systems (BBS), chat rooms and multi-user domains (MUDs) allowed groups of people to interact electronically. He defined virtual community as:

> social aggregations that emerge from the Net when people carry on…public discussions long enough, with sufficient human feeling, to form webs of personal relationships in cyberspace. (Rheingold, 1993: 3)

Rheingold suggests that typically a virtual community will form when groups of people share a common interest, a health issue, political persuasion, scholarly pursuit, lifestyle or hobby. As the community develops, members contribute to on-going discussions, form links with others in the group and forge friendships.

Virtual communities cover a huge range of interests and connect diverse groups, from people talking about surviving cancer or dealing with bullying to groups that discuss TV shows and popular culture.

Individuals in these groups feel a sense of connection and belonging through their shared communication and early research into online communities identified their ability to build supportive relationships and strong community ties (M. S. Furlong, 1989; King, 1994). Scholars like Rheingold (1994) and Negroponte (1995) championed a theory of the internet as a free and boundless medium that would merge disparate technologies and allow new communities to develop:

> computer-mediated communication…will do by way of electronic pathways what cement roads were unable to do, namely connect us rather than atomize us, put us at the controls of a 'vehicle' and yet not detach us from the rest of the world. (Patton, 1987:20)

These communities were seen as socially beneficial in the context of loss of community debates; many believed that the internet could make up for the lack of community in the 'real' world. Rheingold studied the Whole Earth 'Lectronic Link (WELL), founded in 1985 and now one of the oldest virtual communities. The WELL was a bulletin board system (BBS) that Rheingold argued could (and did) foster a strong sense of community. He illustrates this with a number of examples in his influential text *The virtual community: Homesteading on the electronic frontier* (Rheingold, 1993) and, reflecting on the WELL as a community almost two decades later, gives the example of Philcat:

> a fellow who used the handle 'Philcat' logged in one night in a panic: his son Gabe had been diagnosed with leukaemia, and in the middle of the night he had nowhere else to turn but the friends he knew primarily by the text we typed to each other via primitive personal computers and slow modems.
>
> By the next morning, an online support group had coalesced, including an MD, an RN, a leukaemia survivor, and several dozen concerned parents and friends. Over the next couple years, we contributed over $15,000 to Philcat and his family. We'd hardly seen each other in person until we met in the last two pews of Gabe's memorial service. (Rheingold, 2012)

For Rheingold, many online groups demonstrated the strong bonds and a close sense of belonging that would merit a definition of 'community'. These communities were different from traditional, geographically based communities in the range and fluidity of discourses available to them and of course in their lack of physical proximity and co-presence.

The potentials of this are profound; when distance means nothing, people from all over the world can participate in communities and interact with others who share their interests and concerns. The virtual communities of the early internet grew out of the very human desire to interact. Online community was driven by the hunger for connection, to feel a part of something and to feel a sense of belonging in an increasingly complex 'real' world; a logical response to late modernity as a globalised individual experience (Miller, 2008).

The contemporary internet is littered with various types of community and Armstrong and Hagel (2000) provide a useful summative typology:

1   Communities of *transaction* based on the exchange of goods and services: eBay, freecycle, gumtree and buy/sell Facebook groups (see, for example, J. Boyd, 2002; Ginsburg, 2000).
2   Communities of *interest* based on specific topics that participants want to discuss, from fandom to gardening to politics (see, for example, Baym, 2001; Jenkins, 1992).
3   Communities of *fantasy* in which participants create new environments, identities or imagined worlds and interact in them, from online fantasy sports leagues to MUDs (see, for example, Farquhar & Meeds, 2007; Steinkuehler & Williams, 2006).
4   Communities of *relationships* where participants share personal experiences and form networks of support often around intense life experiences like illness, addiction or grief (see, for example, Broom, 2005; Lingel, 2013).

While academic research has worked to define and understand the manifold ways in which community might be articulated online, critics argued that whatever form virtual community might take, connections made in online textual environments were poor shadows of 'real' community bonds and interactions. Virtual communities were seen as isolating individuals from their real-life communities (Kling, 1996) and it was feared they would detract from face-to-face interactions and worsen problems of community cohesion and civic participation (Blanchard & Horan, 1998):

> While all this razzle-dazzle connects us electronically, it disconnects us from each other, having us 'interfacing' more with computers and TV screens than looking in the face of our fellow human beings. (Broadcaster Jim Hightower, quoted in Fox, 1995: 12)

Proponents of virtual community argued that these kinds of spaces have value at individual and societal level. Not only by compensating for a lack of real-world community, as in the earlier example of Philcat, but by being more meaningful communities because they are based on choice rather than on the luck of geography.

Virtual communities offer the opportunity to foster more authentic, egalitarian and emotionally satisfying forms of social involvement, allowing increased freedom of expression and wider access (Hiltz & Turoff, 1993).

Research also demonstrated that contrary to early fears even prolific users of digital technology were not glued to their computer screens but had significant offline social networks that were not *replaced* by new modes of communication but were *enhanced* by them (Boase, 2008; K. Evans, 2013). Indeed, to return to Fischer's social history of the telephone, the internet much like the telephone is a technology of sociability:

> using the internet has little effect on average user's level of face to face contact...Although access to the Internet may have vastly expanded Americans' acquaintances – the Facebook 'friends' sort of circle – it would not have been a revolution in their personal relationships, just a nudge. (Fischer, 2011: 96)

What these antithetical positions of reinvigorated or destroyed communities fail to acknowledge is that the internet is simply a medium of connection rather than a technology that fundamentally shapes our social relationships. Wellman and Gulia (1999) in their article *Net surfers don't ride alone: Virtual communities as communities* categorised four conceptual weaknesses around these debates about virtual community:

1   As *manichean*, referring to the dualist tendencies of debates to position the internet as either a panacea or a poison without recognising a middle ground.
2   As *presentist*, referring to the point made earlier in the chapter, that debates about community and technology have a longer history than the internet.
3   As *unscholarly* and based on anecdotal rather than detailed empirical evidence.
4   As *parochial*, referring to an assumption that 'online' is somehow a separate and autonomous space, different and other to the 'offline'. (Wellman & Gulia, 1999)

Taken together, these critiques suggest that a more useful discussion might instead focus on how online communities make us feel and what they add to our lives; what Anderson has defined as our sense of 'imagined community' (Anderson, 1991).

(RE) IMAGINING COMMUNITY

Anderson uses the concept of 'imagined community' to understand nations and nationalism, but the notion of imagining communities into being through sentiment, interaction and shared symbols and values also speaks to the imagining of virtual community. Virtual community is also produced and sustained by symbolic strategies, collaborative interaction and shared understandings.

In addition to how virtual communities might make us feel we also need to recognise that, as in Wellman and Gulia's parochial critique, the dichotomy between online and offline is false and arbitrary. As digital technologies become more ubiquitous and invisible in our daily lives we don't consciously think of our online vs. our offline lives and the notion of 'virtual' in opposition to 'real' becomes a rather strange turn of phrase. We interact and have a sense of community and belonging across a continuum of physical and digitally mediated spaces.

Virtual communities are not a separate and independent reality but are imbued with the socio-cultural-economic baggage and contexts of our daily lives (Kendall, 1999; O'Brien, 1999; Wellman & Gulia, 1999). So, how can we understand our experiences of digitally mediated community given the complexities of defining what they are or might be?

One answer is to think outside of the entanglements of community and think about a different way to understand how we form groups online. There has been a gradual shift in scholarly debates away from conceiving of society as made up of bounded communities and towards an understanding of society as a series of fluid networks. This shift reflects, in part, some of the problems with defining community and enables us to think beyond communities as having proximity, permeance or consistency (Lindgren, 2017).

FROM COMMUNITY TO NETWORK

In the mid 1990s Sociologist Manuel Castells (2010) described the concept of the *Network Society*. We live in a society underpinned by the logic of networks. For Castells, networks have always been a feature of society but are now their most important organising structures. Networks have shaped all spheres of social life from the economy to culture in a global society dominated by what he defines as 'informationalism':

> Networks were historically useful for personal interaction, for solidarity, for reciprocal support. But they were bad performers in mobilizing resources and focusing these resources on the execution of a given task. Yet this substantial limitation of networks' competitive capacity was overcome with the development of new information/communication technologies, epitomized by the Internet...The prevalence of networks in organizing social practice redefines social structure in our societies. (Castells, 2000:695)

The connective power of networked computing and the internet means that the potential of networks has been realised. This is not to assume that these networks are necessarily digital. Castells does not position new information technologies as causal factors of social change. Rather, they are the means through which new forms of production and management, new forms of communication media and the globalisation of economy and culture are realised. The rise of the network society is a result of the socio-economic restructuring of capitalism, the cultural and social changes in society since the 1960s *and* the revolution in information technology.

Using the concept of network rather than community allows us to acknowledge a middle ground between understandings of us as individual actors and understandings of us as members of a group. This is not to suggest that the idea of community is irrelevant, rather that two decades of internet research has helped us to work through the complexities and challenges of understanding virtual community. As Rheingold suggests:

> If I had encountered sociologist Barry Wellman and learned about social network analysis when I first wrote about cyberspace cultures, I could have saved us all a decade of debate by calling them 'online social networks' instead of 'virtual communities'. Social networks predated the Internet, writing and even speech. (Rheingold, 2006: 47)

The concept of the network society is closely linked to debates about the rise of individualism considered earlier in the chapter in the discussion of Putnam's *Bowling Alone* (van Dijk, 2012; Wellman et al., 2002). Within a network society Rainie and Wellman have defined this individualism as a new operating system of *networked individualism* (Rainie & Wellman, 2012a). Networked individualism is not oriented around close knit communities or family groups but on looser, more fragmented networks. These networks still offer support and solidarity but are diffuse and sparsely knit, with vague and overlapping social and spatial boundaries.

The important point to remember in this shift of narrative is that the network now orients around the individual. Individuals are at the centre of their own web of social relations, part of a number of communities both online and off, each meeting different social, emotional and material needs.

Most people do not live in tightly bounded groups and as we move between our homes and our places of education, work and leisure we socialise and interact with shifting, fluid networks. Social networks are no longer anchored to a particular place and time and individuals can pursue new modes of sociality in and through digital spaces. We interact with what Castells has called 'communities of choice' with others who share our interests and affinities.

These networks existed prior to the internet but digital social networks (powered by using the internet and mobile phones) are more diverse and give people a new range of ways to solve problems, meet their social needs and interact with the world around them. The role of technology in this transformation is defined by Rainie and Wellman (2012a) as a triple revolution.

1   First, an *internet revolution* has given people communication power and information-gathering capacities that dwarf those of the past. The change in the ways in which we can communicate with other people has shifted the point of reference in society from the household, family or group level to the individual.

2   Second, a *social network revolution* has shifted how people relate to each other, providing the opportunity for people to reach beyond the world of tight groups and participate in fluid and diverse networks.

3   Third, the *mobile(-isation) revolution* means that mobile phones have become key affordances, allowing people to access friends and information at will. We are in a state of hyperconnectivity meaning we are never alone; we are always accessible; we are networked individuals.

Technology has empowered us as individuals by giving us the tools to change the size and shape of our social networks and to change the ways in which we manage our social networks:

> The networked individualism operating system requires that people develop new strategies and skill for handling problems…They need to expend effort and sometime money to maintain their ties near and far; choose whether to phone, visit or electronically connect with others; remember which members of their network are useful for what sorts of things…and forge useful alliances among network members who might not previously have known each other. (Rainie & Wellman, 2012a:9)

The careful management of these networks becomes a feature of networked individualism. This is a theme we will return to in Chapter 4 when we explore how digital technologies shape how we relate to each other socially. For now, I want to return a point I made earlier in the chapter when I suggested that it is not difficult to see how Putnam's arguments about individualised leisure could be applied to digital technologies.

Combining the impact of the triple revolution suggested by Rainie and Wellman with Putnam's focus on technological individualism speaks to contemporary concerns about how our mobile devices in particular are shaping how we interact with each other and the wider world.

PHUBBING

I'm sure you are familiar with the sight of people spending time together, in a pub or at a restaurant, looking at their mobile devices rather than talking to or giving their attention to the people they are with. In 2012 an Australian campaign to give this phenomenon a neologism resulted in the term *phubbing*; a portmanteau of the words 'phone' and 'snubbing'[1]. Phubbing, the practice of ignoring your companion(s) in order to pay attention to your phone or device is now experienced as a norm in social interaction and public life (Chotpitayasunondh & Douglas, 2016; Roberts & David, 2016).

Think about the last time you were out with a group of friends; did you all have mobile devices in hand or on the table next to you? Think about the last time you were waiting at a bus stop or on a train, were most people concentrated on their mobile devices? The idea of phubbing as a part of how we experience digital technologies in public spaces relates to the third aspect of Rainie and Wellman's (2012a) networked revolution, the mobile revolution. While much attention has been paid to virtual community as experienced on the internet, contemporary understandings of how we experience space and place cannot ignore the ubiquity of the mobile phone as a social object:

> Whatever it is called, and wherever it is used, this simple, accessible technology alters the way in which individuals conduct their everyday lives. It has extensive implications for the cultures and societies in which it is used; it changes the nature of communication, and affects identities and relationships. It affects the development of social structures and economic activities, and has considerable bearing on its users' perceptions of themselves and their world. (Plant, 2000:23)

The mobile makes person-to-person communication possible regardless of location or time, shifting public/private boundaries and increasing interactivity and connection across our networks. Phubbing represents a paradox in which we are connecting with people in physical spaces while at the same time being somewhat separate in those spaces and from those connections. This creates a conversational fusion of two places; an absent presence (Katz & Rice, 2002) or what Turkle (2011) has described as being alone/together.

Concerns about the state of community and contemporary civic life have sparked headlines about technology undermining human interaction and destroying the art of conversation (Mount, 2015), creating phone zombies (Gurchiek, 2018) and damaging our emotional health (Lego, 2018). This kind of media coverage reflects the moral panics around new technologies that we considered earlier in the chapter and Alex Haigh, the graduate student behind the initial campaign, plays into these narratives with the 'stop phubbing' website (http://stopphubbing.com/) which provides humorous statistics about the prevalence of phubbing, global comparisons of the worst perpetrators and hints on how to stage an intervention. Similar campaigns have also drawn on ideas of social isolation and technological individualism. For example, Brazilian advertising agency Fischer and Friends created the 'Offline Glass' to combat texting in social spaces. The glass has part of its base cut away meaning it can only stand when supported by a mobile phone as part of its base, thus promising to 'rescue people from the online world' by encouraging them to put their phones down and speak face to face (Bowater, 2013).

A growing body of academic research on the social and psychological effect of excessive smartphone use has reported concerns about internet 'addiction' (Beranuy et al., 2009; Griffiths, 2000; Salehan & Negahban, 2013), depression and anxiety (Lepp et al., 2014; Thomee et al., 2011) and isolation, what Habuchi (2005) has defined as the telecocooning effects of mobile phones. While this notion of telecocooning speaks to Putnam's arguments about the individualisation of leisure, are we more preoccupied by the connections we make with our technologies than with the real people standing right next to them? Are we, as Turkle argues, together/apart and alone/together (2011)?

The idea of *excessive* use and the value of quantifying use as excessive is questionable. Indeed, the whole notion of technology as somehow addictive is problematic. Professor Andrew Przybylsk, a psychologist and Professor of Human Behaviour and Technology, argues that narratives of addiction are alarmist, trivialise how we think about addiction and are not based on empirical evidence (Przybylski, 2020). It is an unhelpful metaphor given that the 'solution' to addiction is to remove the addictive substance. We cannot and are not going to 'get rid' of the internet (Turkle, 2011). It is infinitely more useful to examine the quality and contexts of use rather than simply focus on time spent on a device.

RETHINKING BOWLING ALONE

What is interesting about these narratives around phubbing is that they fail to acknowledge the points put forward by early proponents of online community who argued that digitally mediated communication is not fundamentally changing human communication but is allowing it to take a different form. Again, these debates about the nature of interactions between us and technology in public space pre-date the internet.

Theorists of place and mobility have illustrated similar withdrawals from the public sphere. Using the example of the Sony Walkman and the iPod, work in cultural studies has argued that these mobile devices enabled people to withdraw from their immediate location and engage in their own private sound bubble (Bull, 2000, 2007; Du Gay et al., 2013). So critiques of mobile disengagement, from being plugged into a Walkman to phubbing our friends, are less critiques of mobile devices and more about how we use them to control our environments and our social experiences (Frith, 2018).

Rather than demonising new forms of social exchange and activity, like phubbing, we need to understand them in the context of a network society. The ever-increasing presence of mobile phones mean that the boundaries that separate us from our social networks are diaphanous; we are, as Rainie and Wellman (2012a) argue, networked individuals:

> We are not bowling alone, but texting our friends, seeing who's available, sending the electronic invitation, and waiting for people to show up, scheduling another time because someone can't make it and maybe, if we're lucky, actually getting to bowl. (Hogan in Rainie & Wellman, 2012a: 56)

Wong (2020) provides a vivid example of this in his work on 'hidden' young people who shut themselves in their bedrooms and are assumed to be socially withdrawn. In his study of Hong Kong and Scottish youth Wong argues that the idea of hidden youth comes from research in South Asia that has noted the apparent withdrawal of young people who do not go outside for a protracted period and spend extended periods of time online. Initially conceptualised as a psychological problem, Wong argues that more recent research (Furlong, 2008) has suggested that this 'bedroom hiding' is a coping mechanism for the pressures, demands and insecurities faced by young people. Wong argues that hidden youth are not isolated, withdrawn or cut off from society but experience *diverse* forms of connectedness in online and offline contexts. Online interactions bring enjoyment and sociality with young people relying on online communities to seek solace and alternative forms of social connection (Wong, 2020). These alternative social connections were made highly visible during the pandemic lockdowns where opportunities for digital connectivity were a communicative and social lifeline for many (Chambers, 2023; Morris & Orton-Johnson, 2022; Orton-Johnson, 2021; Shah et al., 2020).

We will look at our social relationships in these networks in more detail in Chapter 4 but in the context of this chapter do we need to rethink Putnam's notion that we are isolated from 'community'? Rather than community and civil life being eroded perhaps we can understand it as evolving in and through networks.

We may not be participating in local bowling leagues, but we might be active in (and with) networks of people who share our passions and beliefs. Phubbing may simply be a way in which we are reconfiguring and (re)navigating how we think about public and private space in a cultural landscape where mobile devices have become ubiquitous mobile media portals (Goggin & Hjorth, 2009).

FROM COMMUNITIES AND NETWORKS TO SPACE AND PLACE

Earlier in the chapter we saw that late modernity has been characterised by a disembedding of time and space (Giddens, 1991) and that virtual community is, in part, about removing geographic and temporal boundaries. This section of the chapter will consider the inverse argument; that digital technologies are shaping our local geographies, enabling us to experience *physical* places as *digitally* mediated. This digital mediation is facilitated by the ubiquity of mobile devices. This is not to suggest that mobility is a uniquely digital phenomenon. The ability to carry media has existed since the 'first time someone thought to write on a tablet that could be lifted and hauled – rather than on a cave wall, a cliff face, a monument that usually was stuck in place, more or less forever' (Levinson, 2004:16), rather that mobile devices can shape our understandings of place.

In common with the concept of community, 'place' is a contested term but can be understood as a combination of location (the where), locale (the material settings) and sentiment (the feelings and emotions evoked by a place); place is constituted through our bodily experience of architectures, horizons, artefacts and people (Cresswell, 2014; Speed, 2010; Wilken & Goggin, 2013).

The idea of place is particularly important in understanding our relationship with mobile technologies (Evans, 2015; Humphreys & Liao, 2013). Smartphone location-based services (LBS), such as global positioning systems (GPS), google maps and geotagging simultaneously locate us in a geographical place *and* mediate how we understand, experience and navigate that place (Hinton & Hjorth, 2013). This convergence of the virtual and the physical is described by Gordon and De Souza e Silva (2011) as net locality, the ubiquity of networked information introduced to physical spaces by mobile devices. Mobiles help us reimagine and reinforce our experience of place as a 'geo-imaginary and socio-cultural precept' (Hjorth, 2008: 93).

Our physical geographies are digitally represented by vast amounts of data and mobile devices and social media acts as conduits for these layers of information; our physical environment has grown a digital double (Avram, 2014).

Again, this is not to suggest that locative media is new in its potential to link information and place. de Souza e Silva and Frith (2010) cite Jim Spohrer's vision in the mid 1990s of a system called *Worldboard*, that used technology to enhance physical space with digital information:

> The nonphysical information becomes a 'thing' overlaid on physical space and becomes part of that space, not just an augmentation of it...the same place can appear differently according to who perceives it and for what purpose. Depending on the technology available (or the lack of it), people might be able to experience urban spaces in personalized ways. (de Souza e Silva & Frith, 2010:490)

Since 2008 the release of GPS-enabled smartphones has mainstreamed location-based services (de Souza e Silva & Frith, 2010) and the introduction of networked information to physical spaces has made it possible for us to digitally personalise and control our physical environments. GPS-enabled mobile phones track and display our geographic locations, enabling us to navigate through public places using apps that tell us where the nearest bus stop, cash machine, public toilet, supermarket or cafe is. We can filter information about spaces around us by looking at reviews that other people have left about local facilities, places and events and we can use apps that pull real-time photos and videos to create personalised maps of our location. We can 'check-in' to locations on social media platforms, tag where we are and have been and share information about places with others who may be there or wish to visit. Apps such as Grindr or Tinder open up new social/experiential possibilities for geolocation-based social networking and locations become gamified through augmented reality mobile games like Pokemon Go or GPS-based game Geocaching (Humphreys, 2016).

We digitally annotate, augment and document urban landscapes through a variety of mobile applications. These interactions add new dimensions to the spaces in which we are physically present and when we use these digital resources to inform and navigate, we are traversing both physical and informational space.

For example, (Saker, 2017) in his work on location-based social network Foursquare argues that it acts as an exploratory tool allowing users to engage with spaces in ways that intersect the physical and the digital, enabling online self-presentation based on a display of offline physical activities, representing and transforming how we experience place.

DIGITAL PLACEMAKING

When understanding place through social media platforms we can conceive of it as an ongoing process of renegotiation and enactment and datafication, what has been described as digital placemaking (Halegoua & Polson, 2021; Wilken & Humphreys, 2021).

The concept of digital placemaking describes the use of digital media to create a sense of place for oneself, using digital technologies, practices and infrastructures to embed oneself in a space and to foster or maintain a sense of attachment to a place (Halegoua & Polson, 2021).

In their examination of Snapchat as a digital placemaking tool, Wilken and Humphreys (2021) argue that snaps emerge from and seek to capture affective experiences of place and form a kind of 'spatial storytelling' (2021: 58). Snapchat is a messaging service used to create and exchange multimedia messages known as snaps, shared privately between friends or posted publicly as a 'story'. Snapchat also has a maps interface, *Snap Map*, that enables a user's device to locate other users on an interactive map, to see and search for friends' locations, to use a heat map to show what snaps others have shared in an area and to view and add stories to hot spots (areas where there is lot of posting and activity) on the map.

When they were introduced in 2017 Snap Maps garnered much media attention around privacy and surveillance concerns. While these have largely been assuaged by the realisation of their potential to provide location details in emergencies and disasters (Alfalqi & Bellaiche, 2021), we must also be cognisant of the tensions and inequalities they (re)produce.

Dyer (2020) argues that technology, socio-cultural resources and location have become enmeshed. Citing the online sharing of videos of public spaces he notes how social interaction, online and offline, acts as a policing of space:

> 2018 has seen a spate of viral videos shared online of white females phoning for police on PoC for using spaces in ways the white females perceived as incorrect, such as holding a BBQ in a public area (an event documented in the hashtag #BBQBecky) or an 8-year-old child selling bottled water on the street to passers-by (#PermitPatty). The technology in this case provides a documentation of the tensions inherent around the use of these spaces. (Dyer, 2020: 101)

What Dyer (2020) illustrates here is that technology use is not experienced equally, particularly around systemic racial inequalities. Indeed, digital placemaking may exacerbate existing inequities meaning that certain populations experience digital media in place and placemaking in profoundly different ways (Halegoua & Polson, 2021). We will return to the issue of inequalities later in this chapter and in Chapter 8 but for now it is also worth reflecting on the value of technologies of placemaking.

For example, research on migration has highlighted the importance of mobile devices as tools for forced migrants in terms of survival, resistance and empowerment (Labayen & Gutierrez, 2021; Wittenborn, 2020; Zijlstra & Liempt, 2017). The internet, via mobile devices, is used to create a sense of past, present and aspirational future with migrants using mobile devices to build and engage with networks of support, maintain old ties and validate information and establish physical, socio-cultural and political belonging (Dekker et al., 2018; Smets, 2019; Wittenborn, 2020). Labayen and Gutierrez's (2021) work on sub-Saharan migrants' media practices at the Moroccan–Spanish border looks at the role of migrants' technology use and placemaking. They argue that technologies of placemaking are an important form of 'currency' in migrants' journeys with digital practices helping migrants to maintain control in extremely difficult situations. The value of smartphones is evident as they are, along with passports, among the first things to be confiscated by border guards (Labayen & Gutierrez, 2021).

Challenging real/virtual dichotomies

The proliferation of locative media platforms and geo-locational data affords new opportunities to remap and reimagine place (Hardey, 2007). As such, spatial and locative media disrupts the arbitrary dichotomy between online/real and offline/virtual discussed earlier in the chapter. Digitally mediated places are not either/or, they are geographically rooted but also ephemeral. Locative media shapes our relationship with place as lived *and* imagined, psychological *and* geographic (Hjorth, 2012).

In moving through digitally mediated physical landscapes we knowingly and unknowingly contribute our own spatial information and data. In doing so we alter our experience of digital place, and we shape the digital information space that others encounter when they use the same platforms in the same place, what Hardey (2007) calls a new 'synergistic relationship' linking individuals to data and their localities. As well as linking individuals to data and location, mobile applications are increasingly being used to share our location with friends, broadly defined as location-based social networks (LBSNs). This use of location-based services as a tool for real time and real space social networking will be explored in Chapter 4 on digitally mediated relationships.

DIGITAL INEQUALITIES

This is not to assume that the navigation of these spaces is equitable. As we saw earlier in the chapter, proponents of virtual community highlighted the potential of online spaces to transcend social divides while critiques pointed to the digital pervasiveness of well-established inequalities. Similarly, as we think about the potentials afforded by net locality, we must be cognisant of the social implications of digitally customised public spaces.

de Souza e Silva and Frith (2010) argue that access to available technology will shape how different people might be able to experience urban spaces.

The 2016 Pew Research Centre survey of 14 advanced economies found a sharp digital divide around reported smartphone ownership; younger people, those who are well educated and people with an income above their country median were more likely to own a smartphone compared with older, less educated and poorer members of their societies (Poushter, 2017).

More recent mobile ownership statistics show this gap lessening. As of 2021, 88% of all adults in the UK had a smartphone, with 96% of those aged 16–24 owning a smartphone device compared to 78% aged 55 (Hiley, 2021).

Globally, the Alliance for Affordable Internet paints a different picture reporting that nearly 2.5 billion people live in countries where the cost of the cheapest available smartphone is a quarter or more of the average monthly income (Woodhouse, 2020).

Unsurprising as these findings may be, the question of access to technology has implications for how a digital divide might impact on negotiating cultural and social difference in public spaces:

> Individuals equipped with these technologies have the opportunity to interact with a space that is markedly different from the space perceived by individuals who do not have access to the technology. For example, two individuals may be walking side-by-side down a crowded street, one individual perceiving the street as a physical space while the other perceives the street as a hybrid space. The physical space is unchanged for the individual excluded…while the [other]…perceives the physical space overlaid with digital information. (de Souza e Silva & Frith, 2010:499)

This kind of digital exclusion is meaningful if, as Frith (2018) and Dyer (2020) argue, physical spaces are experienced differently by people if they access digital information through their smartphone. If some are structurally excluded from augmented activities and information then this may lead to new kinds of differentiated spaces that, in turn, may harm our collective experience of public space and how we conceive of community in a networked society (de Souza e Silva & Frith, 2010). These issues of inequality and division are explored in more detail in Chapter 8.

STUDYING COMMUNITY: METHODOLOGICAL CHALLENGES

I began the chapter by suggesting that defining the concept of community was an ongoing challenge for sociology. This challenge is also a methodological one. Communities are complex and multifaceted and do not easily lend themselves to one standardised mode of analysis (Crow, 2018), as Amit argues:

Invocations of community do not present analysts with clear-cut group-ings so much as signal fields of complex processes through which sociality is sought, rejected, argued over, realised, interpreted, exploited or enforced. (2003: 14)

As a result, the study of community has always drawn on a diverse set of methods; interviews and surveys, documentary analysis, oral histories, visual methods and social network analysis. Ethnographic methods in particular have informed much of community studies and this section of the chapter will explore the methodo-logical challenges and opportunities of using ethnography to study digital articu-lations of community.

Ethnography

Traditional ethnography as a methodological approach combines qualitative methods of enquiry as a means of gaining an in-depth and detailed understand-ing of a culture, a social group or a social process. While ethnography is defined by a researcher's interests, background and theoretical orientation, it is a flexible, evolving and interpretive approach that is concerned with an understanding of the symbolic word of the participants and the meanings attached to their interac-tions, relationships and identities (Hine, 2000; Pink, 2015). This understanding comes from an immersion in a setting, ongoing activity or lifestyle and ethno-graphic researchers spend time observing, participating in and interacting with people as they go about their daily lives and routines (Hammersley & Atkinson, 2019).

Ethnographic immersion enables researchers to explore the mundane and everyday activities that are fundamental to the formation and maintenance of community; taken-for-granted practices and interactions that, in their familiar-ity, may be rendered invisible, intangible or insignificant to the members of the community or to methods that rely on recall. Ethnography provides a nuanced account of a culture, from reflexive and engaged observations (Martey & Shiflett, 2012).

It is perhaps not surprising then that the need for familiarisation and immer-sion in an unknown setting drew researchers of virtual community to ethnogra-phy as a method. Early ethnographies of the internet established online spaces as ethnographic field sites and, as we saw earlier in the chapter, a body of litera-ture focused on the study of virtual community and the communicative crea-tion of social meaning. For example, Baym (1997), in her study of the formation of online community in the soap opera fandom groups r.a.t.s (rec.arts.tv.soap), found that the group cohesion of r.a.t.s was based on shared forms of expression and informally circulated, group-specific acronyms, vocabulary and norms. In order to understand these emergent and shared norms ethnography as a method provided the richness and context required and was a natural extension of the ethnographic tradition.

Digital ethnographies of online community

This kind of ethnographic approach has attracted a variety of labels; digital ethnography (Pink, 2016), cyberethnography, netnography (Kozinets, 2019) virtual ethnography (Boellstorff et al., 2012; Hine, 2000). Each maintain a dialogue with traditional ethnography and what they have in common is an interest in studying the spatially and temporally dispersed ways in which technology is experienced in use. They focus not on relations that are tied to a specific place or identity but on being methodologically responsive to the fluidity of digitally mediated interactions.

This does not mean that the object of research is limited to *online* behaviours, interactions and relationships. As the earliest ethnographies of online community evidenced, digital communities extend beyond digital spaces. For example, Kendall's (2002) research on the online forum BlueSky was conducted via a range of face-to-face and online encounters in recognition of the importance of understanding the ways in which our offline realities and identities shape our online realities and identities and vice versa.

In the same way that studies of community have focused on understanding meaning and context in community settings, research on online communities recognised the importance of contextualising online interactions and practices. Online communities do not exist in an independent reality and are affected by participants' patterns of participation and their offline lives. Researchers need to familiarise themselves with the various social, political and cultural identity contexts of the groups they seek to study (Kendall, 1999: 80).

In order to understand the lived experience of our technology use we need to conceive of digital spaces as a cultural phenomenon that can be studied as a place and a way of being. The fluidity of these phenomena mean we are unable to know in advance where the spatial boundaries of a technology may lie (Hine, 2015; Kendall, 1999; Markham, 1998).

Digital ethnography and the boundaries of the field

The flexibility of ethnography as a method is ideally suited to the task of navigating these complex boundaries. This emphasis on tracing or following is at the heart of ethnography and digital traces of networked behaviour are a rich source of data for ethnographers seeking to explore multi-sited and multimedia spaces and communities (Møller & Robards, 2019).

Digital ethnography adapts to manage a field site that is unbounded, distributed and fluid. Digital ethnography recognises the integration of digital technologies into everyday life and the need to avoid rigid and artificial boundaries that obscure these complexities. However, this is not to suggest that traditional ethnography can easily and clearly define the boundaries of a field site and the challenge of boundaries has long been a staple of offline ethnographic enquiry:

> In a world of infinite interconnections and overlapping contexts, the ethnographic field cannot simply exist, awaiting discovery. It has to be laboriously constructed, pulled apart from all the other possibilities for contextualization to which its constituent relationships and connections could also be referred. (Amit, 2000:6)

The 'field' is not a predetermined place awaiting ethnographic discovery; rather it is defined as part of an ongoing process of research (Hine, 2000; Rutter & Smith, 2005) that recognises that culture happens everywhere rather than in neatly bounded sites (Martey & Shiflett, 2012). It is important to highlight the continuity with traditional ethnographic methods here and to recognise that in our complex social worlds the boundaries of the field are necessarily unclear (Atkinson & Hammersley, 1998). But with that caveat of continuity, it *is* the case that the networked technologies and revised definitions of community, outlined in this chapter, have disrupted and challenged what we conceive of and construct as field sites.

Where is the where?

In the same way that online communities challenge our conceptualisations of space by being a-spatial (with membership based on connectivity and choice rather than geography), digital ethnography also challenges spatial and temporal boundaries and is, necessarily, partial, interstitial and highly reflexive. It is no longer necessary or possible to conceive of ethnography to be located in a particular place, as Hine suggests:

> If culture and community are not self-evidently located in place, then neither is ethnography. The object of ethnographic enquiry can usefully be reshaped by concentrating on flow and connectivity rather than location and boundary as the organizing principle. (Hine, 2000: 64)

The digital ethnographer faces an ever-shifting continuum of ethnographic spaces and interactions that cannot be accurately categorised as entirely on or offline as they impinge and interact with each other. The digital traces that ethnography must pursue are those readily visible and available on and in digital platforms and spaces but also those that arise though the process of ethnographic engagement and exploration (Hine, 2015). These traces form what Møller and Robards (2019) call the building blocks of online presence that constitutes online sociality and community.

Digital ethnography demands that we follow this flow; to try and define and contain any method as virtual or internet based is to limit yourself with and by this definition. Again, this is not to imply that traditional ethnographies do not face similar issues, but these spaces provide the digital ethnographer with a new form of ethnographic engagement and a new layer of ethnographic participation:

> This provides a symmetry to the ethnography, as the ethnographer learns through using the same media as informants…This presents an opportunity for rethinking the shaping of the ethnographic object and reformulating the grounds for ethnographic engagement with the field. (Hine, 2000: 10)

In defining the site of research all ethnography needs to be driven by the research topic, rather than assuming or arbitrarily drawing boundaries. The ethnographer needs to explore the different modes of communication and physical/technological locations in and through which their topic of interest plays out. Digital media have changed the repertoire of ethnographic practices as field sites span multiple spaces and objects of interest as social presence and participation is distributed and networked (Møller & Robards, 2019). As such, the ability of mediated ethnography to incorporate social interactions, material structures and digital mobile practices affords us new ways to understand our mediated lives.

CONCLUSION

The analysis of communities and social relations has emerged as a clear and consistent theme in the study of digital technologies. Key ideas in this chapter can be summarised as followed:

- The concept of community has a long and contested history in sociology. The idea of community being in decline enlivened debates about the potential of new technology to provide us with new ways to connect in virtual communities that extend beyond geographic boundaries.
- The concept of virtual communities brings together utopian hopes and dystopian fears about the impact of new technologies on our social lives. Critiques have pointed to the unhelpful binaries and technological determinism that characterise much of these debates.

- Shifting from conceiving of society as made up of bounded communities, more recent scholarly debate has moved towards an understanding of society as a series of fluid networks.
- Despite moral panics about new forms of sociality, digitally mediated communication is not fundamentally changing human communication but is allowing it to take a different form.
- Digital technologies are also shaping our local geographies, enabling us to experience *physical* places as *digitally* mediated. This digital mediation is facilitated by the ubiquity of mobile devices. This offers us new opportunities to (re)imagine place.
- Virtual ethnography has emerged as a tool to explore spaces and interactions across multimodal field sites.

Further reading

Rheingold, H. (2000). *The virtual community, revised edition: Homesteading on the electronic frontier*. MIT Press.

The chapter introduced the work of Rheingold and his utopian provocation of virtual community. His text remains a frequently cited starting point for understanding digital sociability and for those interested in the history of virtual communities: this remains an important read. The book traces virtual communities from the 1960s to the 1990s with the 2000 edition updating the original 1993 version to address, to some degree, critiques of his work that question the separation of virtual and offline as separate spheres.

Chayko, M. (2020). Rethinking community in communication and information studies: digital community and community 'to go'. In *Rethinking community through transdisciplinary research*, pp.99–110. Palgrave Macmillan

In this very readable chapter Chayko argues that technology-rich societies are constantly engaged in community-building activities. She argues that communities are being recast and reconceived as portable and examines the social implications of living in a digital world where community can be taken 'to go'. She discusses the methodologies used in her own study of online community emphasising community as digital and physical. The chapter comes from a book that focuses on interdisciplinary understandings of community and includes a wider section on digital communities in flux.

Rainie, H. and Wellman, B. (2012). *Networked: The new social operating system* (Vol. 10). MIT Press.

This chapter outlined a shift in thinking from communities to networks when understanding social life online. Rainie and Wellman's book provides a very accessible overview of the triple revolutions – the internet revolution, the mobile revolution and the social media revolution – that they argue have converged to shape new social configurations into what they call a networked operating system.

Thomas, L., Orme, E., & Kerrigan, F. (2020). Student loneliness: The role of social media through life transitions. *Computers and Education*, *146*, p. 103754.

While not explicitly about communities online the research reported in this article reflects on many of the issues raised in this chapter and, looking ahead, issues discussed in Chapters 3 and 4. Focusing on loneliness and poor mental health among students transitioning to university, Thomas et al. argue that social media can play an important role in facilitating offline relationships and maintaining ties to old friends as students form new communities.

Hine, C. (2015). *Ethnography for the internet: Embedded, embodied and everyday*. Taylor and Francis.

Along with her 2008 book *Virtual Ethnography* this is key reading from any student wanting an insight into the complexities of the digital as a field site and a research tool. Hine provides a practical guide to how we can think about ethnographic methods to give us a critical stance on the impact of new technologies in our lives.

For those interested in Digital Ethnography Zoe Glatt's very detailed reading list is an invaluable resource https://zoeglatt.com/wp-content/uploads/2023/04/LSE-Digital-Ethnography-Collective-Reading-List-April-2023-1.pdf

---

NOTE

1.   http://adage.com/article/news/mccann-melbourne-made-a-word-sell-a-dictionary/244595/

3

THE DIGITALLY MEDIATED SELF: IDENTITY AND SOCIAL MEDIA

The previous chapter focused on how sociology can understand digital articulations of community, space and place. Having established that digital technologies afford us the tools to manage the size and shape of our social networks, this chapter explores how digital technologies and the digital culture we inhabit have the potential to shape how we understand ourselves and our identities within these social networks. As you read this chapter, I encourage you to think about the following questions:

- How do we construct our identities as individuals?
- In what ways is identity a performative social act?
- How has identity been enacted in and through digital spaces?
- What does it mean to have an identity online?
- How has visual social media culture shaped the ways in which we 'do' identity?

IDENTITY AS SOCIAL

Like the concept of community, the concepts of self and identity are central to sociology and have been an enduring and contested focus of sociological concern. Long before digital technologies and social media platforms got us thinking about how we 'do' or experience identity online, symbolic interactionalist perspectives had established the concept of identity as a fluid, negotiated and reciprocal relationship between the self and society (Fine & Stryker, 1982). Identity is conceptualised as a social construct enacted through our interactions and relationships with others. Identity provides a link between us as individuals and the world in which we live.

The symbolic interactionalist perspective marks a shift from conceptualisations of identity that assume that our identity comes from a clear, consistent, authentic and stable set of characteristics that make up the 'self' (Thurlow et al., 2004; Woodward, 1997). Challenging the idea that a unified self can exist outside of social interaction, American sociologist Cooley used the concept of the 'looking glass self' to define the self as a product of our social interactions (Cooley, 1902). We understand the self as it is reflected by the 'generalised other'. In other words, we understand ourselves by imagining how we appear to other people. Based on this imagining we make a judgement about how other people perceive us and through this process we imagine how other people feel about us. This results in an emotional response, in Cooley's words, 'some sort of feeling such as pride or mortification' (1902: 189).

Cooley argued that we play an active role in this process, engaging in continual self-evaluation, thinking about how we are perceived by others and working to shape those perceptions. We are active in constructing and managing our identities and presenting them in different ways depending on the circumstances in which we find ourselves. Our identities, rather than being stable or fixed entities, are constructed through sets of symbols and representations that we draw on in our interactions with others (Mead, 1934). We find meaning in social interactions and these meanings enable us to engage in reflexive understandings of the self (Mead, 1934; Stets & Burke, 2000). We experience our sense of self indirectly through our interactions with others and through our reflections on how others perceive us. As such, identity is profoundly social (Mead, 1934).

Goffman and the presentation of self

In his conceptualisation of identity construction and human interaction, sociologist Erving Goffman argued that we present the self for the purpose of interacting with others. In his work *The presentation of self in everyday life* (Goffman, 1959), he uses the analogy of dramaturgy and performance to argue that social interaction is like a play in which we try to convey an identity consistent with our expectations and understandings of the situation we are in and the people we are with. Our stage and our audience.

Using the metaphor of a theatre Goffman argued that we have front-stage and back-stage behaviours. The front stage, what Goffman described as the front region, is where we give our performance. As actors on the front stage we are conscious of our performance and aware that we are being observed by an audience. In our performances we aim to adhere to cultural standards of appropriate behaviour, emphasising aspects of the self that give a good impression while supressing aspects of our performance that might discredit us.

In contrast, the privacy afforded by our back-stage area allows us to behave in different ways. The back region allows us to relax from our front-stage roles, to contradict the impressions given by our front-stage performance and to prepare for the next front-stage performance.

Some of the roles we play may contradict each other and some performances are only meant for certain audiences. This means we engage consciously and unconsciously in identity work (Snow & Anderson, 1987).

For example, I give a certain kind of performance as an academic lecturing to students at university. I dress smartly, I speak more slowly and clearly than I do in general conversation and I adhere to the professional and formal nature of the occasion. This is a very different performance to the more informal relationships and interactions I have with colleagues at work or with my friends. My back-stage performance at home with my family, is a different kind of identity again. Our social lives demand that we perform myriad different roles to different audiences.

For Goffman, we rely on these stages and performances in order to construct an identity that is appropriate to the expectations, contexts and demands of different interactional situations. Identity, rather than being a fixed, unitary label, is a series of performative acts that vary depending on context and location (Goffman, 1959).

Our performances help us to navigate and manage our social interactions. As part of our performances we communicate through deliberate conscious expressions. Elements of our performance are purposefully selected to present and communicate our identity in a particular way; for example, the clothes we might choose as being appropriate for different social situations, a wedding, a funeral or a job interview. This is what Goffman describes as our public display. Accompanying these public displays are a wealth of other, often non-verbal cues and expressions that we 'give off', that also tell our audiences about who we are, the colloquial language, the bitten nails, the nervous mannerism or the confident stance.

It isn't very hard to see how the work of Goffman resonates with our understandings of self-presentation in digital contexts. Digital spaces have provided us with new opportunities for self-presentation. In the same way that Goffman argues that physical settings inform our face-to-face encounters, online spaces shape and frame certain kinds of identity performances. As Jenkins suggests:

> This virtual world is, indeed, a stage, and Goffman's dramaturgical model
> has surely found a new world to conquer. (Jenkins, 2014: 265)

A field of literature has emerged that has taken Goffman's concepts of impression management, the presentation of self, and front- and back-stage performances, and applied them to digital contexts and the reflexive ways in which we present ourselves online (Baker, 2009; Baker & Walsh, 2018; Blackwell et al., 2015; Goulden et al., 2018; Hogan, 2010; Lincoln & Robards, 2014; Marwick & boyd, 2011).

Symbolic interactionalist understandings of the self provide a way for us to understand the complexities of our own identities and the identities of others and to understand how we manage and navigate our lives. Identity connects the personal with the social, engaging us as individuals with the society in which we live and the social, cultural and economic structures that shape our experiences of that society. What this chapter explores are the ways in which the digital shapes our identities and our understandings and experiences of social life.

Identity and a disembodied self

When we think about how we interact online, what is interesting about interactional understandings of identity is that, historically, they have assumed a notion of the social that is co-present and embodied. Indeed, Goffman, considering the telephone, argued that conversing over the phone was an inferior departure from the norm of face-to-face interaction, not sufficiently rich in the visible social cues that characterise physical co-presence (Bullingham & Vasconcelos, 2013; Goffman, 1964) Face to face we are able to see and hear a front-stage performance, we can pick up on the non-verbal social cues that form part of that performance.

Online the usual features we associate with the presentation of the self, the accent we have, the way we dress, or the eye contact we do or don't make are less meaningful because the usual physical cues and methods of presentation that Goffman wrote about are dissolved. The dramaturgical analogy of life as a stage, with individuals as actors, is replaced by the metaphor of the screen, with individuals as terminals. Goffman's stage, in other words, becomes a network. As Baudrillard suggests:

> We no longer exist as playwrights or actors but as terminals of multiple networks. These are processes where the stage becomes that of the infinitesimal memory and the screen. The public stage, the public place have been replaced by a gigantic and ephemeral connecting space. (Baudrillard, 2007:16)

How can we understand the digitally mediated self without the embodied social clues that Goffman argues are vital for the accomplishment of social life? To begin to answer these questions we need to consider the history of how identity has been enacted and negotiated in and through digital spaces, and how the move from a text-based internet to the visual medium we know today has shaped our digital identities.

A (BRIEF) HISTORY OF ONLINE IDENTITY

Common with the introduction of other new technologies (from the printing press to the telephone and the television) the advent of digital media was accompanied by an interest in how new media forms might impact social life. Journalists, theorists, politicians and academics from a wide range of disciplines engaged in ongoing debates about how computer mediated communication (CMC) might shape our understandings of self and identity.

Through these debates we can trace a history of digital identity as something that, in the early days of the internet, was experienced through disembodiment, deception and anonymity, to more contemporary understandings of identity as a performative and public digital mediation.

I use the term digital identity here to highlight the distinction between *online identity* and *identity online* (Thurlow et al., 2004). Online identity implies that we have an identity online that is different and distinct from that of our 'offline' identity. Using identity online or digital identity aligns more closely with the symbolical interactionalist emphasis on identity as performative, situational and interactional.

Identity in a text-based internet

The early internet was solely text based. It was accessed through command lines and green-screen terminals and was in many ways the preserve of early adopters, hobbyists, geeks and academics. As such, early digital representations of self relied primarily on text; we wrote ourselves into being online (Sundén, 2003).

As we have seen in the first section of this chapter, understanding identity as a social process invokes a notion of human agency; we have some control in constructing our own identities. This control, however, is shaped by the social structures in which we find ourselves. We may be limited in our identity performances by our physical bodies or by our material and economic conditions (Woodward, 2005). In contrast, in text-based online communities, users were free from these structural and physical constraints and a theme characterising much of the early research on digital spaces was one of emancipation and liberation from the body and the inequalities of our everyday lives.

Early scholarly interest in the potentials of CMC pointed to the ways in which textual online interaction created places where new types of human relationships could unfold. Utopian potentials were explored as research mapped the affordances of new disembodied social spaces.

This cyberculture research focused on text-based online communities, such as MUDs (a term used originally to describe multiuser dungeons, later also described as multiuser dimensions or domains), bulletin boards, chat rooms and text-based adventure games. These platforms were conceptualised as sites in which users could play with aspects of their identity.

An overarching theme running through these literatures was with the disembodiment of the user. Cyberspace was envisaged as a place where previously fixed categories of identity did not apply, freeing up offline personas from rigid categories of gender and sexuality (Rheingold, 1993; Stone, 1996).

Donna Haraway's cyborg provided a metaphor for this new way of looking at identity. In 'A Cyborg Manifesto' Haraway argued that the cyborg subject occupied a place where traditional dichotomies (nature/technology, human/machine, man/woman, physical/non physical), what she describes as antagonistic dualisms, could be broken down and previously oppositional concepts could simultaneously reside. The metaphor of the cyborg highlighted the ways in which traditional identity politics had ignored and essentialised the social construction of race, gender and class, and provided a way to re-inscribe and dismantle difference through the mutability of digital boundaries (1991: 50).

While Haraway did not conceive of the cyborg as a metaphor of equality and liberation (pointing to the patriarchal and militaristic narratives surrounding the concept of a cyborg) much early scholarship did orient around this notion of digital spaces as a panacea to the structural constraints of the embodied and stratified 'real' world.

The promise of new electronic communication was characterised by three key themes. The first, as we saw in the previous chapter, was concerned with the existence of an online or virtual community and the communicative creation of social meaning within online groups (Jones, 1997; Rheingold, 1993; Smith & Kollock, 1999; Wellman & Gulia, 1999). The second emphasised the therapeutic, experimental and recreational aspects of CMC (Danet, 1998; Turkle, 1995). The third focused on gender reproductions and representations online (Danet, 1998; O'Brien, 1999). A key division in these debates came from those for whom this disembodiment was viewed as an emancipatory opportunity for role play and experimentation and those who viewed these new mediums as spaces that had to overcome the problems of disembodiment.

Disembodiment and identity play

Disembodiment was viewed by some as an opportunity to experiment with identity play (Danet, 1998; Turkle, 1995). In her book *Life on the screen: Identity in the age of the internet*, Turkle argued that cyberspace was a new medium in which our ideas and fantasies could be explored through multiple and fragmented identities. Her research looked at text-based multiplayer virtual worlds (MUDs). She highlighted the importance of anonymity in these text-based environments; spaces that encouraged people to create different personas and alternative identities that were unrelated to their 'authentic' offline gender, race or sexual orientation. MUDs were spaces in which users could perform fictional identities in fictitious worlds. Through role play, individuals were able to cycle through and explore different identities and their implications and to express and explore different aspects of the self.

For Turkle, identity in MUDs was about multiplicity, heterogeneity, flexibility and fragmentation (Turkle, 1995). This represented a postmodern way of understanding the self, challenging and subverting traditional ideas about identity as tied to notions of authenticity. Spaces where the self was decentred and multiplied without limit (Turkle, 1995).

This analytical interest in disembodiment, identity play and fantasy online emphasised the importance of anonymity and the dynamic, playful and disinhibiting effects of the medium (Reid, 1991; Stone, 1996). The ability to explore potentially infinite personas and the ability to hide one's identity and be a voyeur was a key feature of debates about technologically mediated relationships and identities.

From disembodiment to an embodied internet

The text-based MUDs in which these studies of early internet users took place, tended to be populated by white, middle-class, technically minded men (Robinson, 2007). As the internet and its users diversified, research shifted away from the idea of identity fragmentation and deception, acknowledging that the earlier literature placed too much emphasis on identity differences and deception, as Baym argues:

> Judging from the scholarly attention paid to anonymous CMC interaction and its uses in identity play, one would think most online interaction is anonymous and few people ever act as themselves. The reality seems to be that many, probably most, social users of CMC create online selves consistent with their offline identities. (Baym, 2015: 55)

Research at this time emphasised the importance of identity consistency between 'real' and digital mediums, highlighting the collaborative identity work we do online; sharing and interpreting new interaction styles, emoticons and norms in our attempts to overcome the ambiguity of identity in disembodied spaces

(Reid, 1991). The liberatory narrative of the early cyberspace literature was challenged and there was a growing recognition that the internet served to reinforce
and maintain, rather than overcome, offline inequalities and stereotypes. Much
of this work focused on gendered stereotypes, for example Kendall drawing on
Goffman, pointed to the purely performative nature of identity play online:

> The electronic medium that makes gender masquerade possible and con-
> ceivable for a wider range of people also enables both the masqueraders
> and their audiences to interpret these performances in ways that distance
> them from a critique of *real* gender. The understanding that the limitations
> of the medium *require* performance allows online participants to interpret
> online gender masquerade selectively as *only* performance. (2002: 107)

What she argues here is that identity play online is not transformative in the
way that Turkle suggests. Rather it is a strategic performance in an online context that mirrors the kinds of performances Goffman argued enable us to manage interaction. She points to the social, economic and cultural structures and
inequalities that shape our performances and emphasises that these endure in
online contexts.

When we perform an identity online, we are not leaving behind the power relations and structural frameworks that shape our physical interactions and identities. They simply take on a digitally mediated form. Debates about online identity
had failed to sufficiently recognise this and treated the 'online' as an isolated
social phenomenon:

> They usually ignore the fact that people bring to their online interactions
> such baggage as their gender, stage in the life cycle, cultural milieu, socio-
> economic status, and off line connections with others. (Wellman, 1997: 446)

The view of the internet as a utopian, liberatory space has been well critiqued in
over two decades of work that has highlighted the race, class and gender inequalities and divides that are embedded in the design, use and distribution of digital technologies. Research has pointed to the ways in which 'identity tourism'
and experimentation primarily involved privileged groups reinforcing stereotypes about different ethnicities and genders (Armentor-Cota, 2011; Boler, 2007;
Carstensen, 2009; Nakamura, 2002).

As Chapter 1 argued, the ubiquity and mundanity of the digital in our everyday lives means that the anonymous textual environments of the early internet
have largely been eclipsed by highly visual digital platforms and applications.
The distinction between online and offline identities is less salient and issues of

disembodiment, anonymity and identity play are no longer the dominant narratives for understanding digital identity. Contemporary understandings of digital identity reject online/offline, virtual/real dichotomies and point to a blending of identity, where the offline and online self-inform each other (Baker, 2009; Baker & Walsh, 2018; Bullingham & Vasconcelos, 2013).

SOCIAL MEDIA AND DIGITAL IDENTITY

In the mid-1990s the internet started to shift from a primarily textual medium to include websites and applications that hosted pictures, photographs, audio, video and interactive media. As graphical browsers were introduced, image and sound became part of the internet experience. Smartphones and faster and more ubiquitous internet connections mean that image and video files have become a dominant form of digital communication. The internet is now a highly visual medium (Marwick, 2015; Walker Rettberg, 2016). This visual turn was followed in the early 2000s by a range of sites, applications and tools, broadly defined as social media, that facilitated image and video sharing, blogging and microblogging, networking and collaboration. In a little over 2 decades social media has become a ubiquitous part of our daily lives and created an infrastructure that allows us to share digital content and connect and communicate across global networks (boyd, 2010; van Dijck, 2013a). Social media technologies afford us diverse spaces and tools with which to perform our identities, encouraging the constant broadcasting, via social media platforms, of the (often) mundane activities and experiences of our daily lives:

> Many of the habits that have recently become permeated by social media platforms used to be informal and ephemeral manifestations of social life. Talking to friends, exchanging gossip, showing holiday pictures, scribbling notes, checking on a friend's well-being, or watching a neighbor's home video used to be casual, evanescent (speech) acts, commonly shared only with selected individuals. (van Dijck, 2013a:7)

Social media involves a self-referential narrativisation of self and experience. We can conceive of social media as a complex ecosystem of platforms that are based on profiles as a public presentation of the self. We can create rich textual and visual images of ourselves and our social worlds that can be shared globally with friends and strangers.

Previously in this chapter, we saw that early research on the internet focused on the ways in which online environments provided opportunities for us to experiment and play with identity. While these text-based environments lacked the visual clues of Goffman's performance the more visually rich environments of contemporary digital spaces point to a need to re-engage with Goffman's notions of self and performance (Bullingham & Vasconcelos, 2013; Jacobsen, 2010). The rest of the chapter does this by exploring three examples of social media culture: selfies, fakebooking (faking Facebook posts) and Finstas (fake Instagram accounts) as contemporary exemplars of the presentation of self.

SELFIES

A 'selfie' is a self-portrait, typically using a smartphone or web cam, taken in a reflective object or from arm's length and shared on social media. In 2013, the word selfie was added to the *Oxford English Dictionary* (along with gif and unfriend) and was named *Word of the Year*. With over a million selfies uploaded to social media every day they have become a ubiquitous feature of contemporary western societies and the internet abounds with advice, tips and tools for achieving the perfect selfie: from selfie sticks and selfie hairbrushes to illuminated phone cases for perfect selfie lighting and selfie drones to capture aerial 'dronies'. In March 2018, a Museum of Selfies opened in Glendale, California exploring the history and cultural impact of the selfie as a defining feature of modern society.

As a cultural phenomenon, the selfie has become the focus of considerable media and academic attention. These debates are often accompanied by a sense of mockery and disdain for a practice which is couched in narratives of vanity, narcissism, superficial attention seeking and a desperate need to receive the validation of others (Murray, 2015). Narratives around selfies seem to overwhelmingly frame them in reductive, pathologising and overly determined ways (Warfield et al., 2016). Yet, as Senft and Baym note, despite their seeming ubiquity the practice of taking selfies 'remain[s] fundamentally ambiguous, fraught, and caught in a stubborn and morally loaded hype cycle' (Senft & Baym, 2015). They are not simply images – they are a set of social practices.

What this section of the chapter will argue is that selfies are a profoundly social phenomena that need to be understood beyond a focus on the individual and the individual act. As C Wright Mills (1959) suggests, in order to understand social processes, we must acknowledge the social and historical structures in which they are formed and in which they interact.

The history of selfies

The selfie is not a new form of expression. Self-portraiture has a long history spanning cave painting, classical and modern art, sculpture and carving (Rettberg, 2014).

The first photographic self-portrait is believed to have been created by Robert Cornelius in 1839. He set up his camera at the back of his father's shop in Philadelphia, creating his portrait by removing the lens cap, running into the frame and sitting still for five minutes before running back and replacing the lens cap.[1] Understanding photography as a social act also has a long history. Susan Sontag in *On photography* in 1977 notes the cultural role of a photograph:

> Recently, photography has become almost as widely practiced an amusement as sex and dancing – which means that, like every mass art form, photography is not practiced by most people as art. It is mainly a social rite, a defense against anxiety, and a tool of power. (Sontag, 1977)

Portrait photographs have historically been central objects in documenting identity and articulating the self (Jones, 2006; Lury, 2013; Rocamora, 2011). What differentiates the selfie from its pre-digital form is its ubiquity, accessibility and purpose. We can see a shift in the photograph as a cultural object that acts as a marker of memory, to an omnipresent public display of identity (Marwick, 2015 2015b).

Selfies are not consumed as objects of reminiscence, they act instead as objects of identity to be consumed by others; shifting the audience from family and friends to a potentially global network (Schwarz, 2010). Digital cameras, smartphones and social media allow us to share photographs making the selfie a performative social act. Photo sharing platforms such as Instagram, populated by selfies, open up spaces of visibility for using selfies to perform to an audience (Marwick, 2015; Routh, 2015).

Social media has prioritised the image, encouraging users to be conscious of how they present themselves using visual material. This emphasis on the visual aligns with broader debates about contemporary society as increasingly 'image saturated' or 'hyper-real' (Baudrillard, 1994) and there has been a renewed focus on the use of the photograph as a means of self-presentation.

The curation of selfies

There is a growing body of literature that has explored a range of selfie practices. Research has explored the ways in which selfies are used as a way to find a new form of celebrity, what Marwick has defined as 'instafame', in the attention economy (Marwick, 2015). They have been positioned as tools of subversive frivolity in the practices of Instagram influencer culture (Abidin, 2016a). Studies have documented how selfies have been used to make ill health visible (Tembeck, 2016), and to express practices around self-harm (Seko, 2013). They have been studied in the context of sexuality and intimacy (David & Cambre, 2016; Miguel, 2016) and as objects of expression and empowerment in the context of gender representations (Tiidenberg & Gómez Cruz, 2015), breastfeeding (Boon & Pentney, 2015) and body image (Chua & Chang, 2016). They have been conceptualised as a digital exploration of identity (Avgitidou, 2003), as objects of empowerment and, conversely, objects of consumerism, commodification and normative discourses (Gill, 2012; Tiidenberg & Gómez Cruz, 2015). This echoes earlier work on the ambiguous role of photographs as objects of self-expression and identity as well as of control, surveillance and classification (Lury, 2013; Rocamora, 2011).

In understanding selfies as a social act, we also need to understand the ways in which they are performative. Selfies are created and curated to present what Goffman (1959) described as a desirable image. Selfies are self-referential and present an idealised 'image' of the self (Schiano et al., 2002; Sessions, 2009; van Dijck, 2008) that is filtered to enhance and subtract aspects of identity (Savolainen et al., 2022).

Selfies, as images that capture a moment, imply spontaneity and reality. However, the purpose of a selfie is to share. They become part of our social media feeds and they portray and construct our identity in particular ways. Selfies are aimed at an audience and in sharing selfies we are, to use Cooley's term, reflexively understanding the self as it is reflected by the 'generalised other'. Selfies are edited back stage (to draw on Goffman's terminology) and an edited self is placed on the front stage in order to perform the self online (Georgakopoulou, 2016).

The selfie represents an act of agency and identity work as individuals choose how to present themselves and their image. This is in direct contrast with more traditional photography, as Sontag notes:

> In deciding how a picture should look, in preferring one exposure to another, photographers are always imposing standards on their subjects. (Sontag, 1977)

Selfie takers do not have a photographer's standards imposed on them and instead make conscious choices about how to present themselves to the world, engaging in identity 'labour' to do so (Marwick, 2013). The selfie is not accidental, it is approved by the taker then embedded in their social networks (Saltz, 2014). Framing selfies in this way, as an act of making the self visible in participatory digital culture, shifts the narrative of selfies away from narcissism and vanity (Maddox, 2018). As Rettberg argues:

> our fascination with creating digital self-portraits is indicative of our collective coming of age where we as a culture are discovering that we have voices online and can express ourselves rather than simply accepting the mass media's view of the world. (2014: 463)

Rettberg (2014) employs the term filter as an analytical tool that does more than describe the ways in which we might enhance images using the filters provided by photo apps. The concept of a filter helps us to understand how we manage our presentation of self across digital platforms of representation. By filtering we digitally add and remove elements of the image, changing its colour, texture and content. We curate and manage the style of our images as we take them and as we present them (Rettberg, 2014; Savolainen et al., 2022).

When taking selfies we are conscious of the cultural rules and conventions of the genre; the best angles to employ and the most appropriate facial poses and expressions. For example, when we present our selfies we employ filters that blur, wash, brighten, highlight and add hues to our images in conscious and reflexive ways (Marwick, 2015). An array of culture resources and instructables can help us in this representation work and the internet is littered with Instagram filter cheat sheets, filter hacks and selfie apps.

The notion of constructing and carefully managing our identities, as we perform them through selfies, maps on to Goffman's conceptualisation of the idealised performance. We conceal things about us that are incompatible with the idealised version of self that we wish to perform and we minimise, omit or redact images in order to perfect our performance (Baker, S.A. & Walsh, 2018). We purposefully conceal elements of the performance that are incompatible with an idealised version of the self that we wish to present.

Filters and visual effects form part of what Marwick (2015: 144) calls a normative presumption of digital manipulation. Marwick's notion of normative presumptions is worth reflecting on here. Selfies are a relatively new phenomena and shared cultural understandings and expectations of how, when and why selfies should be taken and shared are emergent and mercurial. For example, ideas about where and when it is appropriate to take selfies are shifting and contextual. In 2013, US President Barack Obama, UK Prime Minister David Cameron, and Denmark's Prime Minister Helle Thorning-Schmidt took an impromptu photograph of themselves at the memorial service for the late South African President Nelson Mandela and were widely condemned for being inappropriate. Similarly, a trend for tourists to take selfies at locations such as Auschwitz, Chernobyl and in front of war memorials has resulted in debates about where and what is appropriate. Shifting contexts aside the presumption of manipulation means that we understand that selfies and Instagram images are manipulated in order to present an idealised identity performance.

The normativity and ubiquity of these adjustments are, conversely, highlighted by the hashtags #nofilter, #nomakeupselfie and #celebratetheimperfect. #nofilter images are posted and labelled as 'authentic' and unaltered by virtue of having no filter. Reade (2021) in her study of women's use of Instagram argues that the portrayal of 'authenticity' online involves posting of 'raw' images and text that are governed by norms and understandings of how young women should conduct themselves in a postfeminist, neoliberal and commercial context (2021: 549). These rules of authenticity demand a balance of openness and self-disclosure; inspirational images combined with representations of less desirable aspects of the self. 'Instarealism' celebrates a presentation of the flawed 'real' self:

> Women are revolting. In a small but influential corner of Instagram – the very platform that champions digital enhancement – a deliciously ironic beauty rebellion is taking place. (Pollitt, 2015)

Several high-profile examples of Instarealism have played out in mainstream media. In 2015, Essena O'Neil, an 18-year-old Australian model with over 612,000 followers on Instagram, made international headlines when she quit social media, deleted over 2000 photographs from her Instagram feed and renamed her account 'Social Media Is Not Real Life' (Hunt, 2015). She described Instagram as a space of manipulation, self-promotion and 'contrived perfection made to get attention'. She then recaptioned over 100 photographs to highlight the 'reality' of her Instagram feed highlighting how long it took her to get the photograph, how she had not paid for many of the clothes she was wearing and how the seeming perfection of her life was an illusion.

However, these kinds of accounts and the concept of authenticity as a conscious construction play into demonising narratives about the dangers of social media, or the vanity and narcissism of young women, while the structural inequalities and cultural standards of gender relations and beauty ideals are rendered invisible. As Vivienne argues, 'a proliferation of carefully composed and aesthetically pleasing self-portraits by mostly attractive young white women hardly constitutes social change' (Vivienne, 2017:7).

SELFIES AND SOCIAL INEQUALITIES

Given the identity work done by selfies it is important to reflect on the ways in which they are imbued with well-rehearsed social and cultural baggage. Early internet research demonstrated the myriad ways in which gender representations online tend to reproduce offline stereotypes. The cultural scripts we bring to our online lives mean that rather than playing in a wonderland of imaginative creativity we replicate long-standing and highly traditional gendered identities (O'Brien, 1999; Slater, 1998).

Much of the journalistic coverage of selfies has focused in particular on young women and their apparent narcissism (Murray, 2015). For Burns, these narratives matter as they act as a form of social control that maintains gendered power relations and legitimises normative models of conduct:

> Once the selfie is established as connoting narcissism and vanity, it per-petuates a vicious circle in which women are vain because they take selfies, and selfies connote vanity because women take them. (Burns, 2015:1720)

Döring et al. (2016) in their study comparing gender stereotypes in selfies and in magazine adverts drew on a sample of 500 publicly available Instagram self-ies of men and women. They measured the degree of gender stereotyping in the selfies using categories of gender display (Goffman, 1979; Kang, 1997). The cat-egories focused on feminine touch, the ritualisation of subordination (measured by posture and imbalance), licensed withdrawal (measured by withdrawing gaze and loss of control) and body display. They matched these categories with three social media-related categories (kissing pout, muscle presentation, faceless por-trayal). Their results revealed that male and female Instagram users' selfies not only reflected traditional gender stereotypes but were even more stereotypical than magazine adverts. Here, user-generated content did not lead to a reduction in gendered representations and instead gendered stereotypes were imitated and replicated (Döring et al., 2016).

While user-generated content provides the opportunity to subvert, challenge and play with mainstream representations of masculinity and femininity this study provides an illustration of the structural and cultural barriers that may inhibit digital displays of diverse and non-normative identities. Gendered selfies are a logical consequence of the internalisation of female sexual objectification within a misogynistic, heterosexual, patriarchal culture; 'the male gaze gone viral' (Agger, 2012). Levelling accusations of narcissism and vanity at gendered prac-tices of self-representation fails to acknowledge more complex social and cultural divisions at play. Selfies can be seen as a digital opportunity to carve out cultural space:

> To call it narcissism is to take an individual, psychological approach as opposed to a sociological one which asks: 'What is the culture offering girls and women as a way of visibility?' (Murphy, 2013)

Conceiving of selfies as digital opportunities allows them to be seen as a democra-tising form of self-expression available to the masses. As such, they can be a pow-erful tool for shaping and re-shaping the narratives and images that dominate our mainstream media landscapes. Selfies as a form of visible self-representation can help to reimagine conversations about media, gender and sexuality (Abidin,

2016a; Albury, 2015). Some body-positive feminists and queer theorists argue that selfies can be empowering (Vivienne, 2017), while other forms of feminist resistance such as the hashtag #FeministSelfie enable women and girls to challenge and subvert gendered expectations of beauty and presentation of self (Routh, 2015).

Selfies have been positioned as tools for challenging dominant narratives and representations of gender and ethnicity. The underrepresentation in mainstream media of Black and minority ethnic groups has denied access to self-expression in these media, so selfies provide an important and visible cultural space:

> The reason it is revolutionary and empowering to see selfies of beautiful Black women is because proper representation of people who look like me is nowhere near the point of over saturation...Social media allows for people of color, queer folks, fats, femmes, trans* folks, and differently-abled folks to find proper representation of ourselves sans gatekeepers...The fact that people who are maligned, marginalized, and strategically erased find the courage to make the deliberate choice of seeing themselves as beautiful, is both astonishing and miraculous. (The Feminist Griote, 2013)

To those who have historically been denied self-representation in media, the selfie holds liberatory and democratic potential. This is not the liberatory potential of disembodiment that I outlined at the start of the chapter. This is a liberatory potential that comes from web 2.0 platforms that enable anyone with a network connection to participate in digital culture (something explored in more detail in Chapter 5).

There is a note of caution to sound in this emancipatory narrative around selfies. As Senft and Baym (2015) argue, celebrating *all* selfies as empowering makes as little sense as denigrating them *all* as disempowering and narcissistic:

> it is equally easy to imagine how someone could go from feeling empowered by producing or viewing a particular selfie to feeling socially, politically, or economically disempowered by its circulation. Such disempowerment might occur online in the form of being disciplined for taking selfies wrong; as racist, misogynist, homophobic, racist, ageist, or ableist attacks; as online bullying; or under the guise of a malicious meme that 'borrows' a photo generated for an entirely different audience. It could occur offline, too, as happens when someone finds himself fired at work after being targeted by a revenge porn episode; victimized by doxxing (where personal documentation is hacked and released online); or, worse still, becomes the target of stalking or physical violence. (Senft & Baym, 2015:1598)

Existing debates do not provide us with an adequate conceptual understanding of selfies. We can start to understand them as a complex and often contradictory form of visual identity work. Selfies are not simply about the self, they are produced and consumed in the context of cultural filters that shape, in highly systematic ways, how we see and enact subjectivity and visibility (Grindstaff & Torres Valencia, 2021).

The selfie creates and constructs personal narratives and provides a cultural context that helps us with the construction of our identities. But selfies also highlight tensions between compliance and resistance in identity performances (Savolainen et al., 2022) and power relations and inequalities in visibility and representation 'in the context of the new gaze economy of digital culture' (Grindstaff & Torres Valencia, 2021).

FRAMES AND IDENTITY PLAY

Returning to Goffman may help us to understand the presentation of self online in this visual medium. The idea of front and back regions first introduced in *The presentation of self in everyday life* (1959) were elaborated on by Goffman in his later work Frame analysis (1974). Goffman's terminology changes from stages to frames and he argued that, like stages, frames make social interaction meaningful. Frameworks define and allow participants to interpret human interaction and understand social situations. Frames provide us with culturally determined definitions of reality that enable us to make sense of objects and events and to navigate our social world. What Goffman is suggesting is that people use guiding frames of reference in order to classify their experiences.

In describing frames Goffman goes beyond simply front- and back-stage areas and argues that we have a continuum of formality. In very formal situations, like a wedding, funeral or job interview, the frame is consciously and deliberately structured by the participants for a certain effect. The more formal a situation the more the performer(s) will try to hide the process of performance. In contrast, in more informal performances the roles can be more relaxed to allow for more collusion between participants. This might seem like a rather odd theoretical interlude, but while frame analysis has primarily been applied to social movement studies, policy studies and communication studies in order to explain social processes, it is of value here in understanding contemporary online identity play.

In his discussion of frameworks, Goffman introduced the notion of benign and exploitative fabrication. Benign fabrication is organised for the benefit of those it deceives, which Goffman suggests is often thought to be morally justifiable. Exploitative fabrication is organised for the benefit of the fabricator alone.

Goffman argues that exploitative deceit is actually very difficult to perform, in part because of the cognitive strain of managing multiple layers of identity work. In contrast, with benign fabrication we participate in performances where we are willingly 'transformed into collaborators in unreality', these are 'voluntarily supported benign fabrication(s)' (Goffman, 1974: 136). For Goffman, this benign fabrication represents an involvement and engagement in a frame or experience with an understanding that it isn't necessarily 'real' (Rettie, 2004). Participants collaborate in finding a way to frame their understanding of an experience in a way that enables them to participate in meaningful ways.

I introduce this very simplified notion of frames here to point to the way in which they might help us to understand online identity as part of wider social and cultural narratives around online performances of the self. We share a cultural knowledge that selfies and our presentation of self on social media is not 'real' or 'authentic' and we collaborate in a frame that supports our online identity work. This enables us to participate in this identity work while acknowledging the artifice. The next section of this chapter will illustrate this using the example of Fakebooking and Finsta accounts.

Fakebooking

In 2013, Dutch student Zilla van den Born used Facebook to document her five-week trip around South East Asia. In reality she had never left her home city of Amsterdam. Using photoshopped images she documented her 'travels', posting pictures of herself eating exotic food in Asian restaurants, visiting Buddhist temples and snorkeling in turquoise water. After being waved off by family at the airport she returned home and spent 42 days manipulating images and posting them to her Facebook timeline. She went to extraordinary lengths to perpetuate the illusion, which was fed to her friends and family who she skyped from her bedroom, decorated to look like a Thai hotel room:

> I did this to show people that we filter and manipulate what we show on social media – we create an ideal world online which reality can no longer meet. (Hooton, 2014)

Much like the Instarealism accounts discussed earlier in the chapter, the practice of Fakebooking represents another form of identity curation. The airbrushed version of life that is presented through our social media fields can be conceptualised as a benign fabrication. We know that the life stream, as presented on social media platforms, is curated and we understand that they are not 'reality' but a series of snapshots and fragments. While van den Born was using the practice to highlight the hyper-curation of our identity profiles and social media feeds, the practice of editing and de-tagging pictures, changing 'check-ins' and sharing links create 'small stories' (Georgakopoulou, 2016) that combine to form a mediated presentation of self.

Multiple identities, Instagram and Finsta accounts

We perform our identities online across multiple platforms and to multiple audiences. This is a complex set of social tasks. This section of the chapter looks at Finsta accounts (a portmanteau of the words 'fake' and 'Instagram') as an example of identity work that seeks to manage these demands. Before considering Finsta accounts, the next section of the chapter links with the previous section on selfies to position Instagram as the digital home of the selfie.

Instagram

Launched in 2010, Instagram is a social networking app that enables its users to share photos and videos from mobile devices. Uploaded images can be edited using a range of filters and can be curated and organised by using tags and location information. Posted images appear on users' news feed and can be viewed by their followers. A user can decide who will see a post by either sharing publicly or defining pre-approved followers. The app has a direct friendship model (Baker & Walsh, 2018), meaning that users choose who to follow and gain their own followers without an expectation of reciprocity.

Instagram has grown rapidly since launching; as of February 2023 it has around 1.3 billion monthly active users with more than 50 billion images shared (Datareportal, 2023). Instagram is characterised by images of idealised and highly curated identity performances. As with the curation and construction of selfies more generally, Instagram users may spend considerable time editing their photos and coming up with captions for their images and stories.

As this chapter has outlined, digital spaces allow for different gradations in editing and presenting the self (Bullingham & Vasconcelos, 2013). One of the ways in which we participate in these gradations and editing is by running multiple, simultaneous accounts each performing a different aspect of the self. Choosing to host multiple accounts across social media platforms demonstrates an intentional decision to show different, sometimes contradictory, aspects of the self to selected audiences. What Goffman would define as a benign fabrication that shares an understanding of a frame or experience that isn't necessarily 'authentic'.

Van Dijck (2013b) argues that users have a need for multiple 'stories' about themselves across different social networks and will do different identity work across these networks. For example, I use Facebook to connect with close family and friends, I am aware of who my audience is and perform an informal presentation of self. Facebook serves the purpose of a personal self-presentation. On X I follow and have followers who are entirely unknown to me in a personal capacity and I use the platform in a more professional context with a corresponding professional presentation of self. I use Instagram to share images that sit somewhere in-between my known and unknown audiences on Facebook and X.

Each construction of self entails a strategy aimed at performing a social act or achieving a particular social goal (Van House, 2009). These performances are structured, or framed to use Goffman's terminology, by the digital architecture of each platform.

In their discussion of bloggers who host multiple blog accounts, Bullingham and Vasconcelos argue that the purpose of multiple accounts is to allow the creation of different personas to suit each blog. This ensures that the content of the blog does not compromise what they define as the offline identity or the primary online identity of the blogger (Bullingham & Vasconcelos, 2013). The primary account performs to what boyd describes as the 'super public' (2006); the audience that you do not know, while secondary accounts are often restricted to private and carefully selected audiences. This means that individuals can post an 'unedited self' in a secondary account without the fear of losing face on their main account. The secondary accounts enable a form of identity management that is highly conscious and selective of its audience.

Many Instagram users have a second private account – a Finsta (as opposed to their real Instagram account or Rinsta) to share content that they know won't be judged in the same way as their primary account. A Rinsta account may host the more curated, quixotic, filtered and performative images (Darr et al., 2022) while the visual narrative of the Finsta is candid images or intentionally unattractive presentations of self. These posts are viewed as more authentic and 'true' (Kang & Wei, 2020; Taber & Whittaker, 2020).

A Finsta account enables the user to have a more personalised and private account and to avoid the scrutiny of unknown or unwanted audiences. Finsta accounts have fewer more select audiences with each account representing a segment of the self that an individual wants to perform to a specific audience depending on their relationship to them. With each account comes a different audience, and therefore with each account comes an adjusted version of the self.

By operating multiple accounts, Instagram users are actively working to define how their online self is perceived. Each account represents a different audience and a different identity performance. Users then adjust their performances according to context in the same way that Goffman argues we adjust our performances in face-to-face interaction, conscious of our setting and our audience.

This is not the decentred identity play that Turkle describes but it does speak to her notion of identity fragmentation. The need for a multiple, composite self has increased with the advent of public communication moving to an online space (van Dijck, 2013b).

Media coverage of Finstas has echoes of the rhetoric surrounding selfies. Rather than narcissism and self-obsession, the narratives accompanying Finstas resemble a moral panic (Cohen, 1972) focused on young people's digital media practices. Tales of secrecy and deviance dominate media coverage that describe Finstas being used for 'scandalous and overtly sexual behaviour' (Patterson, 2016) or to deceive prying parents who view their child's Rinsta without realising they are not privy to the private, 'more honest' Finsta account (Williams, 2016).

A more realistic analysis would be to consider Rinstas and Finstas as simply another way in which we use social media as a communicative tool in our interactions and as part of our identity project.

The phenomena of maintaining accounts across a range of social media platforms for different identity work has been well documented (van Dijck, 2013b). By presenting different aspects of the self on different platforms users can present multiple stories or versions of the self. Each story relates to a different part of their identity and can address a different audience.

In part, this speaks to issues of authenticity outlined earlier in the chapter in discussions of Fakebooking and Instarealism. Research has shown that young people in particular value authenticity and a congruence between social media presentations of self and offline identities (Darr et al., 2022). This, in turn, relates to having to juggle a desire to be authentic online with the uncomfortable reality that we may not want to be authentic with all of the audiences (friends, families, colleagues and strangers) that see our online performances. Rinsta and Finsta accounts help young people navigate some of these complexities in balancing self-presentation and authenticity (Huang & Vitak, 2022).

Rinsta accounts are used for what is recognised as the stereotypical and expected social media activity of showing the 'best bits' of life and receiving external validation for images of major life events or for sanitised, filtered and enhanced images (Darr et al., 2022; Huang & Vitak, 2022) In contrast, Finsta accounts are used for less polished performances of the self (Kang & Wei, 2020). Without pressure for perfection they are perceived to be less artificial and calculated (Huang & Vitak, 2022).

There are obvious parallels here with Goffman's front- and back-stage performances and having two distinct spaces for self-presentation enables both real and authentic performances to trusted friends as well as a presentation of self to wider audiences.

In providing these distinct spaces Finstas and Rinstas can enable self-validation and self-expression critical to the social development of young people, in particular for those from historically marginalised populations (Williams, 2022). Williams, in her study of adolescent Black females' use of social media, highlights the influence Instagram has on the identity expression of Black adolescent girls. She argues that Rinsta accounts are used to present a confident performance oriented around appearance, while Finstas revealed a more vulnerable and private expression of identity as a personal space for documenting thoughts, feelings and experiences. Williams argues that Finsta accounts provide an important outlet for expressions of racial and gendered pride while also acting as an outlet for uncensored adolescent expression. This helps mitigate against the harmful effects of more Rinsta social media usage oriented around mainstream constructions of beauty and perfection:

> Through Instagram, Black female teens are able to find the value of forming an opinion and the power of sharing it with others...In using Instagram as a space in which to express and shape who they are, these participants demonstrated a conscious control and intentional ownership of their online space. (Williams, 2022: 96)

Carving out more intimate online spaces accessible only to chosen audiences is conceptualised as an *intimate reconfiguration* of social media (Xiao et al., 2020). In this reconfiguration Finstas become spaces of content considered not worthy or suitable for the aesthetic of a Rinsta; a place for taboo, stigmatised or risqué content that is 'not safe for work' (NSFW) and a way to be vulnerable in expressing uncomfortable and difficult emotions (Xiao et al., 2020). Darr et al. (2022) describe these practices as 'spilling T' (expressing strong honest opinions) and 'shit posting' (sharing content that is unimportant and unsuitable for Rinsta). Finsta accounts form active resistance to the norms of the mainstream Instagram environment which are viewed as inauthentic and form a space in which authenticity can be validated and acknowledged by friends (Darr et al., 2022; Kang & Wei, 2020).

The way in which we use these tools is fluid and emergent. To return to the earlier discussion of Rinsta and Finsta accounts, the work of Tao and Ellison (2023) highlights how content sharing practices change over time as teenagers become young adults. Their research suggests that online behaviours mirror our development, shifting as we mature and transition through life stages and shifting contexts (Tao & Ellison, 2023).

They illustrate this by drawing on the '#casual Instagram' trend which invited posts that are not curated and advocated posting without reflection on how a post would be received. The trend emerged from the TikTok community, favouring an aesthetic of the more prosaic aspects of everyday life rather than the inauthentic Instagram norm (Haimson, 2016). In part, this shift was in response to the global pandemic and lockdowns, stuck inside we had little to post about beyond the mundane and everyday, so the sharing of more quotidian activities moved from Rinsta to Finsta. However, the trend also reflects the ever-emergent norms that flow across social media platforms.

What Tao and Ellison's work highlights is the limitations of Goffman's analogy in its application to Finsta and Rinsta accounts. Even pandemic lockdown 'casual images' are a carefully curated and constructed aesthetic that just happen to look relaxed and unpretentious. What Tao and Ellison argue is that in both kinds of accounts self-presentation is intentional and strategic. Rather than thinking of front and back stage perhaps it is more useful to think of multiple accounts on a single platform enabling users to 'partition' audiences (Haimson et al., 2016).

It is not simply that Rinsta accounts are for engaging with large audiences to receive positive affirmation for highly curated self-presentations. Nor that Finsta accounts are simply spaces where more authentic, problematic and less desirable selves can be revealed to highly curated subsets of larger networks. Instead, we need to think about the liminal spaces between the two and the shifting ways in which we employ these as self-presentation tools (Tao & Ellison, 2023).

SOCIAL SURVEILLANCE

The way in which we conceive of our audience(s) is of key importance here. Marwick uses the term social surveillance in suggesting that our social media presence is characterised by watching and an awareness of being watched (Marwick, 2012).

Marwick argues that while the role of technologies in surveillance has been well documented at a macro level, we also need to reflect on the ways in which social surveillance has created a set of practices through which surveillance of and between individuals is digitised and normalised through social media (Marwick, 2012). This form of surveillance has been conceptualised as a collapse of context for social media users who rely on an imagined audience to manage their interactions with invisible, heterogeneous and potentially large populations (Litt and Hargittai, 2016). For Marwick (2012), this is a domestication of surveillance practice that has a power that exists in mundane day-to-day interactions, that flows through social relationships and that takes place between individuals.

The presentation of self on social media platforms faces the challenge of this merged audience of family, friends, colleagues and acquaintances from various contexts of our lives (Marwick & boyd, 2011; Papacharissi, 2010; Pearson, 2009). This can challenge the front- and back-stage areas of our identity performances and, as Papacharissi suggests:

The individual must then engage in multiple mini performances that combine a variety of semiological references so as to produce a presentation of the self that makes sense to multiple audiences, without sacrificing coherence and continuity. (2010: 307)

As symbolic interactionist work has shown, this kind of multiple performance across many stages is not uniquely digital. We are engaged in performances as we move through our daily routines. We perform our identities at home and at work, with friends and strangers, face to face and on the phone. In contemporary society these performances are also now digitally mediated, so it makes sense that our identity work takes place in and through social media. As van Dijck argues:

social media are not neutral stages of self-performance – they are the very tools for shaping identities. (van Dijck, 2013a)

RESEARCHING THE VISUAL ONLINE

Earlier in this chapter, I noted the shift from text-based interaction online to the very visual and embodied internet we understand today. Social media is rich with visuals and GIFs, and selfies, emojis and memes populate a growing number of platforms and apps explicitly framed around images. Social media images visualise culture and act as tools of digital participation, they help us to communicate and share online, to perform identity and to participate in our digital landscapes in playful or disruptive ways (Massanari, 2013; Nissenbaum & Shifman, 2017; Shifman, 2013). The proliferation and ubiquity of networked images has created a profoundly visual social media (Leaver et al., 2020; McCrow-Young, 2021).

This chapter used the example of selfies as a social tool of identity and communication. The complexities of selfies as a social phenomenon are mirrored by the methodological challenges faced by researchers who want to study the visual in digital contexts. The visuality in social media demands methodological negotiation and reflection, yet there has been a lack of attention paid to the methods we might use to track, analyse and understand social media as image-based intertextual spaces (Highfield & Leaver, 2016).

One early project employing computational and data visualisation methods to analyse large numbers of Instagram images was the project *Selfiecity* from Tifentale and Manovich (2015) and the Software Studies Initiative lab. Their project assembled a dataset of 656,000 selfies taken in New York, Bangkok, Moscow, Sao Paolo and Berlin during a one-week period in December 2013. The final sample included 3200 photos, identified by Mechanical Turks and the researchers as true single person selfies. Using face analysis software these images were compared, measuring facial characteristics between cities, genders and ages. The project visualised the data in a number of ways including video montages of selfies from each city, graph-like image plots composed of individual photos, an interactive visualisation app as well as more conventional statistical and comparative summaries of the data (Tifentale & Manovich, 2015). The project emphasised the complexities of selfies as both shared digital images and as a social phenomenon serving multiple functions. Importantly, the project also pointed to the methodological challenges we face in understanding them:

> New image-making and image-sharing technologies demand radically new ways of interpretation and analysis in what we might think of as a post-digital age, and Selfiecity is an attempt to explore and map these new representational forms. (Tifentale & Manovich, 2015:120)

One of the reasons that studying social media images is so methodologically challenging is that while they represent and visualise social practices, their meanings and the ways in which they are generated and disseminated are complex. Images online take many different forms and the analysis of digital images must recognise and take into account their specific qualities. Rose (2016) suggests four key sites where the meanings of digital images are made, each with their own technical, compositional and social modalities: 1) *the site of production*, relating to how the image is made, the technologies involved, the genres invoked and the socio-economic conditions under which it was produced; 2) *the site of the image*, referring to the meaning composition and affective experiencing of the image; 3) *the site of the image circulation*, referring to how images move and circulate, how this might change the meaning of an image and the technical, social, political and economic conditions that shape that movement; and 4) *the site of the audience*, referring to the social identities of those watching and consuming images and how audiences may shape and develop the meanings of these images.

Defining the visual

A key issue here, aside from the sheer volume and scope of images online, is that the ways in which digital images are distributed and circulated mean that traditional models of visual analysis and comparisons with the sampling and analysis of print images may not apply (Hand, 2017). What Rose highlights is the ways in which digital images are multi-sited, multimodal, intertextual, often transient and embedded in a range of digital networks and contexts that shape how we can understand and explore them. So, for example, in order to understand a selfie posted on Instagram a researcher would seek to analyse its production, site, circulation and audience but also the textual contexts and classifications of the image.

Researchers therefore face the challenge of defining what a visual object in social media is. Social media sites are assemblages of users, algorithms, and data requiring us to think carefully about the empirical object of research and to understand the inherent bias that comes with embedded algorithms and the snapshots of data and content that social media provide us with (Marres, 2017; Pearce et al., 2020). In this sense we need to be attentive to what Rogers defines as a distinction between 'medium research', the study of a platform's structure and affordances and the data we can access from the API and 'social research', the stories that can be told about a phenomena outside of these platform effects (Pearce et al., 2020; Rogers, 2017).

A further distinction can also be made between approaches that view images in 'realist' or 'constructionist' terms, each constructing different ontologies of the image (Hand, 2017). A realist understanding of images approaches them as representative evidence of the social world they portray, with the content of an image corresponding to what it represents. Conversely, constructivist approaches point to images as partial constructions of the social world. This positions the images as a research object in different ways for the social researcher:

> These approaches construct different ontologies of the image: on the one hand, the image is an evidential document of something else (communities, identities, events), where on the other hand, the image is more like an inter-textual site of discursive relationships. (Hand, 2017: 220)

This dichotomy of realist/constructionist conceptualisations of images has important implications for how we structure research questions and for the methodological tools we seek to answer these questions.

Sampling images

Selfiecity provided an example of a large-scale project employing multiple researchers and analysing tens of thousands of images through automatic and manual methods. In image-rich social media environments how can smaller scale projects conceptualise sampling as a process? The question of sampling is not a problem faced solely by those studying social media images and negotiating complex issues of representativeness, authenticity and exhaustiveness are enduring concerns (Hand, 2017). However, the sheer quantity of images online across a range of platforms can be overwhelming.

One solution is to constrain a sample to a particular timeframe or location. Hand (2017) uses the example of studying visual representations of race across social media platforms during particular events like protests or following instances of racially motivated violence. In this exemplar we might employ the use of a platform's own classification system – for example X hashtags. This could also result in thousands of images, however, and researchers need to have a clear sense of the appropriate and relevant hashtags that are being employed at a particular time in relation to certain events. Researchers would need to identify the 'right' hashtag, which may be the hashtag that is trending or that is most popular, but they also need to be sensitive to the ways in which hashtags may change, adapt and be embraced and resisted over time, in different contexts and across different platforms.

Each decision will result in different content, a different sample and different data. This data will also be shaped in ways that may not always be visible or obvious as the algorithmic processing and ordering of images will shape how we can understand the meaning and contexts of our data (Hand, 2017):

> To study social media is not just to study users and networks, content, information, and interactions: it is to study the platforms and their contexts, their affordances and changes, including with relation to other social media platforms. (Highfield & Leaver, 2016:51)

As such, the study of digital images is both medium research and social research as we explore how platforms shape and develop their own norms and practices (Rogers, 2021). Citing the example of images associated with #climatechange on Instagram and X, Rogers suggests that the study of the visual gives us insight into how an issue is being framed or presented as well as highlighting different platform vernaculars:

> When sorted by popular posts tagged with #climatechange, Instagram may portray more individual 'small actions' ('teens plant trees'), whereas Twitter may have more of the charts and figures of science, or the memes of politicians (French Premier Macron's 'Make our planet great again'). Depending on the platform used to access the issue, the question of who acts, and how it is visually displayed, is answered differently. (Rogers, 2021:6)

The concept of a platform vernacular refers to the emergent norms, cultures and structures that establish practices and shared meanings as people participate across social media genres and in specific online contexts and points to the need to consider the interplay between the medium and the social in our research design.

Scraping and the use of APIs

One methodological approach is to scrape image data. Scraping is a technique for the automated collection of online data using code to capture and download targeted data from the web (Marres & Weltevrede, 2013). The potential of scraping has been subject to something of a methodological hype in the context of debates about the computation turn towards big data in the social sciences. This has been accompanied by concerns over privacy and ethics in the aftermath of the Cambridge Analytica scandal (Giorgi, 2022). Outside of these debates, Marres and Weltevrede (2013) emphasise the methodological value of scraping as a practical tool of digital research. Scraping allows the organisation of ephemeral content for cultural analysis offering 'a rich picture of this type of content as a social and cultural entity' (Bainotti et al., 2021a).

A primary tool for harvesting this 'big data' is the use of APIs. An API (Application Programming Interface) provides direct access to a platforms back-end structure. Back-end structures are where platforms store and organise data and some platforms make this data available through their APIs (Pearce et al., 2020). Researchers can use software scripts to access the API and automate the retrieval, storage and manipulation of digital data left by the users of a service (Lomborg & Bechmann, 2014). Importantly, as a back-end application the use of APIs enables researchers to access data that is not public or that would usually require a login and password.

While APIs make data more publicly available an important caveat to note is that they are not fully open and do not provide access to the full databases of social media platforms. The commercial value of social media data means that access to data is highly controlled and regulated and most of the major social networking sites are making it increasingly difficult for researchers to access. For example, in 2020 Instagram permanently disabled access to its API, a positive step for users' privacy but a challenge for social researchers who must deal with changing platform policies and emergent and shifting ethics around user privacy (McCrow-Young, 2021).

McCrow Young argues that the changing nature of what platforms like Instagram allow researchers and third-party scrapers to access means that a creative approach combining manual and automated data collection is often required. In her work on Instagram and responses to the Manchester Arena attack in 2017, she proposes what she defines as connective visual mapping. Connective visual mapping is a methodology that uses a number of digital tools to collate and analyse visual data taking into account the 'nuanced and dynamic site of the networked image and its environment' (McCrow-Young, 2021). She maps macro data (hashtag and account tag data) to gain an understanding of platform vernaculars and combines this with an analysis of micro data in the form of close examination of indivdual images:

> The processes of accessing, archiving, and anonymising Instagram data in this study highlight the fluid nature of commercial social media platforms and the challenges of dealing with Instagram posts as units of analysis. Rapidly changing – and predominantly commercial – digital environments require the use of new and often unconventional tools...which inevitably carry risks as they lack decades of academic scrutiny and refinement. (McCrow-Young, 2021:31)

The work of McCrow-Young highlights the need for researchers to be adaptable and reflexive as we navigate commercial tools, platforms and gatekeepers as part of the research process. Use of APIs as a methodological tool have limitations in scope; for example, the data collected from APIs has an in-built bias toward those types of users that are the most 'active' content contributors. This may hide or render invisible other types of participant, activity and data (Lomborg & Bechmann, 2014).

Equally, while a large volume of data can be collected and can give us a good idea of *what* people are doing online this data is less able to provide us with answers about *why* people behave in certain ways or about the meanings users ascribe to their use. Using APIs as research tools therefore shapes the kinds of research questions we can ask and answer and may need to be complemented with other methods in order to provide a richer, more contextualised understanding of social media use (Lomborg & Bechmann, 2014).

Ephemerality, ethics and the visual

One challenge posed by social media images is their ephemerality. Increasingly, social media platforms enable participants to share content that disappears after a specific period. For example, Snapchat content is shared with specific people or groups, rather than being public by default, before becoming inaccessible to recipients. Similarly, Instagram stories is an in-app feature that allows users to post videos and photos that automatically disappear after 24 hours. While beneficial for users' privacy this ephemerality has methodological implications. There is the possibility to archive and store ephemeral images by using tools to capture, scrape or archive. For example, the Instagram Scraper developed by the Digital Methods Initiative at the University of Amsterdam retrieves Instagram images for specified hashtags, locations or usernames. However, the logic of Instagram stories or snapchats as fleeting digital moments is challenging from a methodological perspective demanding new approaches to accessing and analysing these kinds of images.

In particular, the shifting temporalities of epehmeral images pose ethical questions about how (or indeed if) an image intended to be 'of a moment' should be archived for study (Highfield & Leaver, 2016). Settings and practices, policies and social and cultural norms around privacy are emergent and mercurial with definitions of what can be considered public or private online in contested flux. These ethical questions have rather blurry boundaries and vary across research settings and contexts. Social media users may post images to a particular hashtag or group without an expectation that it will be viewed by a much larger audience. Although posted publicly users may not have intended for their images to be stored or disseminated widely.

The act of highlighting these groups through research may amplifly visibility in unanticipated or problematic ways. For example, Leaver and Highfield (2016) in their study of #ultrasound selfies on Instagram noted significant privacy issues where users were sharing, on publicly accessible accounts, personally identifiable metadata about the person being scanned and their foetus. While an argument coud be made that images published to public websites are ethically available to research, the lack of explicit informed consent is problematic. There are no easy answers to these questions and a sensitivity to the ethical implications of methodological choices when using digital images is necessary (Rose, 2016).

Analysing digital images

Given the discussion so far about medium and social research (Rogers, 2017), we might choose to analyse social media images in the contexts of the broader discourses and sign systems of which they are a part (Hand, 2017; Rose, 2016). Semiology, content analysis and discourse analysis enable us to explore and decode the ways in which images are constructed and circulated in particular social contexts and wider societal discourses. For example, earlier in the chapter I noted the work of Döring et al. (2016) whose study comparing gender stereotypes in selfies and in magazine adverts drew on a sample of 500 publicly available Instagram selfies of men and women. Their content analysis of posts found that gender stereotypes observed in mass media were imitated or even exaggerated by young people in their selfies on Instagram suggesting that the ubiquity of gendered selfies may be a logical consequence of societal inequalities and structures.

Similarly, work on 'Fitspiration', a term used on social media to describe fitness inspiration content designed to motivate people to exercise and pursue a healthier lifestyle, has emphasised the potentially objectifying messages of fitspiration in relation to body image (Tiggemann & Zaccardo, 2018). In studies of social media as a source of information about health behaviour norms, work by Carrotte et al. (2017) and Tiggemann and Zaccardo (2018) employed content analysis to study public hashtags across social media platforms.

Carrotte et al. (2017) used three randomly generated timeslots and searched for the tag #fitspo across Instagram, Tumblr, Facebook and X. Tiggemann and

Zaccardo (2018) sampled images by selecting the first 600 images returned from a search of the hashtag 'fitspiration'. Using these different sampling strategies both argue that the highly visual nature and mobile formats of social media produce highly gendered body images. These images might be analysed in the context of broader discourses of the 'disciplined' female body and symbolic representations of a very limited body type (Carrotte et al., 2017; Hand, 2017; Tiggemann & Zaccardo, 2018).

As well as providing examples of ways in which we might sample social media images these studies return us to the realist/constructionist dichotomy outlined in the earlier section *defining the visual*. Social media images are analysed as constructions that symbolise or represent gender stereotypes and body ideals and are understood as 'inter-textual sites of discursive relationships' (Hand, 2017: 220).

While debates about realism and constructivism are beyond the scope of this methodological reflection, it is important to note that for researchers of social media images, the mobility, transience and temporality of the visual forces us to contextualise an image in the wider socio-digital landscapes of its creation and circulation. In other words, we need to think carefully about how our methodological approaches to the study of the visual online take account of the interplays of platform affordances, shared cultural vernaculars and fluid inter-textual meanings that differ from photographic, film or print images:

> Social media researchers have to think about what specific images 'do' socially over time and space and how this might be accessed and assessed given the multiplying audiences. In addition, the dynamics of social media are such that the question of 'what people do' with images becomes paramount to understanding compositional and interpretive issues. In other words, the 'meaning' and 'doing' aspect of images being researched will partly be an outcome of everyday practices and cannot be assumed by appealing to the history of a prior medium. (Hand, 2017: 220)

Understanding digital images then involves widening out our definition of the digital to incorporate the material and physical spaces and interactions in which digital images flow while acknowledging the practices in which they are embedded.

The methodological opportunity here is that the study of visual images is accessible via a range of methods that can be employed to explore and understand social media images, their intertextuality and their socio-technical construction: from large-scale, quantitative analysis of particular content forms to interviews and observations of individual users or communities of interest (Highfield & Leaver, 2016). The challenge is in trying to understand the diversity of images and the multi-modal meanings that they might articulate as they are produced, circulated and viewed.

CONCLUSION

The concepts of self and identity are central to sociology and have been an enduring and contested focus of sociological concern continuing with more contemporary debates around how self and identity are digitally articulated. Key ideas in this chapter can be summarised as followed:

- Symbolic interactionalism provides us with a starting point for understanding self and identity as profoundly social. Goffman's dramaturgical analogy presents the idea of an identity performance and digital spaces have provided new spaces for these performances.
- Early debates about online identity were grounded in how we write ourselves online in text-based digital environments. Here, the impact of disembodiment and online deception and anonymity were highlighted with research focused on identity play and the suspension of fixed, rigid and visible markers of identity online.
- Later conceptualisations of online identity emphasised the continuity of online and offline performances of self and challenged the dichotomy of online/offline as separate and distinct spaces of identity construction and performance.
- Social media has created a visual medium affording us new spaces to perform our identities and present a narrativisation of self and experience, shared globally with friends and strangers. Social media is a space for identity performances; we use them as communicative tools in our interactions and identity work.
- One form of self-presentation, the selfie, has become a cultural form and an object of identity that we curate and present as a social act shared with a generalised other. Selfies are imbued with social and cultural baggage and act as objects of both social and cultural conformity and subversion and resistance.
- Our social media presence is characterised by watching and an awareness of being watched that normalises digital interpersonal social surveillance.
- Digital images are a medium and a tool for social research as we explore how platforms shape and develop their own norms and practices.

_____ — **Further reading** —————

Bailey, M. (2021). *Misogynoir transformed*. New York University Press.

This chapter argued that the identity work in selfies is imbued with cultural baggage, challenging the liberatory potential of online spaces of representation with long-standing social inequalities. In this book, Bailey introduces the term *misogynoir* to define anti-Black and misogynistic representations of Black women in digital spaces. Through ethnographically rich and diverse case studies she traces the ways in which Black women have used social media platforms to confront misogynoir.

Hogan, B. (2010). The presentation of self in the age of social media: Distinguishing performances and exhibitions online. *Bulletin of Science, Technology and Society*, *30*(6), pp. 377–386.

In this article, Hogan articulates the ways in which Goffman's presentation of self provides a lens through which we can understand differences in meaning and activity of online participation. Importantly, Hogan distinguishes between performances as subject to continual observation, and exhibitions as subject to selective contributions and third-party curators. In doing so he extends the presentation of self analogy, incorporating an exhibitional approach alongside the concept of dramaturgy, taking into account the affordances of social media platforms.

Leaver, T., Highfield, T., & Abidin, C. (2020). *Instagram: Visual social media cultures*. John Wiley and Sons.

This chapter argued that Instagram has become synonymous with selfies and self-representation. For students interested in Instagram this book is a great introduction to how to understand and study visual social media, exploring Instagram as a platform and a culture. The authors argue that Instagram is a conduit for communication and the book offers a history of Instagram as a platform as well as an exploration, through a range of examples and case studies, of its cultural impact.

Abidin, C. (2016). 'Aren't these just young, rich women doing vain things online?': Influencer selfies as subversive frivolity. *Social media+ society*, *2*(2), p. 2056305116641342.

In this article, Abidin takes seriously the phenomena of selfies, challenging discourse that selfies are merely frivolous acts. Focusing on influencers the author examines, through ethnographic research, how they shape the social media ecology through their gendered labour, reappropriating the selfie as an act of subversive self-branding and self-actualisation.

Janetzko, D. (2017). The role of APIs in data sampling from social media. *The Sage Handbook of Social Media Research Methods*, pp. 146–160.

The *Sage Handbook of Social Media Research Methods* is an excellent resource for any student looking to engage with social media research and to understand the breadth of methodologies covered by this term. This chapter is intended as a brief overview of some of the issues around social media data and for a more detailed discussion of APIs in social media this chapter by Janetzko is a good starting point. In it he provides an accessible overview of APIs as well as raising critical questions about the completeness of data drawn through public APIs.

NOTE

1. http://www.loc.gov/pictures/item/2004664436/

4
DIGITALLY MEDIATED RELATIONSHIPS

The previous chapter focused on how sociology can understand digital performances of self and identity. The chapter concluded with the concept of social surveillance; a set of practices through which surveillance of and between individuals is digitised and normalised through social media (Marwick, 2012). Having established that digital technologies have the potential to shape how we understand ourselves and our identities as part of social networks, this chapter looks in more detail at how we manage these audiences. In other words, how are our interpersonal relationships mediated through digital spaces and interactions?

Digital technologies provide us with unprecedented connectivity to our friends and acquaintances. The ways in which digital technologies are influencing relationship dynamics has, unsurprisingly, been the focus of ongoing academic and popular debate and a large body of research has painted a rich picture of how they are shaping contemporary cultures. We use digital technologies to strengthen and maintain existing relationships as well as to extend our social networks beyond our geographic location. As we saw in Chapter 3, the last decade has seen social media sites become a ubiquitous part of our personal lives. This digital sociality has resulted in new ways of understanding and articulating identity but has also contributed to new ways of understanding, experiencing and, importantly, displaying friendship and intimacy.

In this chapter, we move from discussions of community and identity to think about new kinds of intimacy. This chapter focuses on interpersonal relationships exploring the ways in which our social media practices have created an intimate public sphere in which we want and need to be continuously connected; a culture of connectivity in which we increasingly feel dependent on our devices and apps (Miguel, 2018; van Dijck, 2013).

As you read this chapter, I encourage you to think about the following questions:

- How do digital technologies shape how we manage our social relationships?
- How have social media technologies been domesticated?
- What do we mean by mediated intimacy?
- How does the digital connect us?
- What new kinds of digitally mediated social relationships and connections can we identify?

A CONTINUITY OF CONCERNS

The idea that technologies can help us to form and maintain relationships has a long history. This history has been accompanied by enduring concerns about their potentially detrimental effects on our interpersonal relationships. For example, in his social history of the electric telegraph, Standage (1998) argues that we can identify many affinities between the development of the telegraph and the development of the internet. Both impacted the ways in which we can connect and communicate and both were accompanied by concerns about their potentially deleterious consequences. Standage describes the relationships and romances that blossomed over telegraph communications and highlights the scepticism and concern with which these new relationships with 'strangers' were met by friends and family.

It isn't hard to see parallel concerns around digitally mediated relationships online. Indeed, there has been a pervasive tendency to see digital connectivity as something detrimental to the quality of human relationships. Narratives about digital technologies and their impact on interpersonal relationships express concerns that real and meaningful relationships (i.e., relationships sustained through face-to-face communication) are being replaced with virtual and superficial ones (i.e., relationships sustained through digitally mediated communication). Ironically, the internet is littered with advice and sensational warnings about replacing real-life intimacy with online interaction; for example: *9 reasons technology has ruined relationships, friendships and your life* (Mullins, 2014), *How social media is taking away from your your friendships* (Chesak, 2021), *6 ways social media is ruining our friendships* (Williams, 2015), *7 ways technology is killing your relationships* (Kahn, 2015). These kinds of click-bait and sensationalist warnings ignore the social histories of communication technologies that evidence their role in supporting and maintaining pre-existing social relationships; for example, Fischer's (2011) work on the telephone shows we tend to use this technology to call people we already know. Similarly, our online interactions largely solidify and reinforce our existing social relations and networks. Rather than dichotomising, valorising or demonising 'online' vs 'offline' connections it is perhaps more useful to emphasise the interconnected nature of digital and face-to-face relationships (Raghunandan, 2018).

From strangers to friends

As we saw in Chapter 3, early literature around computer-mediated communication (CMC) focused on the anonymity of disembodied spaces. Scholarly interest in the potentials of CMC pointed to the ways in which textual online interaction created spaces where new types of human relationships could unfold (Turkle, 1995). This emphasis on identity play and deception was tempered by later work that highlighted the fact that users of CMC created online selves that were largely consistent with their offline identities (Baym, 1998: 55).

Rather than most people creating new relationships with strangers online, empirical evidence suggests that we tend to use online spaces to maintain relationships with people that are already known to us in offline contexts. Social media enables users to connect with heterogenous social ties and build social capital (Ellison et al., 2007; Johnston et al., 2013; Lambert, 2016). These relationships are characterised by media multiplicity and we are connected across a range of digital platforms (Baym, 2015; Haythornthwaite, 2005).

A culture of connectivity

As our lives are increasingly embedded and enmeshed in digital technologies, digital platforms act as social intermediaries, used to socialise, communicate and connect with friends and strangers (Rosenfeld & Thomas, 2012; van Dijck, 2013b). The ubiquity of these technologies and our reliance on social media connectivity was highlighted on Monday 4th October 2021 when an internal technical issue rendered Facebook and its family of apps, including Messenger, Instagram and WhatsApp, inaccessible for around 6 hours, affecting billions of users worldwide (BBC, 2021).

While #facebookdown trended on unaffected platforms like X, users relying on Facebook apps to conduct their daily lives keenly felt the impact of their absence, providing a highly visible demonstration of our collective economic, cultural and social reliance on giant corporations of centralised social media:

> In such moments of dysfunction, the technologies come out of the woodwork and become unmistakably and painfully visible through the

> desolation of the 'could not reach server'-messages that replace significant portions of what constitutes 'life'. (Lindgren, 2021b)

These kinds of outages, and the feelings of disconnection and frustration that accompany them, highlight our dependence on digitally mediated connectivity. For many this dependence had already been starkly realised during the self-isolation measures put in place in response to COVID-19 lockdowns; digital technologies were our social and communicative lifelines as the temporal rhythms of daily life were disrupted in unprecedented ways and we became digital by default (Livingston, 2020).

While outages and lockdowns provide examples at the extreme ends of a spectrum of connectivity, they highlight the myriad ways in which digital technologies connect us. We struggle to imagine being without our devices. As part of my *Digital Culture* course my students and I engage in a digital detox experiment designed to highlight our reliance on communicative devices and platforms. Our abstinence is usually short lived and accompanied by feelings of failure for being unable to last much more than 24 hours without succumbing to the attention-demanding pings of our notifications. What we are experiencing, however, is not failure. Rather, we are experiencing the ubiquity and domestication of devices that have become a constant presence in our lives.

Connectivity via digital devices is integrated into our routines and mediates our interactions and interpersonal connections: a co-presence defined not by geographic or physical boundaries but by a psychological state of digitally mediated intimacy (Hjorth & Richardson, 2016).

DIGITALLY MEDIATED INTIMACIES

The sociological literature provides us with a range of definitions of intimacy and we can trace shifting understanding of intimacy as rooted in local communities and families, to post-traditional intimacies that take more individualised forms, variously defined as 'pure' relationships and elective intimacies (Chambers, 2013). This shifting conceptualisation broadens and extends definitions of intimacy to include the range of people we are intimate with and the various modes through which that intimacy occurs (Attwood et al., 2017).

While an exploration of sociological understanding of intimacy is beyond the scope of this chapter, the shift in the *modes* through which intimacy occurs is central to an understanding of digitally mediated intimacy.

The concept of mediated intimacies emerged from literature on social media that emphasised the personal connections made in and through online spaces (Baym, 2015). The concept draws together understandings of intimacy as a set of *practices* that enable, generate and sustain the reciprocal sense of being close and special to someone (Jamieson, 2011), with understandings that human actors are connected, co-constituted and mediated *in* and *by* digital technologies (Attwood et al., 2017). We connect in and through a polymedia environment in which a diverse range of digital tools enable us to communicate with each other to develop and maintain social ties. As such, digital technologies have become 'infrastructures of intimacy' as we form connections with other people and with devices, apps and platforms (Paasonen, 2017).

Social media technologies encourage us to share many aspects of our lives; the places we visit, the activities we participate in, the friends we are with and the things we like and dislike. These practices create and foster intimacy (Andreassen et al., 2017). In this sense social media practices find common ground with practices of intimacy as both enable and encourage us to share, to reveal ourselves and to connect with others. Social media use extends intimacy beyond the private sphere of the home, blurring the boundaries of public and private life through practices of intimacy that are conducted in the public sphere with a more broadly defined range of participants (Andreassen et al., 2017a; Chambers, 2013).

The concept of intimacy is increasingly important in contemporary understandings of the 'project of the self'. We struggle with the hyper individual nature of post-industrial society, balancing our need for connection and social bonds with our increasingly mobile and individualised lives (Bauman, 2013; Chambers, 2013; Miguel, 2018). We develop 'personal communities' as we move home or school, travel, attend university, move jobs and navigate life transitions (Pahl, 2005; Spencer & Pahl, 2006). These networks offer support and solidarity but are diffuse and sparsely knit. They have vague and overlapping social and spatial boundaries and are characterised by loose fragmented networks that are not oriented around close-knit communities or family groups.

It is not hard to see how, with this geographic dispersion of networks, social media speak to our desire to connect by facilitating different kinds of mediated relationships (Chambers, 2013). Rainie and Wellman define this as *networked individualism* (2012a); digital social networks that help us to maintain diverse and geographically dispersed relationships, affording us a sense of belonging and connection.

MOBILE INTIMACY AND HYPERCONNECTIVITY

Perhaps one of the most profound ways in which intimacy is mediated is through our mobile devices. The ubiquity of mobile phones means that the boundaries that separate us from our social networks are increasingly diaphanous. In 2022 there were an estimated 7.26 billion mobile phone users which translates to 91.69% of the world's population owning a smartphone (Turner, 2022).

The mobile revolution (Rainie & Wellman, 2012b) enables us to be networked individuals with always-on connectivity assumed, expected and provided by our mobile devices. Personal mobile devices facilitate accelerated forms of sociality and they have become key affordances, allowing us to access friends and information at will (Lash, 2002; Wajcman, 2008):

> Whatever it is called, and wherever it is used, this simple, accessible technology alters the way in which individuals conduct their everyday lives. It has extensive implications for the cultures and societies in which it is used; it changes the nature of communication and affects identities and relationships. It affects the development of social structures and economic activities, and has considerable bearing on its users' perceptions of themselves and their world. (Plant, 2000:23)

This access to our networks comes in part from the way in which we have embodied our mobile devices. They are intimate technologies (Bell, 2006) that, for many of us, are never far away: in our pockets, next to us on tables and by our bedsides. As such, our mobile devices are personal intimate tools for increased connectivity that provide a myriad of social benefits. They enable us to maintain and strengthen existing relationships through mediated interactions and to connect and reconnect with geographically dispersed friends and family. Our embodied mobile devices afford support, interaction and intimacy as we mediate relationships through our devices and via our social media networks (Lin et al., 2012).

One consequence of our embodied devices is that we become hyperconnected. Hyperconnectivity is a state of always-on, accessibility, a constant possibility of connection and an expectation that we always are, and should be, contactable. This fosters an enhanced sense of connection to our networks imbuing them with a heightened sense of intimacy (Wajcman et al., 2008), what Rainie and Wellman describe as a 'cocoon like zone of intimacy' (2012a: 96).

In practice, this cocoon of intimacy is often rather mundane and every day. We use our mobile phones for micro-coordination – 'when will you be home', 'could you pick up some bread', 'where shall we meet', 'I'll be 10 minutes late'. But even these prosaic connections intensify a sense of linked and connected lives and micro-connections have become not only mediated *markers* of intimacy but actually help to *constitute* intimacy (Wajcman et al., 2008).

Ambient Intimacy

Technologies mediate and constitute intimacy by providing tools and platforms through which we can make personal connections and the concept of intimacy is central to our understanding of social media (Hinton & Hjorth, 2013). Using the concept of ambient intimacy, Hinton and Hjorth (2013) suggest that digital technologies create a state of continual 'always on' presence. Being able to digitally follow each other provides us with a sense of mediated ambient intimacy that makes us feel connected and close to one another (Lin et al., 2016).

> Each little update – each individual bit of social information – is insignificant on its own, even supremely mundane. But taken together, over time, the snippets coalesce into a surprisingly sophisticated portrait of your friends' and family members' lives. (Thompson, 2008)

These mediated acts of (often) micro ambient intimacy mean we can keep in touch with people in ways that might be impossible, geographically and temporally, in our day-to-day lives. Social media platforms give us a window into the everyday activities of friends and family, enabling us to bypass routine conversational catchups and providing us with opportunities to communicate to our networks our moods, our activities and the details of our lives. For example, Snapchat and Finsta accounts are used to check in with friends, exchanging small moments of our daily lives that are too vapid for Instagram (Bayer et al., 2016; Kang & Wei, 2020).

The often-banal interactions, mediated via digital technologies and on social media sites, act as social glue creating a continual ambient awareness that allows us to maintain a presence in someone's life and they in ours. We can stay connected to friends and family while we wait at the bus stop or when watching TV, filling 'dead' time by maintaining ambient intimacy with and in our networks.

In this sense our micro connections are not (just) mundane posts or messages about our pets, children or lunch; they are a way to feel connected and emotionally closer to people who we don't share our daily lives with.

The Cost of Hyperconnectivity

Paradoxically, the technology that promises to connect us also threatens to overload us. As well as facilitating connection and ambient intimacy, the embodiment of our mobile devices also creates new demands and new expectations. Our connectivity is socially liberating but at the same time socially taxing. Turkle (2016) describes this as a tie to our 'intimate machines'. We are tethered to devices that trap us in their demands of perpetual contact (Baym, 2015). While the possibility of constant connection afforded by our digital devices can facilitate new forms of intimacy, they also increase the burdens of expectation:

> Digital hyperconnectivity has recast social relationships, lifting them out of the here and now, disciplining and re-formatting them, and infusing them with new obligations, new expectations, and new anxieties…It has brought us into intimate relations with ever-more powerful, ever-more seductive devices. (Brubaker, 2020:727)

In the context of hyperconnectivity, in relationships and friendship groups a failure to deliver regular messages may no longer be excused by absence but instead might be read as evidence of lack of care. For example, the absence of a social media presence may be felt or interpreted as invisibility or recalcitrance (Blatterer, 2010; Bobkowski & Smith, 2013). A sustained visibility and presence online may become a necessary task in reaffirming and maintaining one's place and presence in peer networks, as social networking sites act as key venues for representing intimacy and for displaying and performing friendship (Livingstone & Brake, 2010).

For adolescents this mediated peer connection has been found to be particularly important with digital devices perceived as essential. Not having a phone means missing out on conversations, on sharing messages and on the digitally mediated small talk that ensures peer connectedness and peer acceptance, the absence of which can amount to social exclusion (Mittmann et al., 2022).

Hyperconnectivity creates a mediated social environment in which we face multiple demands. We present and perform our identities online across a range of platforms to multiple audiences. These performances and interactions do not occur in an online void but are framed by the expectations, contexts and lived realities of our offline interactions and relationships. Our online and offline interactions inform each other while also forcing us to negotiate blurred boundaries between our public and private lives. Our hyperconnectivity connects our materially located spaces and relationships with the blended audiences and spaces of our digital networks.

DIGITAL INTIMACY AS PUBLIC INTIMACY

Digital technologies are woven into the fabric of our lives and social media sites mediate friendships through self-representation and peer interaction. As this chapter has outlined, digital spaces and mediated intimacies provide new ways of 'doing' friendship and of fostering and sharing intimacy (Chambers, 2013; Nayak & Kehily, 2013; Raghunandan, 2018). While sharing has always been part of practices of intimacy (Jamieson, 2013) the sharing that is mediated by digital technologies is a *public* practice of intimacy, occurring in networked public spaces

(Miguel, 2016). These practices function to demonstrate friendship and intimacy and act as public performances of friendship, shared bonds and shared histories, as well as being performative in excluding those who do not share these intimacies (Lambert, 2016).

Public intimacies, performed in front of networked publics (boyd, 2010), blur the boundaries between our public and our private lives. As well giving rise to the kinds of social surveillance practices discussed in Chapter 3, these are spaces in which intimacies are shared and experienced:

> intimacy is increasingly being performed in public through social media... the social media environment complicates the negotiation of privacy concerns with social and emotional desires to be accomplished within these network. (Miguel, 2018:28)

This is not to argue that our social relationships have been transformed by technologies. Rather, they have adapted to new social media environments while remaining embedded in existing practices and social norms (Miguel, 2018). Social media platforms, with their emphasis on sharing, connection and display, offer us ways to represent and articulate imtimacy in public spaces, encouraging us to reveal (valuable) personal information. The public performance of intimacy, played out publically across social media, has important implications for our understandings of privacy and public/private boundaries – themes that will be considered in the next sections of this chapter.

Networked publics

boyd (2010) conceives of networked publics as publics that are restructured by networked technologies. This is not a deterministic stance implying that digital technologies have fundamentally changed our relationships; rather, it is a recognition that the ways in which we are networked and mobilised, with and through media, have shifted (Varnelis, 2012). For boyd, these shifts comprise the spaces that have been constructed as a result of digital technologies as well; what she defines as the 'imagined collective' that has emerged from the intersection of people, technology, and practice (2010: 39).

The distinct properties of networked publics are their *persistence, searchability, replicability* and *scalability*, each creating a set of dynamics that shape how we understand our interactions in these publics (boyd, 2010). Our online interactions are persistent in that they are automatically recorded and archived and remain available beyond the temporal point of their creation (Davis & Jurgenson, 2014). Even after content is deleted, we cannot know if something we put online has been saved as a screenshot, downloaded or stored in some digital or physical way. Our content is also replicable and can be duplicated, is searchable and can be found and is scalable in its visibility.

boyd is not suggesting that the ability to record interaction is a new or uniquely digital phenomena, rather she is highlighting the nature of digital recording that transforms interactions from ephemeral by default to persistent by default (2010: 46). Similarly, the reproduction of images, text and other media is not an inherently digital phenomena but the reproduction of content in digital environments is easier and, importantly, content may be altered and replicated in ways that people do not easily realise. The internet has also introduced new possibilities for distribution creating unprecedented scalability. Digital technologies amplify the potential audiences of our performances involving participants who would otherwise not be party to these practices of intimacy (White et al., 2018). This creates the possibility of unanticipated visibility. The potential for visibility is in part a result of the searchability afforded by digital technologies with search functions enabling us to find people and content more easily within these networked publics.

The invisible audience and content collapse

These four properties of networked publics have important implications for how we can understand our digitally mediated social relationships. The first of these is the inability in mediated spaces to know who is listening to or watching what we share and what we say, what boyd (2010) defines as the invisible audience. While many may wish to garner attention when they post online (wanting to go viral to monetise content or seeking an audience to support political campaigns or activist causes) many of us post to social media with a smaller and particular audience in mind (friends, family or colleagues). The concept of an imagined audience enables us to think through the contexts and framing of our social media posts and interactions by imagining who may be looking at our content:

> Audience is critical to context. Without information about audience, it is often difficult to determine how to behave, let alone to make adjustments based on assessing reactions. To accommodate this, participants in networked publics often turn to imagined audience to assess whether or not they believe their behaviour is socially appropriate, interesting, or relevant. (boyd, 2010:50)

The concept of an invisible audience enables us to contextualise and position our online performances, but also highlights the ways in which our public performances may be visible to people that we don't know or didn't anticipate were looking at us. This creates what boyd (2010) defines as context collapse. While we might have a sense or a hope of who our audience is in online settings, the nature of a networked public means that we often have to contend with audiences made up of different groups of people who come from different contexts in our lives.

Many of us consciously try and manage these collapsed audiences as we make decisions about what is appropriate to post on platforms where close friends, distant acquaintances, family members and work colleagues may converge. Jokes and comments may fall flat, be misunderstood or cause unintentional offence as we judge and misjudge what is appropriate across an audience that reflects different social contexts and expectations.

This, in turn, creates new emotional demands, requiring us to think about the dilemmas of un-friending, possibilities for embarrassment, problems caused by being tagged in a photo and the scope for misunderstanding and offence. As a result, we must invest time and energy in negotiating digitally mediated practices of intimacy:

> Having to make new kinds of choices, such as when and when not to spy on others, whether to accept or reject a friend request or whether to 'cull' social ties from one's network. This is the skilled labour of intimacy in the digital era. (Lambert, 2016: 2571)

The colliding of contexts can also be problematic when the scalability and persistence of digital media creates an environment in which our content is available and easily searchable.

While there are many offline social situations in which divergent contexts converge, online there are countless examples of the consequences of actions that are normatively appropriate in one context being revealed to members of another audience where norms and expectations are different.

In one instance of a phenomena defined as 'Facebook firing' (Hidy & McDonald, 2013; O'Connor & Schmidt, 2015), 24-year-old US high school teacher Ashley Payne was forced to resign after an anonymous emailer complained to the school about a photo posted to her Facebook profile of her holding a glass of wine and a mug of beer while on holiday in Europe. The school principal had been contacted by a parent concerned by Payne's 'unacceptable' online behaviour promoting alcohol use. Ashley had fallen foul of a networked public, where our personal and professional lives and the many situations in which we find ourselves are meshed together often with problematic consequences:

> The ability to bring various social situations together on social media has proved to be both highly beneficial at times and disastrous, too. Messages

intended for one person or group sometimes leak out into others, leading to high-profile embarrassments that garner media attention and sometimes serious harm to individuals. (Davis & Jurgenson, 2014:483)

Duffy and Chan (2019) cite a similar case in which American cheerleader Bailey
Davis was fired as a cheerleader for the New Orleans Saints after posting an image
on her private Instagram page of herself in a one-piece bodysuit. Her subsequent
complaint to the Equal Employment Opportunity Commission highlighted the
gross disparity in treatment of the cheerleaders and players in the Saints Social
media policy and raised important questions about the politics of digital surveillance and the inequalities in who gets surveilled (Duffy & Chan, 2019).

Through our sharing practices on social media we may act as though our audiences are known and bounded when in reality the affordances of networked publics mean they are potentially limitless, spanning multiple contexts within and
beyond our social networks and connections (Davis & Jurgenson, 2014).

There are well-documented examples of context collapse and the impact of
networked public scalability, none perhaps more notable than the racist tweet of
Justine Sacco. Justine Sacco, a former public relations executive, was travelling to
South Africa from the USA in December 2013. En-route she posted to X – to her
170 followers – about her journey. At a layover at Heathrow she tweeted about
England, 'cold and bad teeth' and before boarding her flight to South Africa she
tweeted 'Going to Africa. Hope I don't get AIDS. Just kidding. I'm white!' (Tsikata,
2015). After tweeting she turned off her phone for the flight. During the flight
her tweet was picked up by several online media outlets and after 3 hours began
to trend on X. While she was inaccessible and airborne anger over her tweet went
globally viral in a X firestorm that was both an ideological crusade against her
racism, but also a form of idle entertainment. As her flight continued a hashtag
began to trend worldwide #HasJustineLandedYet with her ignorance at what was
happening lending the episode a dramatic irony, as one X user described, 'I don't
think America has watched a landing this closely since Apollo 13 re-entered the
earth's atmosphere in 1970 #HasJustineLandedYet' (Chaudhry, 2016).

On arrival she was fired from her job and was a figure of world-wide sham-
ing as a result of her 'toxic disinhibition' (Chaudhry, 2016). Sacco's text demonstrates clearly boyd's properties of networked publics in its rapid and mass
circulation of text spreading far beyond the intended and expected audience.
A form of viral call out culture that has become a feature of contemporary networked publics:

Social media is so perfectly designed to manipulate our desire for approval,
and that is what led to her undoing. Her tormentors were instantly con-
gratulated as they took Sacco down, bit by bit, and so they continued to

do so. Their motivation was much the same as Sacco's own — a bid for the attention of strangers — as she milled about Heathrow, hoping to amuse people she couldn't see. (Ronson, 2016:270)

In such cases of unanticipated disclosure to unanticipated audiences, the invisible audience is only revealed following ill-timed, careless or incendiary posts that fracture the social norms and conventions that we usually adhere to when we present ourselves. The background expectancies we use to understand and interpret the social world are breached (Garfinkel, 1967) and the fragility of social order online revealed.

Duffy and Chan (2019) describe these digital *faux pas* and the cultural anxiety surrounding them as grounded in an *imagined surveillance* across an expansive social media ecology including Facebook, Instagram, LinkedIn, Snapchat and X. They argue that for young people in particular this is couched in discourses of employability that highlight the high stakes of one's social media activity. This is particularly challenging in the context of debates around authenticity and identity (discussed in the context of Rinsta and Finsta accounts in the previous chapter). How can we be consistent in our identity performances, maintaining various digitally mediated 'selves', each played out in different ways across different platforms?

Context collapse may result in these kinds of breached norms and viral calamities but it also enables the kind of ambient intimacy that fosters connectivity and is an important way of maintaining weak ties, making new connections, and obtaining social and professional resources (Davis & Jurgenson, 2014).

Public/private boundaries

Networked publics complicate and remediate the boundaries of public/private. Our social behaviours in networked publics are augmented by platforms that largely emphasise the public sharing of information (boyd, 2010; Papacharissi & Gibson, 2011). As such, social networking platforms represent what Raghunandan (2018) describes as a graduation of friendships; social spaces in which family, friends, close confidants, work colleagues and acquaintance are digitally co-present. With friends that we are close to and have regular contact with social media acts as a space of intimacy. However, it also reveals our lives to the weaker ties in our networks who would not be privy to this information in other social contexts, transforming practices of intimacy into curiosities for others.

Debates about privacy are increasingly central to our understanding of digital culture and society and privacy is the focus of Chapter 7 in this book. In the context of privacy as it relates to our social relationships a complex picture emerges of us as individuals actively engaging in processes to manage our visibility and social boundaries in a range of privacy and visibility practices (Tufekci, 2012). Research has highlighted the variety of strategies employed to preserve privacy including deleting content, 'cleaning' social media feeds after they have been viewed by the intended audience, using aliases or multiple accounts (for example the Finsta accounts discussed in the previous chapter) and using coded content (Raynes-Goldie, 2010).

SOCIAL SURVEILLANCE AND INTIMATE SURVEILLANCE

In Chapter 3, I introduced the concept of social surveillance in social media where our presence online is characterised by watching and an awareness of being watched (Marwick, 2012). Social surveillance has created a set of practices through which surveillance of and between individuals is digitised and normalised through social media. This has important implications for how we use social media in our interpersonal relationships.

Research has highlighted shifting relationships of surveillance between parents and their children with the ubiquity of mobile phone ownership and the individualisation of mediated interaction. Mobile devices remove young people's social interactions from their parents' oversight (via the domestic landline telephone) and provide a repertoire of devices and spaces in which they can more autonomously manage their interactions and availability (Ling & Yttri, 2005). Conversely, however, connectivity can also function as a form of surveillance as the expectation of constant availability is experienced by young people largely in terms of scrutiny and control – 'where are you', 'what are you doing', 'when will you be home'. This is a form of surveillance Leaver (2017) defines as routine, affectionate and well intentioned. An intimate surveillance that normalises the idea that parents subject their children to surveillance as an act of care.

While young people's social media use is often scrutinised by parents, research has also highlighted the ways in which young people learn to negotiate the complexities of their own privacy and presence online (Clark, 2013; Leaver, 2017; Livingstone & Sefton-Green, 2016). Part of this process of negotiation draws on understanding and using the affordances of social media platforms and tools to navigate the mutual and participatory surveillance of mediated relationships (Westcott & Owen, 2013).

SNAPCHAT AND AFFORDANCES OF PRIVACY

Snapchat as an instant messaging platform provides us with an interesting example of the ways in which platform affordances and public/private boundaries play out in social media interaction. Snapchat is a messaging app used for creating and sharing multimedia messages called 'snaps'. Unlike social media platforms like Facebook, Instagram or X, with their largely public and one-to-many model of communication, Snapchat affords users more privacy, enabling conversations to take place in smaller more private groups (Utz et al., 2015). Snaps can be sent privately to selected contacts or posted as a private or public 'story'. As a more private space with a focus on person-to-person sharing of 'snaps', Snapchat provides a platform for communication between close personal friends (Utz et al., 2015).

This perception of privacy comes largely from the logic of the Snapchat app. Content is shared with specific people or groups rather than being public by default and the distinguishing feature of Snapchat is that content shared by users disappears after a specified period of time before becoming inaccessible to recipients. Content can be saved by participants in 'memories' but this is visible to sender and receiver (Grieve, 2017; Piwek & Joinson, 2016; Wilken & Goggin, 2013). This bounded and ephemeral nature goes some way towards addressing the challenges of the networked public persistence identified by (boyd, 2010).

While this ephemerality has led many to focus on use of the platform for sexting or cyberbullying, research on 'snapping' has also demonstrated its use in close interpersonal relationships. Snapchat interactions strengthen friendships, facilitate closeness and the sharing of a moment with trusted ties (Bayer et al., 2016; Vaterlaus et al., 2016):

> a 'snap' thus represents a deliberative, shared experience that is temporally bounded. In doing so, Snapchat facilitates a distinctive sharing practice that is both in-the-moment and momentary. (Bayer et al., 2016: 959)

Bayer et al. (2016) argue that ephemeral platforms like Snapchat are visual conversations and a form of proximal sharing that is comparable to mundane forms of social interaction like small talk. They argue that the meaningfulness of these interactions comes from sharing 'insignificant slices of personal life' that, because of their ephemeral nature, focus attention on current interaction (2016: 971). This temporal demand represents an example of the tensions of hyperconnectivity with snaps providing an immediate sense of intimacy and closeness that demands attention and 'presence' in order to maintain and reinforce social bonds.

In offering a space for more private and intimate conversations that are perceived to lack the digital permeance of other online spaces Snapchat acts to reinforce social bonds, forge small networks of close relationships and facilitate bonding social capital (Piwek & Joinson, 2016). Ephemeral social media apps could encourage and foster playful, privacy conscious interaction norms with intimacy achieved through the affordances of the platform embedded in our daily communication practices (McRoberts et al., 2017).

MEDIATED INTIMACY, PRIVACY AND PLATFORM AFFORDANCES

We can identify two contradictory concepts of digitally mediated intimacy and friendship: one emphasising exclusiveness and privacy, the other emphasising connectivity and sharing (Chambers, 2017). This relates not only to our individual understandings of how we navigate and negotiate privacy and intimacy in and through social media, but also to more macro understandings of privacy and data and how they intersect with our human desire to connect. Barnes defines this as the privacy paradox; we express concerns about our privacy and our online activities but we behave in ways that suggest we are willing to trade our privacy for ease, convenience and connectivity (Barnes, 2006).

Think for a moment about your own use of digital apps and platforms. Have you read and are you confident that you understand the privacy settings and the terms of service that you are agreeing to when you download and use apps or sign up to social networking platforms? If you haven't you wouldn't be alone. An experimental survey conducted by Obar and Oeldorf-Hirsch (2020) invited students to join a fictitious social networking service, *NameDrop*. 74% of respondents skipped the privacy policy choosing the option to 'quick join' and while all respondents were presented with the terms of service, 98% missed the 'gotcha clauses' that the researchers included: in joining the respondents unwittingly agreed to have their data shared with the NSA, their employers and to provide the social networking site with their first-born child as a condition of access.

Obar and Oeldorf-Hirsch argue that for the majority of their participants privacy policies and terms of service were viewed as boring and pointless impediments to participation in social networks, with 'I agree to these terms and conditions' the biggest lie on the internet:

> The negative implications of this behavior were suggested by the 'gotcha clause' analysis. Instead of notice components helping users control their

digital destinies and corresponding consequences in both online and offline contexts, the vast majority of participants completely missed a variety of potentially dangerous and life-changing clauses. (Obar & Oeldorf-Hirsch, 2020:143)

Findings like those of Obar and Oeldorf-Hirsch raise questions about the role of SNS providers in facilitating or hindering processes of consent and transferring the burden and responsibility of data privacy and management onto individuals. As individuals we tend to trade off concerns about privacy for the benefits of being part of networked publics. Rather than being excluded or isolated we embrace new opportunities for connection and to be seen and heard by others (Berriman & Thomson, 2015).

Social media sites emphasise principles of openness and their ability to give individuals greater powers to share and connect. But social networking platforms are not neutral spaces in which we 'do' friendship, they are global for-profit corporations whose technical structures and affordances shape how our interpersonal relationships play out online. This is an important consideration when we remember that the business model of most social media sites is one of data harvesting based on our public performances and interactions, as Chambers argues about Facebook:

> The implication is that connectedness is more powerful by being *disclosing*. Invoking a discourse of disclosure and reciprocity, Facebook discourages users from private, exclusive connections by steering them to share highly personal information. Yet is the power to share benefiting Facebook users, advertisers or both? (Chambers, 2017:29)

Ephemeral platforms like Snapchat and encrypted messaging apps like WhatsApp offer a way to subvert the public sharing promoted by social media and avoid having our friendships exploited. But the way many platforms are structured encourages us to find connections, suggests people we may know and shows us the networks of mutual friends that surround us (Bucher, 2013; Chambers, 2017). As such, social media platforms act as engineers of techno-sociality (Miguel, 2018). They help users make choices about who will and who will not be their friends and online friendships need to be understood as a gathering of heterogeneous elements that include both humans and nonhumans. The configuration of friendship online is fundamentally technologically driven and commercially motivated, defined by Bucher as algorithmic friendship (Bucher, 2013).

Social media platforms are shaping how we interact with each other, not as benevolent entities that want us to find connections, but as global corporations that use our very human desire to connect to keep us using their services in order to gather and sell our data and preferences. This is a linking of economies and intimacies that Illouz has defined as emotional capitalism (Illouz, 2007).

Our intimate lives and our relationships are increasingly commodified and quantified. This commodification creates what Andrejevic describes as a social factory that 'puts our pleasures, our communications, our sociability to work, capturing them in order to extract value from them' (Andrejevic, 2010:90). Social media can be empowering for us, enabling us to connect, forge and strengthen bonds in new social spaces but social media companies are underpinned by a contradictory corporate logic of data for profit.

The ubiquity of social media raises important questions about how we can understand interpersonal relationships in a digital society: are they reshaping how we experience friendship or are our understandings of friendship changing to incorporate a set of broader and looser digitally mediated social relationships? As platforms and apps profit from our most basic desires, cynics (and sociologists) might be quick to appropriate the theories of German philosopher sociologist Theodor Adorno to suggest that as social media users we are being manipulated and exploited by corporations in competition for the financial benefit they can glean from our need to connect.

From 'networked publics' to 'refracted publics'

It is useful here to return to boyd's (2010) framework of 'networked publics', introduced earlier in the chapter, in the light of developments in social media. Reflecting on the decade since boyd's work, Abidin et al. (2021) provide us with an important companion framework of 'refracted publics'. They argue that our contemporary landscape of digital media has shifted from the internet cultures in which boyd's work was developed. boyd was focused on exploring platforms, infrastructure and affordances and the way they created a set of dynamics that shape how we understand our interactions in these publics. Abidin et al.'s framework reflects a contemporary digital landscape of data leaks, fake news and the global pandemic (2021: 2).

She defines 'refracted publics' as publics that are born of an internet culture that is characterised by a perpetual content saturation. We are bombarded with a continuous flow of content that makes meaningful consumption difficult. We live in an attention economy where competing content is vying for our attention. We live in a social media culture that is gamified and datafied (we will explore this idea further in Chapter 6) and given this glut of content and information we are increasingly distrustful of often polarised information sources (Abidin, 2021: 4).

Where boyd's networked publics were characterised by persistence, searchability, replicability and scalability, the conditions of Abidin's refracted publics are 'transience', 'discoverability', 'decodability' and 'silosociality' (Abidin, 2021: 2). I reproduce and paraphrase her useful summary of the key differences in Table 4.1.

Table 4.1   Conditions between 'Networked publics' and 'Refracted publics'. Adapted from Abidin (2021: 2)

'Networked publics' (boyd, 2010)	'Refracted publics' (Abidin, 2021)
Persistence	**Transience**
Online content is recordable and archivable	Online content is ephemeral
Searchability	**Discoverability**
Online content can be accessed via searches	Online content is unknowable until chanced upon
Replicability	**Decodability**
Online content can be duplicated	Online content can be duplicated but may make no sense out of context
Scalability	**Silosociality**
Online content has the potential to be highly visible in networked publics	The visibility of online content is intended to be localised and communal

The shift to refracted publics in the context of digitally mediated relationships emphasises the kinds of ephemeral interactions and awareness of privacy that drives users to engage with, for example, Snapchat, discussed earlier in this chapter.

As we have seen in Chapters 2 and 3, and in this chapter, digital media is changing the ways in which we connect and relate to each other. We can transcend global boundaries to create and maintain our social relationships with people, finding and sharing opportunities and resources. Conversely, we can find ourselves exhausted by new demands and victim of more undesirable aspects of online connectivity. Comparing online and offline interactions and intimacies or framing them as either emancipatory or deleterious ignores the social contexts and platform affordances in which these interactions are grounded and is of little analytical value. As social scientists we need to focus on the contexts, structures and affordances of the communicative tools that have become part of our lives and relationships:

> There are no doors where we can check our personal, social, cultural and historical identities and world views before entering. We are not free to create entirely new kinds of communication, selves, relationships, groups, networks or worlds. Nor are we forced into an alternative world of shallow simulations of inauthentic message exchange that take us farther from one another. Digital media aren't saving us or ruining us. (Baym, 2015:1991)

Understanding new forms of connecting and relating requires us to think not only about the possibilities of building different forms of intimacy through digital media but also to acknowledge our acceptance of the normative relations of consumer capitalism in a network society and in our networked and refracted publics.

STUDYING APPS: THE WALKTHROUGH METHOD

This chapter has explored the ways in which social media technologies have become woven into the fabric of our daily lives. The chapter argued that social media platforms and apps act as engineers of techno-sociality; their technical structures and affordances shape our interpersonal relationships (Miguel, 2018). Apps and digital platforms reflect our cultural values and users, developers and advertisers interact in and through apps in ways that shape our daily practices (Cavagnuolo et al., 2022). If we conceive of our mediated lives as being made up of heterogeneous elements that include human and nonhuman actors, then an understanding of these technical affordances is key. Apps guide and shape how we understand and experience our digital media environments but questions about how we can study apps pose new methodological challenges for social research (Light et al., 2016).

Apps are largely closed systems with public access to source code limited or wholly unavailable (Burgess, 2012; Rogers, 2013). This means researchers are unable to examine the structure and underlying code of apps in the same way we can with webpages or more accessible software. Some digital data can be gathered from apps using Application Programming Interfaces (APIs). As discussed in the previous chapter, an API is an interface in a computer program that enables the software to 'speak' with other software, meaning third-party companies can develop apps that integrate with social media platforms like X or Facebook (Lomborg & Bechmann, 2014). Some social media companies use APIs to make data on usage available, allowing researchers to use software scripts to access the API and scrape data for analysis. This 'computation turn' in the social sciences (Berry, 2011; boyd & Crawford, 2012) has opened up new possibilities for the large-scale systematic collection of digital usage patterns that go beyond the limitations of traditional methods like ethnography, interviews or surveys (Lomborg & Bechmann, 2014).

However, even where APIs are accessible for research social media companies structure their APIs in ways that place limitations on how researchers can employ them, due to commercial sensitivities or the design architecture of the app. This shapes the research questions that we can ask of this kind of data. For example,

APIs can collect data about users' location, demographic information, newsfeeds and uploaded materials, but the users generating this data may not be representative of the larger populations of app users. Users who generate the most content and interaction may be disproportionately represented and so data may be skewed towards the most active and visible participants:

> The data collected from APIs has an in-built bias toward those types of users that are the most 'active' content contributors, whereas the data say very little, at best, about the so-called 'lurkers' who may read their newsfeeds and Twitter streams with great interest and on a daily basis but who barely post anything to the stream themselves. (Lomborg & Bechmann, 2014:259)

This inability to know the quality and representativeness of the sample may have serious implications for research questions that focus on, for example, understandings of lurker populations or less active or visible members of a group. While API data may provide a rich picture of patterns of activity and logs of behaviour, it provides very little about the context in which this activity takes place nor about the meaning-making ascribed to it.

The methodological reflection at the end of Chapter 2 focused on how ethnography as a method provides a way for researchers to trace the everyday activities that are fundamental to the formation and maintenance of social life. These ethnographic observations are vital for socio-cultural understanding but are limited in their ability to incorporate detailed understandings of the technical structures and affordances of the apps that facilitate these new intimacies. Conversely, we have the challenge of data gathered from APIs which can provide a large dataset but may be limited or incomplete in scope and lack the symbolic elements and social interpretations that users bring to apps (Light et al., 2016; Rieder & Röhle, 2017). Analysing an app demands that we pay attention to its technological features, its embedded socio-cultural representations and its social and cultural influences (Light et al., 2016).

The walkthrough method, proposed by Light and colleagues (Light et al., 2016) is a method that incorporates the study of the technological features of an app with a critical analysis of the cultural meanings embedded in its design and use. The walkthrough method originates from software engineering and the study of Human-Computer Interaction. Here the method was primarily focused on user testing to improve code quality and usability (Cavagnuolo et al., 2022). Its articulation by Light (2016) employs the method to analyse apps as socio-technical artefacts and to understand how an app and its interface shapes how users experience its functionalities and data flows. Light and colleagues have used the walkthrough methods to explore the use of apps in a range of digital spaces, looking at different sexual cultures (Light, 2016), examining authenticity across different social networks (Duguay, 2016), and studying the creative features of Instagram (Duguay, 2017).

In doing so, they demonstrate how the walkthrough method combines a way to pay attention to the technological characteristics that influence cultural and social dynamics with an analysis of the socio-cultural representations embedded in their design and production. The method maps the app's design and function-ality and by engaging with an app as a critical user the researcher can follow the flows of practice implied and shaped by an app while also analysing how these are culturally coded:

> This method aims to understand what seemingly mundane apps do and feel like. The apps are 'made strange' by moving slowly through them, applying analytical categorization to every design element, allowing a detailed analysis of how entry and exit point architecture shapes the flow of arrival and departure'. (Møller & Robards, 2019:102)

Practically, the walkthrough method consists of two stages of analysis: the analy-sis of the environment of use and the technical walkthrough. These incorpo-rate elements of ethnography as the researcher observes and generates fieldnotes about their experience.

The analysis of the environment of use

This first stage focuses on the vision of the app, its operating model and its governance.

1   The vision of the app refers to the study of the app's purpose, its target users and the concepts that the app conveys. The vision of the app may be communication via its presentation in the app store, via a website, company blogs or marketing materials. These provide a basis for understanding how users perceive and approach the app. Light et al. (2016) use the example of dating apps Tinder and Squirt to illustrate their concept of vision. They argue that (originally) Tinder was presented as an app for people interested in relationships while Squirt, whose target audience is men who have sex with other men, highlights the functionality of communicating with multiple partners at once. Each vision presents different views of monogamous relationship norms that suggest what the app is supposed to do, how it can be used and who it is primarily for (Light et al., 2016).

2   The analysis of the operating model focuses on the business model and income source of an app in order to understand its underlying political and economic interests. For example, apps may use in-app purchases to provide additional functionality or access or may require the user to provide data in exchange for more in app services. Sources of data here include industry documentation, public market information or public documentation and records about the app as well as in-app menus and pricing options (Light et al., 2016).

3   The analysis of the governance of the app explores how an app regulates user activities through rules and guidelines as well as formal terms of service and conditions of use. These enable an analysis of the ways in which an app provider manages and regulates user activity in order to maintain their operating model and sustain the apps vision (Light et al., 2016).

The technical walkthrough

The technical walkthrough is the main component of data collection in the method and consists of three core elements: registration and entry, everyday use and suspension, closure and leaving. Each involves the researcher exploring the app as a user and taking an analytical approach to the processes of engaging with the app, focusing on how cultural discourses around, for example, gender, ethnicity, sexuality or class are constructed and articulated (Light et al., 2016). This analysis is based on the interrogation of what Light et al. (2016) call mediator characteristics, including the app's interface, its functions and features, its textual content and tone and its symbolic representations, all embedded with cultural meanings and referencing cultural texts that exist outside of the app.

1   Registration and entry are the starting points of the walkthrough following how a user registers with an app, e.g., through a second party login such as a Facebook or Google account, online via a website or directly with the app itself. Light et al. (2016) suggest that the expected use of the app is communicated strongly during the process of registration with registration processes highlighting terms of use, preferred practices and suggestions about ideal use via 'how to' guidelines.

2   The second stage of the technical walkthrough is concerned with an in-depth analysis of the features of the app, its interface, functionality and the affordances it offers. This element of the walkthrough focuses on everyday use and the researcher must follow activity flows to explore the possible range of uses and how the app fits into their lives.

3   The final stage focuses on how users leave the app and suspend or close the app. This may be temporarily leaving the app or permanently deleting it. Light et al. (2016) note that different apps try and retain users in a number of ways. They cite the example of Facebook and the social and technical tactics it uses to get users to postpone decisions about how to delete their data; telling users they will be missed by friends and offering options to later reactivate data rather than deleting a profile entirely and permanently. Here the walkthrough enables researchers to understand how apps seek to sustain use, retain users' data and reengage those tempted to stop using the app.

These stages acknowledge the multiplicity of reading strategies that users bring to apps and the fact that users typically engage with interfaces in similar ways and follow similar pathways (Møller & Robards, 2019)

The method provides researchers with a systematic way to study mobile software that Light at al. (2016) argue is often overlooked in analyses of digital technologies. Combining the walkthrough method with other methods and data sources (traditional interviews, survey data or ethnographic techniques) gives us opportunities to combine technical and cultural understandings of the ways in which social media platforms and apps act as engineers of techno-sociality as they shape and are shaped by our use.

CONCLUSION

This chapter has focused on how our interpersonal relationships are mediated through digital spaces and interactions and how we manage the audiences of our identity performances. Key ideas in this chapter can be summarised as followed:

- There has been a historical tendency to see digital connectivity as something detrimental to the quality of human relationships. However, digital technologies play an important role in supporting and maintaining social relationships, connecting us to heterogeneous social ties and building social capital.
- The ubiquity of contemporary digital devices, integrated into our routines and mediating our interactions, has created a state of digitally mediated intimacy. A set of practices that enable, generate and sustain 'closeness' using digital technologies as infrastructures that facilitate connection and the maintenance of social ties.
- Mediated access to our networks also creates a state of always-on hyperconnectivity coupled with an ambient intimacy that both facilitates new forms of connection and increases social demands and expectations.

- Digital intimacies are also public intimacies performed in front of networked publics. This has important implications for our understandings of privacy and public/private boundaries. Networked publics are persistent, searchable, replicable and scalable and as such amplify potential (invisible) audiences who would not normally be party to practices of intimacy.
- Networked publics emphasise the public sharing of information that demand that we engage in practices to manage our visibility and privacy. The affordances of some platforms, like Snapchat, foster new kinds of privacy conscious interaction norms and social media platforms can act as engineers of techno-sociality.
- Methods like the walkthrough method enable us to pay attention to technological characteristics that influence cultural and social dynamics by understanding how socio-cultural representations are embedded in their design and production.

Further reading

Jamieson, L. (2013). Personal relationships, intimacy and the self in a mediated and global digital age. *Digital sociology: Critical perspectives*, pp.13–33. Palgrave Macmillan

In this chapter Jamieson reflects on her earlier work *Intimacy: Personal relationships in modern societies* (1997) in discussing digitally mediated personal lives. She revisits interactionalist accounts of the self in the light of increasingly networked societies and evaluates new forms of networked connectivity and individualism.

Andreassen, R., Petersen, M.N., Harrison, K., & Raun, T. (Eds.) (2017). *Mediated intimacies: Connectivities, relationalities and proximities*. Routledge.

This broad ranging edited collection considers how intimacy, affectivity and emotions are increasingly interwoven with social media. The collection explores how social media construct new types of intimacies using a wealth of empirical examples. Section 2 *Relationship Making and Maintenance* and Section 4 *Becoming and Performing* of the book will be of particular interest to students wishing to explore the ideas raised in this chapter in more detail.

Jaynes, V. (2020). The social life of screenshots: the power of visibility in teen friendship groups. *New Media and Society*, *22*(8), pp. 1378-1393.

In this article Jaynes draws on ethnographic data to explore how teenagers use digital communication in their friendship groups. Using screenshots as an example she argues they act as important digital tools in the process of negotiating power and friendship hierarchies and for establishing peer trust. She argues that the social life of screenshots demonstrates the complexities of the social and the digital in practice, highlighting important questions around power, visibility, and gender.

Chambers, D. (2017). Networked intimacy: Algorithmic friendship and scalable sociality. *European Journal of Communication*, *32*(1), pp. 26-36.

Examining friendships as a form of late modern intimacy, Chambers explores the idea of a crisis of intimacy in a digital era. The article explores how social media are reshaping sociability through algorithmically engineered friendship and cultures of connectivity. Chambers identifies the privacy paradox of publicly exhibited intimacy and discourses of sharing contrasted with exploitative data practices and social surveillance.

Light, B., Burgess, J., & Duguay, S. (2018). The walkthrough method: An approach to the study of apps. *New Media and Society*, *20*(3), pp. 881-900.

For students wanting to explore the walkthrough method in more detail this article provides an accessible and comprehensive overview.

The scope of the chapter does not include the large body of research focusing specifically on online dating, romantic relationships and sex. For more on this aspect of digital intimacy see David and Cambre, 2016; Gershon, 2020; Hobbs et al., 2017; Papacharissi, 2018.

5

CONSUMING DIGITAL CULTURE: PROSUMPTION AND NEW MEDIA FORMS

So far in the book we have discussed ideas about community, identity and relationships and the ways in which technologies have shaped how we interact with the people around us. The previous chapter explored the ways in which, through sharing online, our interpersonal relationships are digitally mediated.

This chapter develops the concept of sharing but moves towards understanding sharing as a cultural phenomenon. This shift of focus explores the ways in which we consume digital culture. In this chapter, I argue that as well as changing the ways in which we interact with each other, digital technologies have changed the ways in which we interact with the media and the ways in which we produce and consume culture. I outline the democratising potentials and affordances of these new models of engagement before reflecting on how the utopian ideas underpinning them have been realised and critiquing the suggestion of participatory symmetry that web 2.0 arguably affords.

As you read this chapter, I encourage you to think about the following questions:

- In what ways have web 2.0 technologies changed how we interact online?
- Why does the ability to participate in online culture matter?
- Who gets to have a voice online and who is excluded?

In 1982, *Time* magazine named the personal computer as 'Man of the Year'. In 2006, their Person of the Year was 'you'. More specifically, the magazine was high-lighting the growing importance of web 2.0, enabling individuals to create and share digital content. Lev Grossman, in the magazines profile of 'you', described web 2.0 as a revolutionary tool for bringing together the individual contributions of millions of people and for making them matter. He emphasised the commu-nity and collaboration fostered by web 2.0 technologies and noted the democratic potentials of new media environments and new forms of user-generated content:

> Who actually sits down after a long day at work and says, I'm not going to watch *Lost* tonight. I'm going to turn on my computer and make a movie starring my pet iguana? I'm going to mash up 50 Cent's vocals with Queen's instrumentals? I'm going to blog about my state of mind or the state of the nation or the *steak-frites* at the new bistro down the street? Who has that time and that energy and that passion?

> The answer is, you do. And for seizing the reins of the global media, for founding and framing the new digital democracy, for working for nothing and beating the pros at their own game, TIME's Person of the Year for 2006 is you. (Grossman, 2006)

In a prescient warning against romanticising the potentials of web 2.0 he added the caveat 'Web 2.0 harnesses the stupidity of crowds as well as its wisdom. Some of the comments on YouTube make you weep for the future of humanity just for the spelling alone, never mind the obscenity and the naked hatred.'

This optimism for, and realism about, web 2.0 provides us with a provocative starting point for thinking about the participatory web cultures that are increas-ingly part of mainstream culture. They have resulted in new forms of social and cultural engagement and data compiled over a decade on from the *Time* Person of the Year award suggests that participatory practices are flourishing: in 2022, in a single internet minute 500 hours of video were uploaded by users on YouTube, Reddit saw 479,452 users engage with content, Instagram users posted 347,222 stories, Facebook users uploaded 147,000 photos and TikTok was installed 2,704 times (Dixon, 2023).

THE WEB 2.0 MOMENT

As the internet becomes an increasingly ubiquitous part of our daily lives it shapes the ways in which we experience and consume culture (Beer & Burrows, 2010). Fundamental to this shaping has been what Meikle (2016) has defined as the web 2.0 'moment'. The term web 2.0 refers to a second generation of the world wide web, characterised by user participation and interaction and marking an evolution of the largely static and read-only websites of the early internet.

There is little consensus about how and what to define as web 2.0. Some dismiss the term as a meaningless marketing buzzword while others argue it is the new 'conventional wisdom' for understanding the internet (O'Reilly, 2009). While definitions vary the centrality of the user is key; we are not simply passive consumers of online content but are active contributors. User-generated content is integral to web 2.0 applications, classified by Constantinides and Fountain (2008) into five main categories:

1   Blogs: websites that allow users to share content on the web. They may be the work of a solo blogger or a small group of bloggers using content management systems like WordPress, or they may take the form of microblogging on platforms like X, or they may be professionally edited multi-author blogs from an institution or media outlet.
2   Social networks: applications such as Facebook and Instagram that enable users to build their own personal profiles and exchange information.
3   Content communities: websites that organise and share particular types of content, for example video sharing sites like YouTube, Vimeo or TikTok.
4   Forums/bulletin boards: websites for exchanging ideas and information usually around specific interests, for example Imgur, Reddit or Mumsnet.
5   Content aggregators: sites that gather content from across the web and put it in one place, allowing users to customise the web content they wish to access, for example Rotten Tomatoes, AllTop or Feedly.

Common across these categories is the idea that we, as ordinary users of the web, can become producers of content in ways that would have been impossible before web 2.0. Rather than static web pages that can only be changed with some knowledge of HTML or code, web 2.0 environments are more accessible, giving us the opportunity to contribute and create online content.

Web 2.0 emphasises and enables collaboration, interaction and participation (Bruns, 2008; Jenkins, 2006). Through our networked digital devices, we can create and share content in models of communication that are many-to-many, rather than between us as single individuals. As a result of our greater connectivity, we have a new collective interactivity and new spaces of cultural production and exchange; changing our 'technological imaginary' about what the web is (Reed, 2018: 38).

New models of consumption and participation mean that as individuals we have the possibility to make our voices heard amongst big media corporations that previously controlled and regulated our cultural consumption:

This shifting of roles, where the reader is also the writer, the student is also the teacher, the citizen is also the politician, and the novice is also the expert, is maybe the most fundamental point made by those who believe that the digitally networked media has made – and will continue to make – the world a better place. (Lindgren, 2017:40)

New media landscapes have been hailed for their emancipatory possibilities for public participation, social inclusion and new levels of democratization (Shirky, 2009). If anyone with a networked computer can participate online, creating and sharing content to a potentially global audience, we are no longer constrained by media gatekeepers as the sole providers of our media content (Leadbeater, 2009; Meikle & Young, 2011; Shirky, 2009).

Web 2.0 and changing understandings of the audience

This is not to suggest that prior to web 2.0 we were entirely passive audiences. We have always been active consumers of media messages, taking our own meanings from the media 'texts' we consume (Hall, 1973). A long history of audience research in the social sciences, summarised by Abercrombie and Longhurst (1998) as a series of paradigms, has conceptualised audiences using simplistic 'effect' models (relating to concerns about the harmful effects of mass media on susceptible audiences and concerns about narrow representations of some groups in the mass media); models of 'uses and gratifications' (relating to the more active meanings and interpretations made by consumers of media messages); and 'encoding and decoding' models (emphasising the ways in which we accept, reject, negotiate, subvert and reinscribe meaning to the media texts that we consume) (Fiske, 1987; Hall, 1973; Procter, 2004).

While the potentials afforded by the advent of web 2.0 technologies have marked a digital shift in our consumption of media, it is important to note the continuity and evolution of practices in cultural consumption, rather than ascribing transformation qualities to new or revolutionary digital capabilities. Similarly, it is important to remember that web 2.0 technologies have not replaced older media forms. We still watch TV and films, we read newspapers and books, we listen to music and consume a range of different cultural products. The difference is that we now consume these in new ways.

Our media has converged as functions of previously distinct technologies are combined in single devices that enable us to access the music we want to listen to on Spotify, watch and catch up with TV on demand, download and read digital books or listen to podcasts and stream films via our iPads, mobiles or personal computers. So, underpinning the participatory potentials of web 2.0 is the concept of convergence; the coming together of things that were separate (Meikle & Young, 2011).

CONVERGENCE CULTURE

The concept of convergence has shaped how we understand the ways in which we participate in new digital spaces. There is a wealth of academic and popular literature around what convergence means, exploring the myriad ways in which new media technologies shape our creative, social and political lives. Broadly, the literature defines four key dimensions of convergence:

1   *Technological convergence*, where technologies integrate or combine. The mobile phone is the iconic example of a device that goes far beyond its original function of making and receiving calls. Our mobile devices combine multiple technologies that enable us to browse the internet, take photographs, stream video and audio, send texts and emails and use geolocating navigating tools.

2   *Industrial convergence* which maps the ways in which organisations are driven by and are driving these technological convergences. We see growing similarities in national and international level regulatory institutions, processes and outcomes, the establishment of universal technical protocols and the rise of global digital companies like Google, Apple and Microsoft as part of the media industry.

3   *Social convergence* referring to the rise of social media and the ways in which these networks have seen a boom in user-generated media content and changing broadcast models.

4   *Textual convergence* in which media is re-used, remixed and reimagined in what has been defined as mashup culture or, for Jenkins (2006), a transmedia model of information dispersed across multiple platforms (Meikle & Young, 2011).

The concept of convergence is closely associated with the work of Henry Jenkins. In his book *Convergence culture: where old and new media collide* (2006), Jenkins explores our relationship to new media and argues that convergence culture is about technological, industrial, cultural, and social change. It is not simply a technological process that has brought media functions together in a single device but is a wider process of convergence that represents a cultural shift in who we are as consumers.

In exploring the relationship between media convergence, participatory culture, and collectivity he argues that we seek out new information and make connections among dispersed media content as processes of media production and media consumption converge (Jenkins, 2006). Our media content is no longer schedule-led and restricted to a particular device but is on-demand and multi-platform. We can customise and collect media in new ways – choosing how to organise our iTunes library or managing our podcast or YouTube subscriptions or binge-watching TV series long after they have been broadcast.

Convergence then is about the interconnection of information and communication technologies, computer networks, and media content. Since a diverse array of content is now being accessed through a range of different devices and platforms, media organisations have developed cross-media content. We have access to a technological websphere with links to additional content and interactive materials: for example, news sites like the BBC provide more than print and audio-visual content and act as media portals. We can press the red button on our remote controls to access additional programming and link to related programmes or content, we can customise our news feeds to receive more stories from our local area and we can comment and feedback on content. This allows us to be much more selective and active consumers as a result of convergences of technology. As Jenkins suggests:

> Media convergence impacts the way we consume media. A teenager doing homework may juggle four or five windows, scan the Web, listen to and download MP 3 files, chat with friends, word-process a paper, and respond to e-mail, shifting rapidly among tasks. And fans of a popular television series may sample dialogue, summarize episodes, debate subtexts, create original fan fiction, record their own soundtracks, make their own movies—and distribute all of this worldwide via the Internet. (Jenkins, 2006:16)

New models of consuming culture have been made possible by the volume and choice of information sources, by the fact that with our phones and digital devices we all have the potential to produce information rather than just consume, by our ability to connect with others who share our interests and by the ease with which digital information is replicable and shareable (Miller, 2011).

FROM CONVERGENCE CULTURE TO PARTICIPATION CULTURE

The concept of convergence is not simply about consuming new kinds of content in new ways. Convergence culture is also about new forms of digital culture and, importantly, as Jenkins points to in the quotation above, new forms of participation. While we have always consumed media from a variety of sources, the key shift identified by the range of concepts under the umbrella of participatory culture is that digital media has given us new tools and new ways in which we can be active contributors to content creation and culture.

What is participatory culture?

Participatory culture is about creating the kinds of online communities of interest we discussed in Chapter 2. Having a networked device, and something to say, gives us the potential to create a community of participants who create and share content with and for each other. In mapping the rise of participatory culture Jenkins defines it as:

> A culture with relatively low barriers to artistic expression and civic engagement, strong support for creating and sharing one's creations, and some type of informal mentorship whereby what is known by the most experienced is passed along to novices. A participatory culture is also one in which members believe their contributions matter, and feel some degree of social connection with one another (at least they care what other people think about what they have created). (Jenkins, 2009:xi)

To again emphasise the continuity of practices, this is not to suggest that participatory culture is in any way unique to digital media. Cultural and political expression has a long history and Jenkins' own concept of participatory culture has its roots in his earlier work on pre-digital fan cultures (Jenkins, 1992). The point is not that contributing to culture is a new or uniquely digital activity, rather that web 2.0 provides new kinds of tools for us to engage in these activities. Social media is a conduit for the sharing of content. We share stories, jokes and memes that are meaningful to us and in doing so we promote, advocate and spread that content. We participate in, create and shape what Jenkins calls spreadable media flows, empowering us as audiences as we become content creators (Jenkins et al., 2013).

Increasing participation on the part of the consumer blurs the boundaries between traditional producer and consumer roles and the concept of participatory culture feeds into wider debates about the nature of media content creation and production as a social, collaborative enterprise (Fuchs, 2014a). These have been variously defined as *prosumption* – the blurring of the roles of producer and consumer (Toffler & Alvin, 1980); the rise of the *produser* – the user as creator and producer (Bruns, 2008); and the *pro-am revolution* (Leadbeater, 2009) dissolving distinctions between amateurs and experts. Common to these various definitions and articulations of participatory culture is the idea that everyone has the potential to produce as well as consume media. This may take the form of tweeting about a TV programme while watching it, posting an Instagram story or a TikTok video, commenting on a news story online or keeping a blog; activities that involve us as users, fans and audiences in the creation of culture and online content (Fuchs, 2014b). These participatory knowledge cultures (Delwiche & Henderson, 2012) involve people collectively classifying, organising and building information:

> Armed with inexpensive tools for capturing, editing, and organising, people tap into a vast ocean of real-time data and multimedia content to promote personal and political interests. Functions once monopolised by a handful of hierarchical institutions (e.g. newspapers, television stations, and universities) have been usurped by independent publishers, video-sharing sites, collaboratively sustained knowledge banks, and fan generated entertainment. (Delwiche & Henderson, 2012:3)

Tapping into data and networks in this way opens up opportunities for creativity, engagement and activism and much of the early literature on participatory culture focused on the ways in which fans in particular contributed to pop culture online (Jenkins, 1992). Participatory culture as an act of leisure and cultural creativity has the potential to have a profound and enriching effect on our lives (Gauntlett, 2013; Lessig, 2008).

Why participate?

The act of creating media and putting it online can serve several purposes. We use social media to document memories through blogging or photo sharing, akin to keeping a digital diary or photo album that we can choose to keep private or to share with members of our networks. We post content to express our creativity, to connect with other people or to give ourselves a voice, using web 2.0 tools to create a global stage for the kinds of presentation of self discussed in Chapter 3; an idea of participation and presentation made explicit in the YouTube tagline 'broadcast yourself' (although interestingly YouTube removed this tagline in 2019 which some argue represents a shift in business model away from the independent content creators that helped grow the platform and a move towards corporate content).

In Chapter 3 we looked at selfies as a way in which Black and minority ethnic groups, who have been underrepresented or denied access to self-expression in mainstream media, have been able to make themselves visible in cultural spaces. The same logic of empowerment applies to participatory acts of content creation. Through new media forms people who are outside of the formal establishments of culture have the possibility to reach global audiences providing the potential for the average person to have an impact on their social world.

This idealised vision of the participatory and democratising nature of web 2.0 platforms and tools is not without tensions and contradictions, and these will be explored later in this chapter. But digital participation does afford us the opportunity to engage in wider social and political commentary, allowing us to speak about issues that are important to us and blogs in particular provide an illustrative example of the ways in which web 2.0 tools enable us to speak to global issues from our desktops.

Blogs as prosumption

Blogs first appeared in the mid-1990s, hosted by free commercial blogging platforms (open-source content management systems like LiveJournal, Blogger and more recently WordPress). They have grown exponentially: 40% of the web in 2021 is built on WordPress, there are an estimated 570 million blogs on the internet and around 7 million blog posts are published per day (Djuraskovic, 2022). With their low barrier to entry, blogs are a relatively easy-to-construct, interactive, flexible and inexpensive mode of self-publication, advertised by the Blogger. com platform as 'push button publishing for the people' (Herring et al., 2005; Jean Kenix, 2009; Papacharissi, 2013). Collectively, they are referred to as the blogosphere, a diverse and varied space of interconnected conversations and individual forms of self-expression (Herring et al., 2005).

A considerable body of academic research has studied the uses and impacts of blogs and while the highly dynamic, diverse and decentralised nature of the blogosphere makes categorisations of blogs difficult, with genres differing wildly in style and content; at an individual level we can think of blogs as reflections of personal experience (Schmidt, 2007).

An interesting example of the transformative potential of an individual blog is given by Clay Shirky (an American writer whose book *Here comes everybody: The power of organizing without organizations* explores how web 2.0 social media tools provides new means for people to collaborate, en masse, outside of formal institutional structures). In his TED talk *How the Internet will (one day) transform government* (Shirky, 2012) he cites Scottish school girl Martha Payne's blog Never-Seconds. In 2012 Martha Payne started documenting her school lunches, taking photographs of the food and critiquing the meal in terms of health, pieces of hair found and an overall Food-o-meter. Her blog went viral after the local council banned her from taking photos of her lunches because of the negative press attention that the blog had attracted. Following the ban Martha posted on the blog that she wasn't allowed to continue to take photos of the food and as the story circulated on the internet the backlash to this censorship came thick and fast. The next day the council removed the ban, following an intervention by the Education Secretary, and later made the decision that schools would offer all students unlimited servings of fruit, vegetables and bread.

One of the comments on the blog made the point that Martha should feel lucky, in a global context, to be offered any school food at all and in response she used her blog to fundraise for a food poverty charity. She went on to raise over £145,813 for Mary's Meals, a Scottish charity working globally to set up feeding programmes in the world's poorest communities. Martha subsequently appeared in numerous documentaries, received awards for public campaigning and fund-raising and wrote a book about her experience.

While examples like NeverSeconds point to the potential for blogs to provide individuals with a global voice, the ability to enact real change and a space in which to raise issues not usually attended to by mainstream media, they have often been idealised as a form of alternative media (Jean Kenix, 2009). It may be empowering to engage with participatory media in this way but democratising narratives need to be tempered by the reality that participatory culture has not fundamentally changed or seriously challenged the power relations and domi-nance of the main cultural industries and major media corporations; what Reed describes as the myth of egalitarian interactivity:

> The occasional exception to the rule – the blog comment or video that goes viral – serves mostly to keep alive the fantasy of a level playing field…A far more level playing field is indeed a potential within the capabilities of the net, but it is an as yet unfulfilled potential that will take collective social action, not just individual luck, to create. (Reed, 2018:44)

I started this chapter by highlighting the volume of content put online in a sin-gle internet minute but the myth of egalitarian interactivity that Reed (2018) identifies, about blogs like Martha's being the exception rather than the rule, raises questions about how many of us are actually content creators or prosumers engaging with web 2.0 technologies in a true participatory culture.

A VOCAL MINORITY

Many of us spend a substantial amount of time on social media but the reality is that a much smaller percentage of us are engaged and creative in the participa-tory ways that Jenkins describes. How many of us are regular bloggers, creating content for the consumption of people beyond our immediate and private social media sphere?

In 2010, Li and Bernoff (Li, 2010) found that of those who use the internet regularly 52% are inactive, 33% are passive spectators and 13% are creators. Over a decade later the creator economy is booming and 2023 statistics estimate that there are over 200 million content creators worldwide (Rayaprolu, 2023). As of April 2023, there were 5.18 billion internet users worldwide (Petrosyan, 2023) so we need to recognise that the notion of use covers a diverse range of activities – from clicking *'like'* on an image to something far more involved and creative:

> For the majority of users, their activity is anything but a communal effort towards a shared cause; they may participate simply to satisfy their individual curiosities or because they are interested in the same product, brand, band or topic…most people who visit user generated content sites are 'driven' there by (viral) forms of social media ('friends' networks) or by plain marketing mechanisms. (van Dijck & Nieborg, 2009:862)

Critiques of the concept of collective participation argue that individuals' engagement, participation and content production is overstated. The ability to participate in and contribute to web 2.0 environments does not mean that people will actually do this and in fact research suggests that only a relatively small number of people, the vocal minority, are active in creating content (Bobkowski & Smith, 2013; Cha et al., 2007; Mustafaraj et al., 2011). A more accurate model is one of consumption rather than creation.

Proactive and creative users are in a minority that highlights profound inequalities in participation (Lussier et al., 2010; Porlezza, 2019), excluding those who do not have the tools, opportunities or cultural and digital literacies from important forms of interaction and access to information (Luyt, 2003).

If use of the internet is largely consumptive, participating as part of consumer capitalism and in the context of leisure (van Dijck & Nieborg, 2009), does this render the creative and democratic possibilities of participation culture redundant? Thinking beyond individual blogs and the limitations of participatory culture, when we take a more macro perspective, we can think of other ways in which participation may have a cultural impact as part of our leisure and consumption habits.

TIKTOK AND COVID, PARTICIPATION AND INFORMATION

Video creation app TikTok was the most downloaded non-gaming app worldwide in 2020 (Shaul, 2020). TikTok surged in prominence and use during the pandemic and provides us with a useful example of the ways in which participation culture, even in a largely consumptive form, can be valuable. As newly enforced social distancing measures interrupted our face-to-face interactions TikTok was one of the many social media platforms that became a space of play and consumption of user-generated content.

Content about COVID-19 proliferated online (Abidin et al., 2021) and the platform demonstrated its viability as means for practitioners to educate and dispel myths about COVID-19 to a broad and diverse adolescent demographic (the largest share of users in the UK is aged 18–24 (26%) (Social Films, 2021); in the USA 63.5% of users are under 29 (Ceci, 2022). Emerging research indicates that while videos by healthcare professionals were in the minority they were among the most widely liked and shared on the platform (Ostrovsky & Chen, 2020), with government accounts used to share guidelines and information (Chen et al., 2021), supporting users seeking and sharing information about COVID-19.

Research has also emphasised the value of audience-centred interactions in public health communication via social media (Asenas & Hubble, 2018). This was evident during the pandemic. TikTok challenges were widespread and popular and UNICEF harnessed this in their use of a video of Vietnamese dancer @im.quangdang doing a 'hand-washing dance' to show how to properly wash your hands to protect from coronavirus, spawning a TikTok dance challenge (Cost, 2020).

Globally, social media influencers were sought after to promote COVID-19 etiquette and normalise new behaviours, demonstrating the potentials of participatory culture:

> This suggests the efficacy of influencers in information dissemination and control in the online space, as citizens worldwide relied on the Internet for information and entertainment during prolonged self-isolation and social distancing measures. (Abidin et al., 2021:124)

While more problematic issues of misinformation, sensationalism and vaccine hesitancy also find a platform on social media (Basch et al., 2022), use of TikTok during the pandemic provides an example of the value of online participation in uncertain and precarious times (Abidin et al., 2021).

YOUTUBE, HUMOUR AND PARTICIPATION

Silva and Garcia (2012), in their discussion of creative participation, focus on online remixes and processes of transformation and redistribution, providing another example of the value of consuming as a part of participatory culture. Connecting cultural participation with political participation and focusing on YouTube videos they argue that YouTube acts as a space for non-conventional participation in the public political sphere.

They emphasise the playful aspects of participation culture in their exploration of remixing and appropriation on YouTube and argue that play can be an expressive practice with political significance. They define this as grassroots participation that interferes in the mainstream mediascape. Highlighting the historical continuity of practices, they argue that while satire and humour have a long history in political and social life, they have been renewed by new participatory media environments.

They use the example of the 'downfall meme' (also known as 'Hitler finds out' or 'Hitler reacts to…') which uses a scene from the German WWII film *Der Untergang* that traces the last 10 days of Hitler's life. The scene depicts the moment when Hitler finds out that Germany's defeat is imminent, and he breaks down in front of four of his highest-ranking generals. In the meme the subtitles of this scene are replaced with new subtitles that bear no relation to the original content of the film. Derivative videos with subtitles in many languages have populated YouTube, typically replacing the original dialogue with subtitles about trivial news, gossip and current events.

The downfall parody has spawned thousands of videos and a YouTube channel @hitlerrantsparodies which acts as an archive and forum dedicated to the parody community (*Hitler's 'Downfall' Parodies | Know Your Meme*, n.d.). The channel hosts one of the most famous videos *'Hitler gets banned from Xbox Live'* as well as more politically oriented additions – *'Hitler is informed Twitter has banned Trump'*, *'Hitler finds out Hillary Clinton has won the presidential election (Alternative Universe)'*, *'Hitler finds out the UK has voted to leave the EU'*.

Silva and Garcia make the point that YouTube videos contribute to the constitution of counter publics, particularly when politicians and public figures become 'victims' of a meme. Thus, the meme follows longstanding traditions of satire in countering messages created in the mainstream media. In the context of institutional politcal communication satirical remixing can be regarded as a new form of political participation arising from playful practices of participatory culture (Silva & Garcia, 2012).

The importance of play as a mode of cultural communication is emphasised across participatory culture literature as a key component of political engagement and social connection (Jenkins, 2006; Milner, 2018). Play 'entices and exhilarates, and most importantly mobilizes participation and engagement through and across culture, politics, community and sociality' (Sujon, 2021).

This is not to assume that the playful creativity of all YouTubers represents politically motivated and engaged acts, but in providing an alternative view, remixing and the use of web 2.0 content and platforms become an accessible form of cultural communication:

> Offering an alternative language for discussing political issues, the parodic satires are in stark contrast with the 'politically correct' forms of debates

previously privileged. Uploaded to a worldwide repository, the videos are accessible to (almost) anyone with an Internet connection. These images hence become part of communication, not in the sense of broadcasting, or even narrowcasting, but of the creation of an imagetic commons, allowing them to be reused, remixed, reinterpreted. (Silva & Garcia, 2012:110)

We can understand these acts of consumption as a form of connection across a global network of communication. When we share user-generated content, like the 'downfall meme', we may not be active creators of content but the act of sharing content with and across our social media networks is meaningful. As Leadbeater argues, 'in the economy of ideas that the web is creating, you are what you share' (2009: 6).

User-generated content that is shared online is about more than the meme, the video or the post. These objects act as tools that enable us to connect and communicate across our social networks. In Chapter 2, I discussed the concept of networks in the context of rethinking ideas about community and I introduced Castells' logic of networks as the organising structure of contemporary society (Castells, 1996). Being connected to these networks through participatory culture, broadly defined as creating and sharing, enables us to conceive of participatory culture as one part of what Castells describes as a space of flows, 'the material organisation of simultaneous social interaction at a distance by networking communications' (Castells, 2010).

BLACK TWITTER AND EMPOWERING CULTURAL SPACES

Jenkins' optimistic blueprint for participatory culture highlights its emancipatory potential for a more democratic and inclusive mediascape (Condis, 2015). The examples discussed so far in this chapter point to some of the ways in which participatory culture may offer new spaces of creativity and engagement. We see new kinds of community formations, new voices represented and empowering cultural spaces emerging that promise a more heterogeneous landscape of cultural production than the disproportionately white, male, middle-class mainstream (Jenkins, 2006).

Brock's (2012, 2020) work on Black Twitter (I use Twitter here rather than X as it relates to scholarship that predates the name change) for example points to the platform as a space where X users who identify as Black perform, share and express Black cultural identity and, importantly, resist mainstream media narratives:

It's a space where mundane black folk can recover, rejoice, or rage without worrying about the gaze of people who have power over them. It also occasionally transforms into a counter-public sphere where issues germane to the black community, and by extension to the U.S., become visible without the gate-keeping of the media or cultural institutions, or the silences of government authorities...If we go back to Ferguson, Missouri, and Trayvon Martin, Black Twitter and Instagram are some of the first spaces online that had really compelling evocations of protest but also support for the protesters in ways that the mainstream media could not, in ways that the beleaguered black national media could not. (Pearson, n.d.)

Brock argues that Black Twitter has revealed alternate discourses to the mainstream, fostering a community and a 'social public' (2012). Similarly, the #BlackLivesMatter hashtag, created in July 2013, has been instrumental in urgent global conversations about endemic structural racism and police killings of unarmed Black citizens (Freelon et al., 2017). This kind of participatory culture has been used to educate and to amplify marginalised voices, mobilising communities into action against injustice. Networked social media impacts on how we communicate, connect and mobilise, blurring boundaries between formal and informal political spheres and widening definitions of political activities (Sujon, 2021).

In many ways these examples illustrate the fluidity and complexity of participatory culture as a concept. Participation can be what Sujon (2021: 150) defines as maximalist or minimalist and we don't necessarily know what we are referring to as participation.

This call for a more critical approach to the concept of participatory culture needs to be sensitive to how culture and structure intersect, considering the socio-economic implications of cultural trends and the divisions and inequalities embedded in their capitalist structures. This would ground our understandings of digital culture in relations of power and inequality, recognising that our capacities for agency and participation are profoundly unequal (Selwyn, 2019; Sujon, 2021; van Dijck & Nieborg, 2009).

Critiques of Jenkins point to his idealisation of community that side-lines the negative potentials and inherent inequalities of online spaces (Fuchs, 2014a). His later work (Jenkins, 2014) acknowledges concerns that networked communications do not necessarily result in more progressive, inclusive or democratic cultures and notes that corporations and individuals within these corporations retain and exert greater power than us as consumers. He also acknowledges critiques of his work that highlight the importance of understanding the socio-economic stratifications of technology access and use that shape how people are able to engage with technology; what Couldry calls the politics of convergence (Couldry, 2011).

Jenkins' response to his critiques is a claim to a *more* participatory culture. He notes that participation is a cultural, political and social act as much as a technological affordance and he highlights the potentials of these practices of collectivity while recognising the complicated and often contradictory outcomes:

> These new platforms and practices potentially enable forms of collective action that are difficult to launch and sustain under a broadcast model, yet these platforms and practices do not guarantee any particular outcome, do not necessarily inculcate democratic values or develop shared ethical norms, do not necessarily respect and value diversity, do not necessarily provide key educational resources and do not ensure that anyone will listen when groups speak out about injustices they encounter. (Jenkins, 2014:284)

For Jenkins, the value and aim of participatory culture is to enable as many people as possible to engage in practices and spaces where inequalities and injustices can be made visible, linking cultural resistance with institutional politics and enabling a more diverse and democratic society. But even in these most utopian emancipatory potentials we need to recognise the structural inequalities at play and acknowledge that participation can be simultaneously empowering and exploitative. While we can make a case that these are new spaces for collectivity, creativity and engagement they can also descend into incivility, passivity, trolling and hate (Delwiche & Henderson, 2012).

TikTok, exclusion and BlackLivesMatter

Inequalities and injustices are not transcended by social media and are deeply embedded in their design and use. The contradictory nature of participatory culture, both empowering and exclusionary, is exemplified by an incident with BlackLivesMatter content on TikTok at a time when activism was surging on social media platforms in response to a global uprising against police brutality and racism in the USA in May and June 2020.

Video creation app TikTok hosts short form videos where contributors post sketches, memes and dances based on audio and music provided through the app, with an emphasis on the creation and remixing of content (Klug, 2020). TikTok as a platform is algorithm driven rather than being modelled around following and followers, the implication being that content from a user with no followers can go viral, so popularity is not based on any individual's social network (Anderson, 2020).

Like social media platforms such as Facebook and X, TikTok has been criticised by its users for the way in which it deals with hate speech and harassment despite user community guidelines and sanctions. However, beyond concerns about the platform as a space giving voice to white nationalists and sexual predators, TikTok has also been criticised for censoring user content based on moderation policies targeting politically sensitive content (Anderson, 2020).

In June 2020, the US General Manager of TikTok and their Director of Creator Community released an apology after users complained that posts with the hashtags #BlackLivesMatter and #GeorgeFloyd were shown to have had zero views (Shead, 2020):

> Recently, our users have voiced tough but fair questions about whether all creators have an equal opportunity for their content to be seen and their experiences affirmed on TikTok. First, to our Black community: We want you to know that we hear you and we care about your experiences on TikTok. We acknowledge and apologize to our Black creators and community who have felt unsafe, unsupported, or suppressed. (Pappas & Chikumbu, 2020)

They stated that a temporary technical glitch had resulted in posts that used the hashtags appearing to be invisible and cited the fact that content with the hashtag had, to date, generated well over 2 billion views. They emphasised that the act was not intentional and stated their aim as a company to be proactive in promoting and protecting diversity, outlining actionable steps to foster an inclusive environment:

> At TikTok we deeply value the diverse voices among our users, creators, artists, partners and employees. We stand with the Black community and are proud to provide a platform where #BlackLivesMatter and #GeorgeFloyd generate powerful and important content with over 1 billion views. We are committed to fostering a space where everyone is seen and heard. (Pappas & Chikumbu, 2020)

Despite this a number of creators claimed that they have not been treated equally on the platform, arguing that community guidelines had not been fairly applied to Black creators who were victims of shadow banning by the platform (McCluskey, 2020). A shadow ban on social media is a sudden drop in views on a user's 'For you' page; the page that users land on when they open the app and the page where content is recommended. Usually, this would be the result of posting content that the platform deems inappropriate: nudity, drugs, violence, hate speech, copyrighted music and fake news. While TikTok claimed that this was not the case in the BlackLivesMatter content, they have previously been accused of (and deny) censoring of content that does not align with Chinese foreign policy, instructing moderators to censor videos that mention Tiananmen Square, Tibetan independence, the banned religious group Falun Gong and the 2019 protests in Hong Kong (Alex, 2019; Reuter & Köver, 2019).

ByteDance, the Chinese parent company of TikTok, make decisions about content censorship that are largely opaque and it is difficult to know what content is being labelled as in violation of their guidelines (Harwell & Romm, 2019). The platform was also forced to admit to supressing content from users it assumed to be vulnerable to cyberbullying. TikTok moderators were asked to make judgements about users' physical and mental traits to identify those who might be at high risk of bullying, notably people with disabilities, facial disfigurements, autism and Down syndrome:

> TikTok moderators maintained a list of 'special users' who were considered especially vulnerable to bullying. These users were generally rated as a risk and their videos were automatically capped...The list names 24 accounts, including people who post videos with hashtags such as #disability or write 'Autist' in their biographies. But the list also includes users who are simply fat and self-confident. A striking number show a rainbow flag in their biographies or describe themselves as lesbian, gay or non-binary. (Reuter & Köver, 2019)

These judgements prevented content from showing on other people's feed or stopped videos from being shown to audiences outside a creator's home country. For TikTok this was an antibullying stance that went wrong and for which they apologised, but it is indicative of the kinds of structural constraints and inequalities embedded in social media that critiques of the concept of participatory culture point to as undermining the ideal of equal participation.

Censorship of content also undermines the potential for users from minority groups to find content that is unrepresented in traditional media. This has important implications as social media architectures could exacerbate existing inequalities and, as a civic space, platforms need to be more accountable for and transparent about their biases and regulations (Are, 2020).

SOCIAL MEDIA, PARTICIPATION AND ONLINE EXTREMISM

This need for transparency is particularly important when we consider one of the implications of the democratisation of communications driven by user-generated content online; the rise of online extremism and hate speech. Hate speech and extremism are not a new or digital phenomena but the networked global reach of the internet and the limitations of platform user guidelines and regulations combine to make social media a breeding ground where hate has thrived (Alkiviadou, 2019; Daniels, 2018; Matamoros-Fernández & Farkas, 2021; Mathew et al., 2019).

> The great virtues of the Internet—ease of access, lack of regulation, vast potential audiences, fast flow of information, and so forth—have been converted into advantages for groups committed to terrorizing societies to achieve their goals. The anonymity offered by the Internet is very attractive to modern radicals, terrorists and vigilantes. Because of their extremist beliefs and values, these actors require anonymity to exist and operate in social environments that may not agree with their particular ideology or activities. The online platforms, from websites to social media and the Dark Net, provide this anonymity and easy access from everywhere with the option to post messages, to e-mail, to upload or download information and to disappear into the dark. (Weimann & Masri, 2023:754)

For example, Weimann and Masrim in their analysis of TikTok content found evidence of fascism, racism, anti-Semitism, anti-immigration, chauvinism, nativism and xenophobia with posts espousing violence, promoting conspiracy theories and glorifying terrorists (Weimann & Masri, 2023: 6). This is not unique to TikTok and social media platforms more generally have been spaces in which minority individuals and groups are targetted and extremist and hateful rhetoric is spread (Alkiviadou, 2019). Social media has become 'not merely a battleground but indeed a real weapon in the conflicts over resources, power and life choices' (Jakubowicz, 2017: 46).

The TikTok terms of service state that a user may not intimidate, harass, promote discriminatory material or post material that is hateful or inflammatory. YouTube states that they remove content promoting violence or hatred against individuals or groups based on age, caste, disability, ethnicity, gender identity, nationality, race, immigration status, religion, sexual orientation and veteran status. Similarly, Facebook community standards disallow hate speech, defined as an attack on a person on the basis of protected characteristics. However, research has highlighted the inability of platforms to impose their own guidelines and sanctions (Alkiviadou, 2019; Daniels, 2018; Ganesh, 2020).

Resolution to ongoing debates about free speech online is difficult, juggling individual right to expression with the potential for online extremism to pose danger. This is coupled with a lack of a global or universally accepted definition of what constitutes hate speech (Alkiviadou, 2019). Social media platforms cannot reply on imposing a single rule to monitor speech as multiple factors need to be assessed, including the magnitude and frequency of postings, the intent of the platform, and the content of the post and platform (Guiora & Park, 2017).

While the emphasis on context and platform is important, understanding the structural underpinnings of these spaces is also critical. Racism is baked into technology and as Daniels (2018) argues, while the rise of the alt-right marks a continuation of a centuries-old racism it is also part of an emerging media ecosystem powered by algorithms. There is a rich seam of research that has highlighted the ways in which race is coded into platforms and technologies and Daniels makes the vital point that racism online is not a 'bug' but is a feature of the system, with algorithms amplifying social media conversations in new ways.

This is an important distinction, emphasising the structural underpinnings of online behaviours rather than foregrounding the interactions, interpersonal relationships and establishment of social norms. This shifts our attention away from thinking of trolling, hate speech and incivility as individual acts and conflicts in anonymous spaces and towards an understanding of racism as part of how social media platforms are designed and governed (Daniels, 2018). This structural concern is echoed by Jakubowicz (2017) in what he calls the political economy of the internet – shaped by large corporations that monetise our connections and data. In his analysis of contemporary racism and the Alt-right online, Jakubowicz argues that the ideology of freedom and the democratic right of free expression underpinning the internet, combined with the anonymity, disengagement, and dis-inhibition of our internet activities has been significant in the growth of internet hate grounded in the hierarchies and privileges of unequal societies.

As this chapter has discussed, political acts of participatory culture are communicative acts that influence our understanding of politics and our understanding of how we relate to civil society. They are creating a new kind of 'personal public' (Asenas & Hubble, 2018) defined not by traditional mainstream news media but by web 2.0 participatory acts. However, rather than democratic spaces for the free exchange of ideas, social media platforms can be angry spaces where 'free speech' has to be curbed and censored (Asenas & Hubble, 2018).

Participatory culture is a complex concept that, in its more utopian vision, sees a public able to collectively participate in civic life with marginalised voices able participate more equally in new networked publics. This model of democratisation is troubled by the dominance and power of new media corporations, the replication of existing offline social inequalities, the need to interrogate social media systems as inherently biased and the complexities of how we manage freedom of expression in mediated environments.

DIGITAL METHODS AND TELLING THE SMALL STORIES

The methods reflection in Chapter 3 looked at some of the ways in which researchers have used social media platforms to scrape data: using hashtags or keywords to gather 'big' data to study events, social causes, social movements, disasters, elections and revolutions (Rogers, 2019). I argued that while this may enable us to collect a large volume of data and can give us a good idea of what people are doing online, it is less able to provide us with answers about why people behave in certain ways or about the meanings users ascribe to their use.

This chapter has considered examples of how social media, as sites of prosumption, also enable us to share the 'small moments' of daily life (Schellewald, 2021). In order to understand digitally mediated sharing and participation as a cultural phenomenon this methodological note will focus on the ways in which digital methods can also help us to understand the micro. Using the example of the qualitative interview this methodological reflection looks at ways in which digital methods can be used to adapt traditional methods to address diverse research questions and research settings in digital spaces.

Small story research

As this chapter has argued, sharing our lives and telling stories online is integral to web 2.0. The use of 'stories' as a design feature of social media is increasingly common across a range of platforms including Snapchat, Instagram, Facebook and Weibo (Georgakopoulou, 2016, 2017, 2022; Page, 2015). Online these stories or micro narrations have become small fragmented units which can be understood as performative, context-specific 'small stories' (Bainotti et al., 2021; Sadler, 2021). With the ubiquity of social participatory media and the convergence of media forms, web 2.0 spaces and platforms have been characterised by their tendency to report the mundane and trivial aspects of ordinary life and are closely associated with the features of a small story:

> Social media environments afford opportunities for sharing life in miniaturized form at the same time as constraining the ability of users to plunge into full autobiographical mode (e.g., the constraint of 140 characters on Twitter). In particular, they offer users the ability to share experience as it is happening with various semiotic (multi-modal) resources, to update it as often as necessary and to (re)-embed it in various social platforms. (Georgakopoulou, 2017:269)

Georgakopoulou argues that small story research is well placed to study how we tell stories on social media. She uses the concept of small story research to focus on the ways in which language shapes and is shaped by social practices (Georgakopoulou, 2017). Small story research draws together a number of methods including digital ethnography, discourse analysis and narrative-semiotic analysis, in order to chart the multiple forms that life writing takes over a range of social media platforms. This technography of stories traces media affordances, uncovers the values embedded in the design of platforms, explores discourses about stories and highlights users' communicative practices (Georgakopoulou, 2022: 270).

The technographic approach of the small story method, like the walkthrough method outlined in Chapter 4, can sensitise us to technological structures and affordances that may shape user experience when narrating the minutia of life. However, these kinds of digitally native methods do not necessarily tell the whole story. Earlier in the chapter I argued that rather than being passive adopters of digital technologies and spaces, users subvert, resist and reshape technological affordances in a range of complex and often counterintuitive ways. We also know that despite the hyperbole around web 2.0 participation, for many, 'use' is characterised by inactivity and more passive forms of engagement. So, questions of why people behave in certain ways or questions about the meanings users ascribe to their use (or non-use) may need to return to qualitative methods that focus on in-depth understandings of users and of their meaning-making, intentions, subjectivities and experiences.

Using 'old' methods in new spaces

Qualitative interviews have long been used by social scientists as a foundational method for in-depth qualitative research, employed to understand the motivations, experiences, perceptions, attitudes and feelings of social actors (Edwards & Holland, 2020). However, the focus on big data-driven approaches to social enquiry have raised questions about the nature and value of sociological methods in the context of a proliferation of digital data:

> A world inundated with complex processes of social and cultural digitization; a world in which commercial forces predominate; a world in which we, as sociologists, are losing whatever jurisdiction we once had over the study of 'the social' as the generation, mobilization and analysis of social data become ubiquitous. (Savage & Burrows, 2007: 763)

For Savage and Burrows (2007) 'knowing capitalism' poses a challenge for some traditional sociological methods, rendering them inadequate for social scientists trying to explain an increasingly complex social world in a neoliberal knowledge economy. In particular, this brings into question the value of the qualitative interview, with data from individual interview testimonies deemed 'inconsequential to greater humanistic and scientific understanding' (Lanford et al., 2019). In part this rests on the problematic assumption that big data, unlike its small counterpart, is a 'naturalistic' form of real and authentic data, providing direct access to people's beliefs and experiences, unfiltered by the bias and influence of the processes of data collection. But all data, big and small, is socially constructed, socially mediated, assembled and interpreted by researchers seeking to understand a phenomenon.

There is a case to be made for the enduring relevance of the qualitative interview and for the creative (re)articulation of the method in digital contexts (Edwards & Holland, 2020). The value of small form, mundane, and minor data is emphasised as important and transformative (Koro-Ljungberg et al., 2017).

Qualitative interviews have always been shaped by technologies, from technologies for recording and transcription, to tools for asynchronous and synchronous text-based interviews and, more recently, the use of e-mail, chat forums and video conferencing platforms. Advocates of online interviews, in their various guises, cite the benefits of convenience, removing barriers of geographical and temporal distance and the financial constraints of bringing researchers and participants together. These logistical advantages make online interviews more flexible and convenient and, as a result of their relative anonymity, they are also of value in recruiting hard to reach populations or respondents and for recruiting for research around sensitive topics (Novick, 2008; O'Connor & Madge, 2017; Opdenakker, 2006).

While online interviews may help overcome some logistical challenges, technical difficulties, poor connection and limited access to the internet and/or connectable devices may constrain the diversity of the research sample, with more vulnerable and excluded people limited in their ability to meaningfully participate. Critics have also voiced concern about the difficulties of establishing a clear sense of trust and rapport in disembodied mediated interactions (Palys & Atchison, 2012).

Video conferencing platforms like Zoom, Teams, Skype, Google Hangouts Meet or GoToMeeting enable the interviewer to pick up on non-verbal, visual cues and communication, fostering personal, emotional, and intimate interaction, alleviating some of concerns around the ability of online interviews to build the same kind of rapport as their in-person counterparts (Deakin & Wakefield, 2014; Lawrence, 2022; Oliffe et al., 2021). As such, technologies incorporating visual and audio communication may replicate, complement, and possibly improve upon traditional interview methods (Archibald et al., 2019). Most recently, during the COVID-19 pandemic, their use re-engaged methodological debates about the value of digitally mediated interviews.

At a time when we were all digital by default, researchers seeking solutions to the challenges of conducting research during physical and social distancing turned to online interviews as an obvious solution. However, conducting online interviews is not simply a logistical decision in response to crisis or distance. Their value is also in their informality as a medium and they may be more suited to some research contexts or respondents who are at ease with the familiar settings and modes of interaction in online spaces. Digital articulation of the qualitative interview help to shift the narrative from in-person interviews as the 'golden standard' (Thunberg & Arnell, 2022), prompting reflection on the ways in which online interviews may complement and augment existing qualitative methods (Archibald et al., 2019).

Qualitative interviews in digital contexts

One example of online interviews augmenting existing qualitative methods comes from Hannell's (2021) work on Muslim fangirls. In her study of how Muslim girls understand their fandom as rooted in a desire to be creative and to engage in participatory storytelling she used online interviews via instant messaging platforms. This enabled her to adopt the style of interaction that the fangirls she was studying routinely engaged in. She also used the instant messaging platforms to encourage her participants to share examples of their fanworks to help her respondents show how cultural production is a meaningful way for them to exercise their public voice.

Similarly, Kunert's (2021) work on female football fandom on Tumblr offered respondents the option of audio chat, video chat, or instant messaging for participating in interviews. The majority of her respondents chose text messages as a format, mirroring their dominant form of communication on Tumblr (which oriented around the exchange of illustrations and match reports via mobile devices) and enabling them to use their Tumblr slang and to forward in-platform links and posts to illustrate points they wanted to make in the interviews.

In both examples the methodological tool employed reflected the participants' activities on the platform, highlighting practices that may have been rendered invisible using other research methodologies. The importance of this methodological understanding of the ways in which textual and visual app-based communication is used in everyday interaction is also emphasised by Anderdal Bakken (2022). She argues that social researchers need to be better equipped to include a range of ways to interact digitally with participants in qualitative interviews. Rather than conceiving of interview methods and digital tools as a means with which to replicate the in-person encounter of the traditional face-to face-interview, we need to broaden use of digital interviewing to include the kinds of text-based asynchronous interaction that is native to many digital apps.

In her work on young people selling illegal drugs online, Anderdal Bakken used text-based app Wickr for interviewing. This was the same digital communication platform used by her target population, making it a natural interview setting. This natural setting challenges traditional understandings of synchronicity in interviewing. For Anderdal Bakken (2022), her text-based interviews were both synchronous and asynchronous, a mix of oral and textual interaction that made use of the affordances of the mobile application she employed. This created an interview setting with almost no spatial or temporal limits. This changes the nature and flow of interaction and can be challenging for researchers and respondents. Interviews may continue over long periods of chat, in unscheduled periods of time creating an 'always on' field site akin to continuous immersive fieldwork:

> app-based interviews are similar to holding conversations during ethnographic fieldwork and not as a more formal interview situation with set limitations of time and space. When using a mobile phone application for interviews, the interview situation itself embeds into the everyday life of the interviewees, as well as for the interviewer. (Anderdal Bakken, 2022:10)

The immersion is enabled by using a platform which interviewees are already comfortable and familiar with, creating new spaces of interaction and new ways of defining, understanding and employing digitally mediated qualitative interviews as a methodology.

Combining digital tools with techniques of qualitative interviewing provides an example of how digital data can also be rich data. This is not to suggest that big and little data are binary opposites or incompatible in terms of the insights they can reveal. Rather the sheer volume of accessible data, made possible by the capabilities of digital methods, may result in an abundance of data that is challenging to describe and interpret in depth (Latzko-Toth et al., 2017). The purpose of this methodological reflection is to not continue an unhelpful dichotomy between 'big' data and 'small' data; rather to highlight some creative ways in which methods can be employed to address diverse research questions and research settings that may not be amenable to traditional face-to-face methods or to approaches more commonly associated with computational social science.

CONCLUSION

This chapter explored the concept of digital sharing and the consumption of digital culture. Key ideas in this chapter can be summarised as followed:

- Web 2.0 is characterised by participation and interaction as users of the web become content creators engaging in new forms of collective interactivity and cultural production. New media landscapes are, optimistically, hailed for their emancipatory possibilities for public participation, social inclusion and democratisation.

- Participatory culture blurs the boundaries between traditional producer/consumer roles opening opportunities for creativity, engagement and activism. However, despite these affordances, critiques of participatory culture point to an overwhelming model of consumption rather than production and highlight profound inequalities in participation.
- Social media platforms provide spaces for non-conventional participation in the public political sphere. Acts of creation and consumption create connections across global networks and can foster empowering cultural spaces. However, in a mediascape where large corporations retain and exert power the politics of participation does not necessarily equate to progressive, inclusive and democratic cultures.
- Algorithms and new networks also amplify hate speech, extremism and prejudice in participatory environments grounded in the hierarchies, privileges and inequalities of society more broadly.
- Studying online spaces and interactions does not always demand or suit digital methods and traditional methodological tools can be effectively employed in an understanding of the digital.

Further reading

Jenkins, H. (2014). Rethinking 'rethinking convergence/culture'. *Cultural Studies, 28*(2), pp. 267-297.

The concept of convergence and participatory culture that has been the focus of this chapter has its roots in the work of Henry Jenkins whose writing on media studies include *Convergence culture, Fans, bloggers, and gamers: Exploring participatory culture*, and *Textual poachers: Television fans and participatory culture*. In this article he responds to a special issue of the journal *Cultural Studies* devoted to 'Rethinking Convergence/Culture' in a discussion that addresses critiques of his concept of participation.

Kaye, D.B.V., Zeng, J., & Wikstrom, P. (2022). *TikTok: Creativity and culture in short video*. John Wiley and Sons.

This chapter used the example of TikTok as a space of cultural production in uncertain and precarious times. *TikTok: Creativity and culture in short video* explores how the platform influences cultures, facilitating creativity, community building and activism. Drawing on a range of timely and interesting case studies the authors explore the challenges posed by TikTok's regulatory and algorithmic mechanisms which foster a sense of individual and collective agency as well as creating a space of disempowerment.

Burgess, J., & Green, J. (2018). *YouTube: Online video and participatory culture*. John Wiley and Sons.

In this book Burgess and Green examine YouTube as an object of study exploring its structures, customs and practices. Chapter 5 in particular relates to the themes discussed in this chapter, focusing on the cultural politics of YouTube and its capacity to enable ordinary people, particularly those marginalised from other forms of cultural representation. They argue that the platform enables participation in popular culture vital for political participation and citizenship.

Beer, D. (2009). Power through the algorithm? Participatory web cultures and the technological unconscious. *New Media and Society*, *11*(6), pp. 985-1002.

In this article Beer sets out a critical agenda to the study of the purported empowerment and democratisation of web 2.0 and participatory culture. Drawing on the work of new media theorist Scott Lash, Beer provides an accessible argument that outlines the power of the new media ontology, pre-empting contemporary debates around algorithmic power and the shaping of cultural experiences.

Hockin-Boyers, H., & Clifford-Astbury, C. (2021). The politics of# diversifyyourfeed in the context of Black Lives Matter. *Feminist Media Studies*, *21*(3), pp. 504-509.

Hockin-Boyers and Clifford-Astbury provide an interesting example of the ways in which we as users of participatory social media can shape our consumption of digital culture to create inclusive digital environments, using the idiom 'diversify your feed'. Using the examples of body positivity and Black Lives Matter they question whether greater engagement with social media help tackle issues of social inequality.

Rogers, R. (2019). *Doing digital methods*. Sage.

While I have focused on qualitative interviews in this chapter, students interested in the study of participatory culture more generally may find Chapter 9 of Rogers' methods text helpful. In the chapter *Memes or virals: Identifying engaging content on Facebook* he takes the meme as a cultural object and discusses how we might treat it as an object of study.

6

DIGITAL LEISURE

The previous chapters in this book have emphasised the ways in which our everyday lives are increasingly entangled and interconnected with digital devices. These technologies have also had a profound impact on how we experience our leisure time. Indeed, the concept of leisure has underpinned many of the ideas explored in the book so far. Leisure brings people together in the kinds of online communities discussed in Chapter 2. The mediated practices of representation explored in Chapter 3 are also leisure practices of sharing and performing identity online. The acts of participatory culture considered in Chapter 5 are leisure activities oriented around user-generated content. The ubiquity of digital information and communication technologies in everyday life has transformed how we experience and understand leisure activities and practices, giving us new online spaces in which to participate in leisure as well as reshaping traditional offline leisure activities.

This chapter does not focus in detail on individual forms that leisure might take in a digital context, for example online gaming, music streaming or the consumption of digital media more generally. These are integral to studies of digital leisure but have become objects of study in their own right and a large literature has emerged concerning, for example, game studies and the sociological study of digital music. Instead, the focus in this chapter is on the ways in which digital technologies blur the boundaries of work and play and shape how we experience our leisure time. Using a range of examples from knitting to travel to wearable sensors the chapter explores the ways in which leisure has taken on new digital forms as well considering the ways that traditional leisure activities have been transformed through digitisation and mediation.

As you read this chapter, I encourage you to think about the following questions:

- How have digital technologies blurred the boundaries between work and leisure?
- In what ways do digital technologies mediate our experiences of leisure?

- How has the digitisation and mediation of leisure shaped how we understand and experience our leisure time?
- How have digital wearables shaped how we participate and experience daily activities?

WHY LEISURE?

The pursuit of leisure has long been regarded as an essential component in our subjective well-being, playing an important role in how we build social relationships, acquire skills and improve our quality of life (Brajša-Žganec et al., 2011; Kuykendall et al., 2018). The field of leisure studies has traced the long history of leisure from Classical Greek understandings of leisure as a cultural ideal to the concept of leisure time as distinct from work in the industrial revolution (Hemingway, 1996; Hunnicutt, 2006). Leisure permeates many aspects of our lives, encompassing sport, travel and tourism, hospitality, media, events, heritage and the arts, with practices of leisure widely reported as beneficial in meeting a range of psychological and social needs. Perhaps because of this scope the concept of leisure has been contested in the sociological literature. Some definitions emphasise the temporal aspects of leisure, while others emphasise its experiential qualities (Wilson, 1980).

Leisure can be defined as a period of time (that is not work), as something that is freely chosen and as a state of mind characterised by freedom, positive affect and intrinsic motivations (Schultz & McKeown, 2018). As such, it can be understood as a multidimensional and multifaceted experience that is a resource for human development, a source of health and well-being and symbolic of quality of life, undertaken for its own pleasure, voluntary and separate from practices of labour (Blanco, 2015).

Blanco defines four kinds of leisure: substantive leisure, active leisure, creative leisure and dignified leisure (2015). Substantive leisure (also defined as serious leisure (Stebbins, 2017)), refers to the systematic pursuit of an activity or hobby where participants develop special skills, knowledge, and experience, pursuing an activity that requires perseverance and commitment. Active leisure relates to activities we proactively choose and desire rather than simply movement or being active. Creative leisure relates to experiences of creativity that are enriching and satisfying. Dignified leisure refers to leisure experiences that bring meaning to our lives through helping others (Blanco, 2015).

Perhaps more important than a unifying definition of leisure is a recognition that there is no leisure outside of society (Rojek, 1985). Leisure is a historical construction and is both a product and a reflection of social, cultural, religious, political, economic and technical contexts (Hunnicutt, 2006). There are considerable cultural and historical differences in how leisure is valued and experienced (Hunnicutt, 2006). In order to understand leisure practices we need to situate them in these historical and social contexts and, as such, leisure needs to be understood as a dynamic and open-ended process (Rojek,1999). Contemporary understandings of leisure also need to situate it in the context of the information communication technologies that have transformed our daily lives (Rojas de Francisco et al., 2016).

Historically, leisure activities have always had a symbiotic relationship with technology. Since the beginning of industrialisation most leisure activities have been profoundly shaped by a range of technologies, from the printing press to the phonograph, from cinema to radio and television (Caldwell, 2012):

> Gains in productivity resulting from technology's use have led to an increase in time and money, the principal commodities that make participation in leisure possible. Whether watching TV at home or taking a holiday flight, leisure-time activities have been increasingly influenced by technology. Technology, as a consequence, has become more and more connected with both the economical conditions for the possibility of leisure and with the actual leisure-time activities themselves. (Poser, 2011:2)

This technology-based expansion of domestic leisure has intensified with the advent of digital technologies that have facilitated a transformation of contemporary leisure practices (Bryce, 2001; Rojek, 1999). Our leisured lives are entangled with digital services, platforms and cultural forms to the extent that a contemporary understanding of leisure necessitates an understanding of digital culture (Silk et al., 2016).

DEFINING DIGITAL LEISURE

The concept of digital leisure is no less contested than that of traditional leisure. Some have employed the idea of mediated leisure to highlight how leisure is increasingly facilitated and influenced by technology (Krotz, 2008; Nimrod & Adoni, 2012; Parry & Light, 2014). Mediated leisure encapsulates the kinds of activities we do online, watching YouTube videos, streaming movies and music or participating in social media channels.

In reality, many digital leisure activities are also associated with face-to-face leisure activities, with digital leisure practices informing and integrating with offline leisure practices and vice versa (Rojas de Francisco et al., 2016). This chapter does not define digital leisure as simply the digitisation and mediation of traditional leisure activities, reading a digitised book on an e-reader, playing a game of backgammon online or listening to music and curating a playlist via Spotify. Nor does it only define digital leisure as the kinds of social, communicative and collaborative activities that have been the focus of the previous chapters of the book, sharing memes in online communities, having a teleparty via Netflix or playing in social media apps. This chapter seeks to explore a definition of digital leisure that encompasses a digitisation of leisure experiences that interact with, enhance and transform traditional leisure as well as leisure practices that have emerged as a result of digitisation.

Digital leisure practices

Digital technologies are a central part of contemporary leisure as wireless connectivity and interactive web interfaces have expanded dimensions of our lived experience (Choi & Dattilo, 2017). The consumption of a range of digital media forms give shape to our leisure time as we embrace them as an integral and embedded part of our lifestyles.

The study of digital leisure practices has often focused on adolescents as the first generation to grow up in an environment characterised by the ubiquitous use of digital technologies. For adolescents, leisure is a key component in personal development (Sivan et al., 2019) and digital leisure for adolescents spans a wide range of activities; connecting with friends and consuming social media, downloading music, uploading videos, sharing photos and using digital technologies as tools for socialising (Valtchanov & Parry, 2017). In this sense digital technologies have provided new spaces and new tools to engage in leisure practices, with the smartphone in particular permeating many aspects of adolescents' lives and shaping how they choose to spend their time. Smartphones are used for *eudemonic* activities: to organise, support and share leisure experiences, such as arranging when and where to meet or sharing images before, during and after events and gatherings. They are also for *hedonic* activities: as a leisure activity in themselves used for streaming and watching films, scrolling social media content, gaming, listening to music and generating and sharing content either alone or with friends. They also act to constrain the leisure of young people, through non-ownership, by creating a lack of engagement in other activities or by encouraging sedentary activity (Allaby & Shannon, 2020; Kil et al., 2021).

Smartphones are central in the leisure lives of young people as a tool for low commitment transitory leisure. In their research on youth leisure and smartphone use, Allaby and Shannon (2020) argue that smartphones 'kill', 'pass', and 'fill' time for young people as a default and passive leisure choice that alleviates boredom.

Phones are used while participating in other leisure activities with young people multitasking across digital platforms, reading messages or scrolling social media while watching a film. This kind of passive smartphone use has also been referred to as 'leisure boredom' (Kil et al., 2021).

Paralleling debates introduced in Chapter 2 about the possible deleterious impact of information communication technologies on community, much of this research has focused on exploring how smartphone use may subsume or replace traditional leisure forms (Katz et al., 2001). However, rather than thinking of 'traditional' and digital leisure as two distinct domains is it conceptually more useful to conceive of a continuum of complementary activities shaped by who and how they are performed (Sintas et al., 2023).

Smartphone use and multitasking is not the sole preserve of young people and much research has focused on the smartphone in particular as a device that can blur the boundaries between home/work/leisure creating flows of networked connectivity (Boswell & Olson-Buchanan, 2007; Son & Chen, 2018). In the context of leisure this blurring of boundaries has been defined as fast leisure (Ortega et al., 2011; Rojek, 1999). Fast leisure is fragmented and ephemeral, ubiquitous and not temporally bounded – micro-games snatched in moments between work, TikTok swiping as the kettle boils or solving wordle puzzles while we watch TV or listen to a podcast:

> a lcisure time that is interstitial, interactive, more selective, shorter lasting, and based on micro formats, and where entertainment, pleasure, relaxation, recreation and fun are what matter. (Blanco, 2015:171)

These kinds of practices and spaces are intertwined with our lives in ways that physical leisure spaces and activities are not (Schultz & McKeown, 2018). When the boundaries between home/work/play are redrawn by our ubiquitous connectivity the distinctiveness of leisure time is eroded; what Sintas et al. (2015) describe as a heterotopic space in which any combination of time, space and activity is possible.

Leisure time is not solely the time we have left when we have completed all of our necessary tasks; residual or left-over time that is free from obligations and characterised by choice (Nimrod & Adoni, 2012). Instead, leisure activities are entangled and intertwined in our daily lives and digital technologies have destabilised leisure activities in relation to time and place (Rojas de Francisco et al., 2016). We browse social media platforms and scroll through Instagram and TikTok as a leisure activity that punctuates our multitasking day. We play online games and communicate with friends and family between work emails, and we consume and curate digital media as part of our leisure time. As such, digital leisure is a gateway to the internet that reconstitutes our understandings of global and mobile internet practices (Rangaswamy & Arora, 2016).

THE DIGITISATION AND RECONFIGURATION OF LEISURE

Digital leisure cannot simply be defined in terms of new digital tools and new spaces, and it is not restricted to the life worlds of a single generation. If we conceive of digital leisure as a range of practices that are mediated in different ways, we can get a richer sense of how digital technologies contribute to, disrupt and reconfigure leisure.

Digitising material leisure: Knitting and social media

One way of defining digital leisure is to look at the ways in which traditional leisure activities have been digitised and mediated (Blanco, 2015). In my own work I have used the example of knitting to argue that social media technologies have become a reciprocal and interconnected aspect of craft as a leisure practice.

In the last decade, there has been a resurgence of interest in knitting as a form of leisure (Parkins, 2004; Turney, 2009). From 'stitch n bitch' groups to pub knitting circles, new public sites for participating in knitting have emerged as part of a contemporary craft movement. Accompanying this renaissance is a growing presence of 'crafters' on the web, with blogs, podcasts and social networking sites connecting a global community of knitters (Orton-Johnson, 2014). Knitters photograph and blog about their projects and yarns, chat and plan face-to-face knit festivals via forums, search for YouTube videos and podcasts to learn new skills, follow 'celebrity' knit bloggers and sell and exchange patterns and yarn via knitting networking sites and visual social media spaces like Instagram. This combination of knitting and social media shifts the popular stereotype of knitting as a leisure pursuit of grandmothers and dull domesticity (Greer, 2008) and challenges the notion of technology as the preserve of the 'digital native' (Bennett et al., 2008).

As a form of leisure, knitting and ubiquitous computing have combined to create an activity that is a mix of the personal and the (networked) social (Rosner & Ryokai, 2009). Social media has given knitters new ways to think about and engage with their craft that, in turn, have become an embedded part of their construction and enjoyment of knitting as a leisure pursuit. By posting and sharing knitting projects on social media sites like Instagram and specialist social networking sites like Ravlery knitting as a leisure activity is remediated and reshaped with, through and in digital spaces and networks.

Launched in 2007, Ravelry is a specialist social networking site for knitting and crochet that incorporates many of the same features as other more generic social networking sites. Members create profiles that can include biographical information such as age and location as well as profile pictures and links to their other websites or blogs. The site also acts as a searchable yarn and pattern database with members active in creating, editing and building a growing collection of shared projects and resources.

Sites like Ravelry add another (digital) layer to the tactile process of knitting, extending and reforming the leisure experience of the knitter. New technologies have enabled people to amplify and extend well-established leisure practices. As such, for leisure practices like knitting, the emergence of an associated participatory web culture can reshape the experience of the craft. The material, tactile processes of knitting are integrated with digital practices of life streaming, and the boundaries and practices of knitting are extended as material handicrafts converge with web 2.0 technologies.

This kind of digitised, mediated knitting represents a point of convergence for academic debates on the nature of online and offline community, on the new forms of production and consumption in web 2.0 environments and on the meaning of identity, connection, participation and leisure in networked societies (Orton-Johnson, 2014).

The study of techno-cultural change marks a territory where distinctions between leisure and technology are increasingly dissolved and knitting as a material craft provides a useful example of the way in which virtual networks and environments have reshaped the consumption of leisure in rich and dynamic ways. Gauntlett (2013) argues that through creating and, importantly, sharing our acts of creativity we feel engaged and connected with the social world, investing it with meaning. For knitters, these newly defined boundaries and practices take a form of leisure popularly associated with old ladies, unwanted Christmas jumpers and the private sphere of the home and provide a forum for presenting knitting as a meaningful leisure activity. I draw on knitting as an example of an activity that could be easily conceived of as highly material and corporeal, in order to illustrate the ways in which digital technologies have enhanced and (re) configured how people understand and experience knitting as leisure.

Similar examples of the digitisation of leisure changing the experience of leisure can be found in other leisure activities. Coward-Gibbs (2021) uses the example of analogue boardgames or table top gaming. While inherently a physical shared experience, analogue gaming has a presence on social media platforms with the digitisation of many popular games such as Settlers of Catan, Puerto Rico and Agricola (Rogerson et al., 2015).

The next section of this chapter highlights how digitisation has shaped traditional leisure practices using a second example, leisure travel, a sphere traditionally seen as inherently distinct from paid work and everyday living which has intersected with social media platforms in ways that transform experiences of travel and tourism.

Digitising global leisure: Influencers and Instagram

Historically, technological advances in transport and travel have been important in opening up access to leisure spaces and enabling international travel (Bryce, 2001). Social media technologies have, in turn, shaped tourism as a leisure practice, changing the ways in which we consume and experience travel as leisure. Instagram in particular has had a profound impact on how tourists interact with and imagine destinations and is a popular channel for sharing images of travel with millions of contributors posting images of their trips, experiences and destinations. Tourists use social media to co-construct their experiences through shared images, videos or written narratives. This becomes a digital display of their travels but also opens opportunities to share and re-experience their tourism through the mediated process of retelling. Much like I argue that social media activity becomes *part* of knitting as a leisure experience, the consumption and curation of travel images on Instagram extends and transforms the experience of leisure travel:

> Personalised digital narratives not only enable people to organise their experiences, the digital storage prompts tourists to continuously reengage with them. As a result, tourists are supported in transforming their experiences into meaningful memories which then contributes to both, shaping personal identity. (Seeler et al., 2019:82)

In addition to helping us engage with our own memories, social media also enables us to consume the travel experience of others, arousing interest in destinations, providing inspiration and acting as electronic word-of-mouth travel advice (Barbe et al., 2020; Smith, 2021).

Along with other Instagram genres, the travel genre has created a space in which social media influencers or micro celebrities can monetise their content and accumulate material and cultural capital (Abidin, 2014, 2016b). Influencers must attract large audiences, foster a connection with their followers and generate interest and interaction around the content they post. Influencers with large-enough followings become entrepreneurs, attractive to businesses and corporations who wish to use their influence as a tool for selling products and services. In the same way that digital technologies have blurred boundaries in other spheres of life, here they blur the boundaries between leisure and work for influencers, disrupting understandings of tourism as escapist leisure, a liminal experience and a break from daily life.

In the context of travel, influencers have become increasingly important in social media spaces where tourists seek travel information and inspiration (Femenia-Serra et al., 2022). Travel influencers use travel selfies and, importantly, the backgrounds and destinations displayed, to gain valuable cultural currency that can boost likes, followers and social capital (Smith, 2021). Many of these are iconic travel images, with tourists frequently queuing at famous sites in order to take the same 'must have' photograph to join a hashtag, Preikestolen (Pulpit rock) in Norway and the leaning Tower of Pisa in Italy being two iconic examples.

This is not a new or uniquely digital phenomena and travel and photography has long been a feature of tourism, but social media practices are increasingly shaping our experiences and understandings of place and leisure. Landscapes and places become 'spectacles' for leisure tourists seeking to boost likes and followers on social media (Smith, 2021); extending Urry's tourist gaze to include digital spaces (Urry & Larsen, 2011). Popular and successful posts imitate those posted by influencers creating a situation in which some iconic landmarks and images become sought after 'bucket list' pictures with capturing the image becoming a primary focus of tourism as a leisure practice:

> When conceived as items to be ticked off a 'bucket list' landscapes are collected as signs buttressing the performance of individual status and desirability, serving as a badge decorating the branded self and as an aesthetic backdrop in the adroit execution of self-advertisement. (Smith, 2021:620)

While social media influencers could be compared to travel writers before them, the global reach of Instagram places influencers in a more immediate role. This can have a material impact on the landscapes and places represented in popular influencer posts. There have been numerous examples of places transformed by their online 'instafame'; the hashtag #SuperBloom for example saw Walker Canyon near the town of Lake Elsinore California overrun by tourists. Dubbed 'poppy apocalypse', the site was unable to cope with the influx of visitors following Instagram influencers posting images of the fields of flowers (Chiu, 2019). This resulted in the temporary closure of the site in a public safety crisis (Gammon, 2019).

A more permanent example of this kind of Instafame can be found at Horseshoe bend on the Colorado River in northern Arizona. This is one example of a landmark that has become a social media destination as travel influencers increase awareness of lesser-known places and spark interest in previously unspoilt locations (Barbe et al., 2020). Horseshoe bend is a site where the Colorado River takes a dramatic u-shaped turn forming a deep canyon. The site has gone from having around a thousand visitors a year to around 1.5 million visitors a year largely as a result of its popularity on social media. Images tagged as #horseshoebend have resulted in tourists flocking to the site, queuing for hours to recreate the icon shots and selfies that they see on Instagram feeds.

It has become the one of the most Instagrammable locations in the USA with its popularity causing concerns about overcrowding and conservation of the area. What was once a trailhead on a dirt site now has two large car parks with a viewing area designed to protect visitors and the environment. The digital popularity of the site has resulted in structural and permanent physical changes (Haubursin Christophe, 2018; Law, 2017).

While there is a longer history of travel and tourism impacting the environment, Instagram and travel influencers give us an example of the ways in which the cultural and physical experience of leisure is digitally mediated. Through online representations leisure travel becomes abstracted from place as landscapes become visual commodities separated from their human and temporal contexts (Smith, 2021). In the same way that online articulations of knitting (re)configure the material practice of the craft, online representations of tourism shape place and have material impacts on the landscapes they represent.

Leisure, activity and digital mediation

The relationship between leisure activities and health is the focus of much research and the use of social networking sites as spaces of leisure has been widely evidenced in relation to fitness activities (Bryce, 2001). Research has documented online fitness cultures related to 'fitspiration' and 'thinspiration' highlighting the ways in which online communities create practices online, developing, circulating and maintaining distinct health and fitness communities (Boepple & Thompson, 2016; Ghaznavi & Taylor, 2015; Jong & Drummond, 2016; Tiggemann & Zaccardo, 2015).

Beyond online representations and the formation of leisure-based communities, we can also identify ways in which digital technologies shape how we participate in activities offline, particularly the ways in which wearable digital devices have framed our experiences of leisure.

Wearable tracking sensors like Fitbit, Apple watch, Jawbone Up, Whoop and tracking apps like Strava and MapMyRun have become a popular part of leisure. Wearable devices and apps are practised as digital technologies of the body using accelerometers and sensors that track user activity, with research suggesting that technological interventions could result in higher levels of physical activity engaging people in fitness as a leisure pursuit (Cho et al., 2021; Fotopoulou and O'riordan, 2016). There is a growing interest in the academic literature about how digital technologies are being used to collect data about our bodily functions and everyday habits, but measuring and monitoring of the self is not a new phenomenon:

> The discourse around wearable devices gives the impression of a radically new technology offering precise and unambiguous physical assessment:

devices that reflect back the 'real' state of the body. Beyond the purely physical, a fundamental claim of wearable devices is that data will bestow self-knowledge: the kind of self-knowledge that will create a fitter, happier, more productive person. This is a seductive promise, but not at all a new one. (Crawford et al., 2015:480)

Crawford et al. use the weight scale as a pervasive and familiar example of the longer history of self-measurement and human subjectivity. Alongside other analogue devices such as the pedometer and pen and paper records, the scale provides an example of the many ways in which technologies have been employed to turn our bodies, minds and habits into data (Sysling, 2020). While self-tracking and body monitoring is not a uniquely digital phenomenon, wearable technologies raise important questions not only about how we understand self-monitoring as a leisure practice but also around how these mediated leisure practices are implicated in what has been termed gamification, datafication and dataveillance (van Dijck, 2014).

Wearables, leisure and gamification

Wearable sensors monitor steps taken, activity level and calories burned. They also track sleep patterns, monitor heart rate and through mobile apps enable users to enter additional information about food intake, blood pressure, menstrual cycle and mood. This data can then be used to chart progress over time, compared with other members in online communities and shared as part of digital social networks.

One of the ways in which this data is made meaningful for users is thorough visualisation and gamification, cultivating competition (with the self and between friends on the app) though the use of points, badges, levels and achievements (Fotopoulou & O'Riordan, 2016). Fitbit for example enables users to virtually explore Yosemite National Park through 'Fitbit adventures'; in solo or multiplayer races users are encouraged to reach new destinations on scenic and iconic trails while collecting treasures and completing mini challenges. These game-like experiences, including threshold targets, narrative storytelling, visual cues, leader boards and goals are designed to encourage, engage and provide social connectivity while emphasising fun and playfulness (Vooris et al., 2019).

Playing games is at the heart of what makes us human (Cho et al., 2021) and the concept of gamification is employed to describe the use of game design elements outside of the context of a game. Gamification is employed in order to influence user behaviour, to motivate, to challenge and to increase engagement and enjoyment. Video games that involve physical activity such as Nintendo Wii,

Sony Eye Toy, Dance Revolution and the Xbox Kinect have demonstrated the benefits of 'exergames' as part of leisure and physical activity (Millington, 2014) and wearable devices that incorporate gamification encourage us to compete with ourselves and other users. Wearables engage us with devices as part of our active leisure time (Windasari & Lin, 2021).

The concept of gamification has been adopted in an understanding of many spheres of social life and in the context of leisure is emphasised particularly in the light of growing concerns about sedentary lifestyles and a lack of leisure time (Vooris et al., 2019). The gamification of daily movement creates a form of leisure in spaces and places that blur the boundaries between home/work/play while also creating a space for leisure in everyday mundane activities:

> Fitbit, Jawbone, Garmin, Microsoft Band, MiCoach, Strava, MapmyRun, RunKeeper, Runtastic, Nike+ FuelBand, Endomondo, Lose It!, Pokemon Go are quantifying, shaping, sharing and augmenting our physical exertions, instructing us as we glide, plod, pedal, trot and chase. (Silk et al., 2016:712)

Gamification, seemingly a playful aspect of wearable devices, also represents a digitisation of leisure that undermines the liberatory idea of leisure as time chosen and intrinsically motivated. Rather than wearable devices enhancing our experience of leisure they erode boundaries of work and play and mask the gamification of labour and data, with leisure and labour collapsed for the benefit of digital capitalism (DeWinter et al., 2014; Wajcman, 2014). Our everyday activities are reconfigured into leisure activities rendering everyday physical behaviours such as taking steps into 'leisure'.

> With *Fitbit,* becoming and staying fit and healthy is a task that occurs around the clock because the collection of data takes place during work, leisure and sleep. No time is wasted; all time is productive, as long as you are alive to generate biological signals. (Fotopoulou & O'Riordan, 2016:61)

This contributes to the creation of a pedagogy about how to live, mediating the body and reproducing dominant discourses about health, levels of activity and healthy bodies, what Fotopoulou and O'Riordan (2016) define as biopedagogy. This biopedagogy in turns creates a moral agenda where users chide themselves for having 'lazy days' or, conversely, are reluctant to participate in activities if they are not being recorded by their wearables: 'if I wasn't wearing my Fitbit it didn't happen'. As such, leisure practices have undergone a digitisation or technologisation. Everyday movements have, for some, been digitised and transformed as steps become tracked. Walking has become a noteworthy 'activity' rather than being *literally* pedestrian (Carter et al., 2018). The implications of this are significant. As leisure activities are reconstituted in these ways, they become datafied and commodified with consequences for privacy and inequality.

The datafication of leisure

Our digital leisure practices are increasingly imbricated within data practices (Lupton, 2016). In using our digital devices and applications we become data subjects as they record our personal data. In the context of leisure, the myriad ways in which leisure and technology are intertwined make this datafication especially salient. The data generated by the digital sensors in our wearable devices is voluntarily generated by individuals and used to analyse progress and share and compare data (Till, 2014). Beyond individual use, however, this data is also uploaded to corporately owned servers, collected as a valuable part of a global knowledge economy and aggregated to provide insights into our habits, behaviours and preferences (Lupton, 2016). The digitisation of our leisure practices generates vast amounts of valuable data highlighting the concept of commodified leisure as a product of capitalism (Terranova, 2012; Till, 2014):

> There is much at stake for companies ranging from Nike, Adidas and Under Armour to Apple, Nintendo, Microsoft and Facebook in remaking leisure activities as necessarily 'digitised' activities. In this sense, it is essential for such companies to ensure the consumer's Sunday morning run, once an ephemeral feat aside from its health, is 'datafied', archived and most of all shared. The same is true of book purchases on Amazon, downloads on iTunes, film selections on Netflix and statements of one kind or another on Facebook. (Silk et al., 2016:716)

Lupton defines this data as 'lively data', generated by the smart devices, wearables and sensors that are part of our day-to-day lives (2016: 709). The cultural phenomena of data tracking has been referred to as the Quantified Self movement (Hjorth, 2018). Data is conceptualised as personal and political. Our devices enable us to reflect, track and monitor our own data but also create our 'data double' connecting us with bigger social networks and social systems (Neff & Nafus, 2016).

In the context of what Zuboff defines as surveillance capitalism (Zuboff, 2019), our digitised bodies and our leisure and consumption habits create highly valuable digital data. The devices and apps we use to monitor our bodies and activities and to share our leisure activities fuel and create surveillance practices in a wider culture of big data. Our data is interpreted and exchanged in ways that are outside of our knowledge and control as users, with our play and leisure obfuscating and/or normalising technological functionalities that we may find problematic or controversial in non-leisure contexts (Silk et al., 2016). This raises important questions about data and privacy that will be the focus of Chapter 7.

LOCKDOWN LEISURE

Earlier in this chapter I made the point that digital technologies blur the boundaries between the domains of work and leisure. By facilitating home access to work, digital technologies contaminate our leisure time (Sintas et al., 2015). These fluid boundaries of leisure and work have never been more prominent than during the lockdowns experienced globally in response to the COVID-19 pandemic. The range of lockdown measures put in place by national governments in order to reduce human contact and slow rates of COVID-19 infection had unprecedented effects on our freedom of movement and social engagements (Day, 2020). While the impact of the pandemic has not been experienced uniformly (Amanatidis et al., 2021; Gammon & Ramshaw, 2021), for many households life has been profoundly impacted as work, education, childcare and leisure unavoidably became intertwined in the home (Craig, 2020; Erturan-Ogut & Demirhan, 2020).

Throughout the course of history, viral pandemics have triggered major social and cultural changes in human behaviour (Jandrić, 2020). The COVID-19 pandemic, occurring at a time characterised by digital hyper connection, has resulted in already ubiquitous digital technologies being employed to adapt economic and social activities to comply with social distancing guidelines and government lockdown rules. A variety of digital tools and applications were used to sustain community networks and personal relationships online, facilitating communication with family and friends through instant messaging apps, social media and video conferencing.

The impact of the pandemic on leisure has also been profound. Restrictions on travel and outdoor exercise resulted in nearly all out-of-home leisure suddenly becoming inaccessible (Roberts, 2020). Pubs, nightclubs, cafes and restaurants closed, alongside heritage sites, galleries, museums, libraries, cinemas, concert halls and theatres, civic and community centres and sports centres and stadiums (Hayes, 2022). Travel and overnight stays were prohibited and access to public green spaces, parks and playgrounds restricted (Morris & Orton-Johnson, 2022; Stoecklin et al., 2021).

Perhaps unsurprisingly, in response to these restrictions, leisure activities became digital by default. People spent more time online and more time consuming streaming services and electronic games (Roberts, 2020). Online tools sustained connectivity and the digitisation of typically non-digital events and activities meant that leisure practices were reinvented. Platforms like Zoom, Google hangouts and Teams became household names, used to host family quiz nights, wine tasting events, viewing parties, board game nights and even yoga and wellness retreats as leisure activities were replicated in the digital sphere (Dunford, 2020).

Use of computer-mediated communication tools increased as people tried to spend leisure time together online (Meier et al., 2021). Across the globe examples of digital technologies facilitating new forms of leisure emerged. Malema et al. (2021) cites the example of the promotion of e-gaming by South African celebrity Cassper Nyovest. Using the hashtag #CassperStayAtHomeGames Cassper challenged celebrities to Fifa games online streaming the matches live on his social media feeds to thousands of viewers who were able to interact with the gamers on breaks between matches.

Similarly, Rendell (2021) highlights the number of artists who used digital media to perform portal shows via web 2.0 platforms. The digitisation of live music is not a new phenomenon but the disintegration of the boundaries of normal everyday life during lockdown enabled portal shows to connect fans around the world. Novel leisure experiences were created as fans watched gigs together and engaged in real-time interaction via platform chat affordances (Rendell, 2021). As well as free gigs provided by bands as 'gifts' to fans, digital technologies also provided an outlet for fans to support an industry threatened by the impacts of lost leisure during lockdown. For example, the live streaming service Twitch TV hosted Stream Aid 2020:

> This Saturday, in response to the COVID-19 pandemic, we're bringing our community and a whole lot of other folks together to do what we do best, #stayhome, play games, and support a good cause. Twitch Stream Aid – a 12-hour charity stream benefitting the COVID-19 Solidarity Response Fund for WHO powered by the United Nations Foundation – will feature some of the biggest names in gaming, music, and sports with special guests and lots of feel-good moments for the greater good." (*Twitch Stream Aid: Go Live to Save Lives on 3/28 | Twitch Blog*, 2020)

This kind of online leisure, the experience of listening to music as part of community, was argued to prevent loneliness during lockdown, embracing togetherness and (remote) intimacy (Lehman, 2021).

Other leisure forms during the pandemic coalesced around the app TikTok. In Chapter 5 I noted that TikTok surged in prominence and use during the pandemic, becoming a space of play and of the production and consumption of user-generated content. As a platform TikTok allows users to create and post short videos of between 3 and 60 seconds using music or soundbites overlaid with a range of audio-visual effect. TikTok was positioned by many as an antidote to the Coronavirus crisis (Kennedy, 2020):

> Since the lockdown, TikTok has become a seething leviathan of user-generated content, chewing down our boredom, our fatigue and our fear and spitting them back at us in 15-second chunks, to be digested ad infinitum. (Kale, 2020)

TikTok became an outlet for creative leisure seeing a rise in content creation as a result of lockdown boredom (de Guzman et al., 2022; Meier et al., 2021). Dance, stunt and lip-synching challenges and collaborative clips featuring duets and transitions were among the participatory challenges and trends that flourished during the lockdowns. The platform launched #HouseofTikTok Hashtag Challenges encouraging users to complete and share a range of challenges ranging from to fitness #WorkoutFromHome, to cookery #CupboardCooking, to keepie uppie #TenTouchChallenge.

Tiktok acted as a channel through which people could play with and reflect on their boredom in the act of what Kendall describes as '[contagious memetic participation' (2021). Kendall points to the #BoredVibes trends common on the platform during lockdown. This saw over 4 million videos posted to the platform using TikToker Curtis Roach's 15-second clip 'Bored In The House' which repeated the lyrics 'Okay, I'm bored in the house and I'm in the house bored (Bored) Bored in the house and I'm in the house bored (Bored)'. The platform hosted a #BoredVibes Challenge to bring people together and 'spread joy'. The expression of ordinary domesticity and boredom as an act of leisure became a form of collective social solidarity and a shared structure of feeling (Kendall, 2021). Binge scrolling content as an act of lockdown leisure provided pleasure in consuming content and acted as a coping mechanism in the face of the temporal and physical changes imposed by lockdown.

In something of an ironic shift, the COVID-19 pandemic not only intensified our relationships with technology but changed many of the narratives surrounding the dangers of a hyper-digitised world. Concerns about screen time, technology 'addiction' and 'obsession' and undesirable outcomes from excessive engagement with technology (boyd, 2015) were replaced with narratives of technology as the essential tool to connect and support us at a time of fear and isolation (Vogels, 2020). However, despite the value of digital connectivity and the frivolity and light relief of playful pandemic leisure on sites like TikTok we also need to note that the ability to embrace technology in this way is a privilege not afforded to many.

The pandemic highlighted and exacerbated stark social, cultural and economic inequalities within and across societies rekindling debates about the digital divide (those who do not have access to digital technologies and those who do not have the digital literacies required to use them). In the context of leisure these inequalities meant that for some any kind of leisure was a privileged luxury, with a total absence of leisure time for those unable to work from home, for those confined in inadequate housing and for those facing an unachievable balance of working and caring responsibilities in tandem with paid employment. These inequalities reflect a longer history of inequalities in leisure that the final section of this chapter will consider.

INEQUALITIES IN LEISURE

As Rojek notes (1999), leisure is rooted in broader social and cultural contexts. As such, an understanding of digitised leisure must recognise that the inequalities that structure wider society are replicated and maintained in online spaces. Inequalities and stratifications are (re) produced in our leisure practices and they are imbued with power relationship and socio-economic and cultural divisions (Silk et al., 2016; Sintas et al., 2015).

Black Instagram and travel narratives

Highlighting a long history, particularly in the United States, of segregated leisure and racialised leisure spaces like swimming pools, parks and playgrounds, Pinckney et al. (2018) argue that access to and meanings of digital spaces and leisure practices are shaped by race and racially charged digital struggles. Digital leisure spaces are racialised, reinscribing and reinforcing racist ideologies and structures (Pinckney et al., 2018). Positioning social media as spaces of digital leisure, Pickney et al. argue that Black people are able to develop counternarratives that resist and challenge representations on the 'world white web' (2018: 271). Digital leisure spaces provide an opportunity for Black people to challenge racial issues and White narratives, to promote racial pride and cultural identity and to engage in activism.

Returning to the example of travel influencers and the internet, Black social media influencers use Instagram to challenge what Arthur (2021) defines as the 'white travel imaginary' of Black nations. Citing the work of Black travel bloggers Jessica Nabongo and Oneika Raymond (the first Black woman to travel to all UN recognised countries and award-winning travel host/blogger respectively), Arthur argues that social media is employed to resist the racial politics that couches the representations of travel to and in Black nations. Shifting the colonial narrative of travel as the preserve of the privileged White person, Nabongo and Raymond use social media to tackle stereotypes and to demythologise travel in Black nations. Using geotags and hashtags like #catchmeinhaiti and #catchmeinashithole they provide alternative narratives of place, impacting traveller perceptions of certain global locales:

> Digital spaces, namely Instagram, have become sites of resisting racist assumptions about locations with predominantly Black populations and a way to reach current and aspirational travellers who may be inclined to dismiss or ignore 'shithole countries' altogether. (Arthur, 2021:391)

For Black travellers like Nabongo and Raymond, Instagram offers a space of resistance and (re) representation, pushing back against a technoculture that has largely been dominated by White voices, imaginaries and stereotypes (Arthur, 2021). These kinds of blogs and influencers have the potential to act as more egalitarian spaces that represent voices outside of conventional structures of power and privilege (Duffy, 2019). However, this kind of 'leisure' activity on social media blurs boundaries between work and play; what has been defined as playbour (Kücklich, 2005). This problematises the idea of leisure as distinct from labour, blurring boundaries of leisure work and activism in complex ways that represents and reinforces life politics:

> the behaviours of Black people in digital leisure spaces do not demonstrate the presence of Black leisure but rather highlight the reality of Black life politics...Black people use digital leisure spaces as a means of both social and political engagement. (Pinckney et al., 2018:284)

This is also reflected in gendered divisions in leisure which map on to enduring forms of gender inequality across work and care domains (Yerkes et al., 2020). Studies from around the globe have identified the gender gap in access to leisure time (Šikić-Mićanović et al., 2021) with leisure identified as a scarce and valued resource in contemporary society (Shaw, 1985).

Marginalised gaming

Gendered differences in play and leisure have been rendered particularly visible by research that has explored the straight White male demographic characteris-ing video game culture (Condis, 2015). Early feminist and queer critiques of video games highlighted the masculine and aggressive nature of much game content and pointed to the lack of representation of women in game production and consumption (Cassell & Jenkins, 2000):

> Understanding how discrimination and inequality shape the experience of gamers who visibly differ from the able-boded, anglophone, cis-het, white 'technomasculine" culture of gaming is crucial given the increasing emphasis on gaming in education and training and the ongoing integration of game-like elements into everyday processes and through gamification and gameful design. (Apperley & Gray, 2020:41)

Intersectional inequalities in gaming reflect and exacerbate existing social inequalities meaning that people of colour, disabled and gender non-conforming gamers are excluded from technomasculine gaming spaces, experiences and communities. This exclusion is particularly important when we consider the gamification or ludification of culture and everyday life (Apperley & Gray, 2020; Raessens, 2006). Research into gaming and gaming culture has unpacked and critiqued representations of women in the *content* of games (as stereotyped, cliched, objectified or entirely absent), men's harassment of women, and structural inequalities in the production and consumption of games (Buyukozturk, 2022).

As gaming platforms have diversified the gaming industry has recognised a broader market and gaming has become more social, casual and pervasive in everyday leisure (Todd, 2015). Numbers of women gamers have increased and the stereotype of the young White male gamer no longer rigidly apply (Cameron, 2019). Women, traditionally more restricted in their leisure time, have become casual gamers playing mobile games like Candy Crush Saga, Pokémon GO and Fruit Ninja. This has been perceived by some as a threat to the masculine identity of the hardcore gamer.

Controversies around these identities in game culture have highlighted persistent gendered divisions in gaming as a leisure pursuit. GamerGate in 2014 has become a marker of culture wars over visibility and inclusion in a traditionally male space (Dewey, 2014). The GamerGate controversy evolved from a series of incidents following a blog post by Eron Gjoni in which he accused his ex-girlfriend, game developer Zoe Quinn, of sleeping with a games journalist in order to get a favourable review of her critically acclaimed game *Depression Quest* (Mortensen, 2018; Todd, 2015). The allegations spread around the gamer community on social media and while notionally there was an outcry about journalistic ethics, integrity and bias, those involved in the GamerGate movement went on to harass, stalk and threaten numerous women developers and feminist cultural critics in a barrage of online and offline hate messages.

Feminist media critic Anita Sarkeesian, who launched a YouTube series on misogyny and representations of women in video games, was also targeted under the banner of GamerGate. Sarkeesian and Quinn had personal information about their home 'doxed', (a practice in which personal information is released online as a form of revenge or punishment) resulting in them going into hiding. This abuse was in response to perceived feminist attacks on the identity of 'gamer':

> As a laboratory of online hate, Gamergate threw into stark relief gaming's political-economic contradictions, where a widening player population provokes vitriol from gaming's allegedly majoritarian, misogynist, and white supremacist 'gamer' identity. (Dyer-Witheford & de Peuter, 2021:376)

GamerGate and the gamer identity controversy does not necessarily reflect the casual players of digital games in the context of digital leisure in this chapter, but highlights gaming culture as a space of gender inequality (Cameron, 2019). This cultural history contextualises the increasing ubiquity of digital games as a mainstream part of digital leisure and everyday entertainment and highlights how leisure technologies can exacerbate and embed gender inequalities and divisions (Apperley & Gray, 2020; Buyukozturk, 2022). Women's leisure as casual gamers, is both segregated and devalued by these controversies (Cameron, 2019). This is not to suggest that there are no hardcore women gamers. Rather it is to highlight the socio-cultural barriers they face in pursuing this form of leisure.

A similar challenge to the identity of 'gamer' can be seen in other marginalised groups. Drawing on Black cyberfeminism, Gray argues that intersecting oppressions in digital spaces mean that, like women gamers, Black gamers face hostile and oppressive realities in games and game communities (Gray, 2017). Using the example of Twitch, a livestreaming service focusing on streaming live video gaming, Gray argues that Black gamers use this space to produce counterhegemonic narratives while playing digital games, making Black gamers visible in spaces dominated by White masculine hegemony:

> Black Twitchers...are not silent, nor are they passive bystanders...Black Twitchers act as agents of social change regardless of their intent. The mere presence of their marginalised bodies disrupts the norm of a space designed for privileged bodies. (Gray, 2017:362)

Gray argues that Black Twitchers challenge the identity of 'gamer' and use gaming communities as sites of empowerment and resistance. In spaces where leisure technologies like gaming combine with social media we can see leisure as a site not simply of play but of cultural and racialised (re)production.

The aim of this chapter has been to reflect on the everyday ways in which technology and leisure interact as part of our day-to-day lives. Digital leisure is not simply the new technologies and new digital spaces that afford us new tools and arenas for play. In adapting our leisure practices to mediated environments we do symbolic, cognitive and practical work by giving technologies meaning, by learning and by incorporating them into our daily lives (Carter et al., 2018). These mediated leisure practices have become part of our daily lives in ways that may enhance our experience of life while at the same time opening us up to practices of dataveillance and exacerbating inequalities.

STUDYING LIVELY DATA AND THE USE OF MOBILE METHODS

Broadly defined as mobile methods, the use of digital devices to study the social world pose new methodological opportunities and challenges for the social researcher. Mobile methods incorporate mobile communication technologies into the processes of data collection and the study of social phenomena. Mobile methods are not simply tools with which to replicate traditional methods; they enable new ways for researchers to follow their object of research (Boase & Humphreys, 2018; Kaufmann et al., 2021).

This chapter has focused on the ways in which the ubiquity of digital mobile devices and communication technologies in everyday life has transformed how we experience and understand leisure activities and practices. Earlier in this chapter I argued that wearable digital devices have shaped our experiences of leisure, highlighting a growing interest in the academic literature about how digital technologies are being used to collect data about our bodily functions and everyday habits. The datafication and gamification of our leisure practices creates what Lupton describes as lively data (Lupton, 2016). This kind of data and the devices that generate it also have potential opportunities for researchers that utilise them as part of their methods (Thorpe, 2017).

Social scientists have an enduring interest in observing social action and the everyday activities that constitute our lives, but what happens when we are offered new digital means and modes of observation? Chalfen (2014) argues that users innovate and engage with their digital devices and applications in creative ways and that the same should be true for social scientists as we extend the 'ways and means' in which 'we see and interpret the social world' (Chaflen, 2014: 299). While many digital technologies are not designed for social research, they can be appropriated for research, emerging as 'research technologies' in particular contexts and configurations of the research process (Pink, 2017).

Thus, the focus of this methodological reflection is not on how we can use data generated *by* digital devices, particularly given the concerns around privacy and surveillance capitalism articulated in the chapter, but rather to explore the use of devices as part of creative methodological toolkits. A methodological creativity and innovation that reflects the multi-dimensional, multi-sensory 'reality' of our social worlds (Brown et al., 2008).

GoPros and wearable cameras as methodological tools

The use of wearable cameras has become increasingly popular, particularly in tourist travel, extreme sports and personal health-monitoring, with footage often shared via social media platforms (Duru, 2018). While this kind of life logging has become part of digitally mediated leisure practices, as tools for social research their use has largely been focused on visual ethnography and on the ability to gather closer, personalised, first-hand data, 'a means to overcome the temporal, textual and sensory limits to the ethnographic explorations of affective everyday phenomena' (Duru, 2018: 943).

A methodological tool grounded in visual ethnography, the use of wearable cameras like GoPros provide a first-person perspective, enable observation at a distance and give an embodied sense of others' perspectives (Pink, 2015). For example, in their study of urban cycling and contemporary urban development, Rick and Bustad (2021) conceive of the city as an urban assemblage and their digital visual research methods, specifically the use of wearable cameras and GoPro video technology, represents a methodological experiment focused on understanding the lived experience of cycling in the city. Their aim was for a methodological approach that maps more closely onto the phenomena being studied, in their case the relationships between humans, movement and non-human environments (Rick & Bustad, 2021). The GoPro was part of an emergent configuration of body, bike, camera, and environment recording that provided them with a video trace through the world. This video trace was made up of 'environmental, sensory, and affective configurations' rather than acting as an objective observational tool (Sumartojo & Pink, 2017):

> the GoPro allows for a collection of visual evidence of how the assemblage of the body, bicycle, camera, and environment also includes the expertise and experiential knowledge of the individual, a knowledge that is embodied through the actions and reactions of the rider. (Rick & Bustad, 2021:256)

This approach is more than simply recording an event, instead the recording plays an active role in the interpretation of an event or experience and in making sense of, in the case of Rick and Bustad, the multiple realities and experiences of urban cycling.

Similarly, Green (2020) employed small wearable video cameras as a methodological tool in her study of children's embodied and sensory experiences in the natural world. To understand how children experience their natural environments Green invited children to put on the wearable camera before going out to play. She argues that the use of wearables as a method is uniquely positioned to provide new ways to understand how children perceive and interact with the natural world and to explore embodied temporal-spatial meanings as children navigate their natural environments (Green, 2020). Using wearable cameras as a research tool also enabled Green to honour children's agency in the research process, helping her to address power imbalances between adult researchers and child participants without the intrusiveness of requiring children to use traditional hand-held cameras.

Like the walkthrough method discussed in Chapter 4, the use of mobile methods with digital recording technologies aim to 'drive along, follow along, ride along, and walk along' (Vannini & Stewart, 2017) with research participants and observe them as they go about their daily lives. In the examples outlined here the wearable camera is used to mediate new ways of seeing for the social researcher and situates the technology as part of the process of knowledge production. Sumartojo and Pink (2017) define this as an empathetic ethnography that extends beyond observation.

The purpose of the digital video is not as a record of social life but instead is a digitally mediated tool to create an extended sharable, collaborative and reflective encounter between researcher(s) and participant(s) (Sumartojo & Pink, 2017). This is established through the process of playback, editing, reflection and discussion with participants after recordings have been made, enabling experiences to be revisited and new connections and observations made (Sumartojo & Pink, 2017). Digital traces created by the GoPro recordings create sharable experiences that can be used to provide new kinds of understanding about how we experience our social worlds.

Using apps to understand the social world

The ubiquity of mobile devices and mobile media apps also afford possibilities for their use as research tools. This is particularly the case when the phenomena being studied is itself mediated by digital devices. For example, Hugentobler (2022) in her study of tourism and memorial sites used Instagram as a methodological device to study how tourists experience entangled online and offline spaces as they use Instagram to engage with sites of cultural heritage. She outlines what she defines as the Instagram interview (Hugentobler, 2022) in her study of visitor experiences of a Dr. Martin Luther King, Jr. Memorial in Washington, DC. Hugentobler argues that the experience of a memorial expands beyond the space and time of the site visit and drawing on the concept of media spaces she argues that visits to heritage sites extend beyond the physical site encompassing digital media before, during and after a visit. Using Instagram location tags Hugentobler sampled recently tagged posts from the memorial and followed and contacted posters in online exchanges via the platform. The chat function of Instagram created a natural and familiar setting for interpersonal communication that benefited from the combination of anonymity and intimacy afforded by the platform:

> The Instagram interview can be used to study intersections of offline and online spaces because it is a medium that bridges that gap…Using Instagram to interview individuals also means reaching them through the platform on which they share aspects of exactly those phenomena under study. (Hugentobler, 2022:257)

Also advocating the methodological value of digital apps and mobile methods for qualitative research, Kaufmann et al. (2021) outline their use of Mobile Instant Messaging Interviews (MIMI) to study participants' everyday life in real-time. Partly in response to the COVID-19 pandemic when in-person research was impossible as a result of social distancing and successive lockdowns, Kaufmann et al. employed MIMIs to try and overcome not only pandemic restrictions but also the increasingly complex nature of our lives as they play out across digital and physical environments. MIMIs enable researchers to connect with participants across 'socio-material-technological spaces' and to gain insights into phenomena that are otherwise hard to research by being inaccessible to other methods or lost in retrospective accounts (Kaufmann et al., 2021).

Like Instagram interviews, MIMIs make use of the private chat functions in apps like WhatsApp that are already ubiquitous and embedded in people's lives. The key difference is in the synchronous nature of the MIMI, employed to keep in constant connection with respondents, to elicit what people are doing, where they are doing it and how they are doing it. This provides an embedded and contextual understanding of social action where the researcher is digitally co-present with their respondent, giving an understanding of their momentary experiences as well as their 'social, physical and affective-emotional situatedness':

> By using popular, well-developed mobile messengers for qualitative data collection, MIMIs benefit from the ease and routinized use of these digital spaces…[and] allows spontaneous (near-)synchronous interactions between participant and researcher while being comparatively unobtrusive. (Kaufmann et al., 2021:3)

In their exploration of casual acts of media consumption, Kaufmann and Peil (2020) used WhatsApp as a tool for MIMI conducting eight day-long studies during which respondents were contacted approximately every hour and asked to report on their current media use. Respondents drew on the range of multimedia forms available to them via WhatsApp (video, screenshots, emojis, filters and hashtags) with follow-up questions exploring their current activities in more detail.

MIMIs foster an informal conversational style, generating rich data that Kaufmann et al. (2021) and Kaufmann and Peil (2020) suggest provides insight into unexpected settings and practices that may be tacit and invisible to respondents. There are disadvantages with the method; the demands it places on the researcher and the participant in maintaining regular connection and the collapse of private and field work spheres for the researcher. Its value, however, comes from the ability to focus on the pervasive, ubiquitous, and 'in passing' nature of our digital media consumption by employing that consumption as a research tool (Kaufmann & Peil, 2020).

While the value of this use of digital methods is self-evident in a study focused on media use where the object and tool of study are closely interlinked, Kaufmann (2018, 2020) argues that it is also of value in studying hard-to-reach or vulnerable groups. In her work on migrant groups and migration journeys Kaufmann argues that mobile methods and smartphones are important tools for researching and engaging with migrants. Studying the mobile and connected everyday life of Syrian refugees in the receiving city of Vienna she used MIMIs to digitally accompany vulnerable sub groups as they navigated their new environments. By using the digital tools and spaces that migrants have already appropriated for their everyday life, she argues that the intimacy and mobility afforded by smartphones provides a method that engages the attention of respondents in their routinely used spaces of digital co-presence. When combined with more traditional methods this data acted as a tool of elicitation and discussion:

> Smartphone data is thus used to reconstruct, together with the participants, the meanings, identities, experiences, relations, practices, and contexts that are connected to the data and the smartphone but can well go beyond it. (Kaufmann, 2020:173)

Importantly, the use of mobile devices can also afford participants some control over what they choose to share potentially leading to greater symmetry in power relations between researchers and vulnerable populations. This shifts the narrative away from the surveillance powers of mobile devices and of big data and emphasises a small data approach to the use of mobile methods that seek to prioritise meaning making and reflection (Kaufmann, 2018, 2020).

CONCLUSION

This chapter on digital leisure has explored how digital technologies shape how we experience and understand our leisure time. Key ideas in this chapter can be summarised as follows:

- Leisure is a construction and reflection of social, religious, political, economic and technical contexts and contemporary understandings of our leisured lives necessitate an understanding of digital culture.
- We can define digital leisure as both leisure experiences that interact with or are enhanced or transformed by digital technologies and leisure practices that have emerged as a result of digital technologies.
- Digital technologies challenge traditional conceptualisations of leisure by creating spaces of fast leisure as we use our ubiquitous connected devices to entertain us and fill time. This blurs boundaries between home/work/play as digital technologies disrupt and reconfigure leisure practices.
- The gamification and datafication of leisure has shaped how we understand and experience leisure activities that are increasingly imbricated within data structures.
- Leisure is a social construction in which inequalities and stratifications are (re) produced exacerbating existing inequalities as well as providing opportunities for resistance.
- Wearable devices and apps can be employed as methodological tools to help us understand the embodied experience of the social world.

—————————————————————— **— Further reading —**——

Spracklen, K. (2015). *Digital leisure, the internet and popular culture: Communities and identities in a digital age*. Springer.

For a more detailed understanding of digital leisure this is a good starting point. The chapters in the book explore how digital leisure spaces and activities have become part of everyday leisure and draw on a range of examples from file sharing practices to the pornification of popular culture online.

Carnicelli, S., McGillivray, D., & McPherson, G. (Eds.) (2016). *Digital leisure cultures: Critical perspectives*. Taylor and Francis.

Another good overview of digital leisure as a field of study can be found in this edited collection that brings together work exploring the ways digital technologies have transformed our practices and experiences of leisure time. The authors in the collection present work on digital leisure ranging from gig culture, sports blogging, gaming and storytelling to older adults' leisure and women's consumption of sexually explicit material.

Lupton, D. (2016). *The quantified self*. John Wiley and Sons.

This chapter explored ideas of datafication and quantification in the context of leisure. For students interested in understanding more about this concept Deborah Lupton's book provides a sociological perspective on self-tracking cultures and personal data trails. Chapters 3 *'An Optimal Human Being': the Body and Self in Self-Tracking Cultures* and 4 *'You are Your Data': Personal Data Meanings, Practices and Materialisations* are most relevant to the ideas explored in this chapter looking at the quantification of the body through wearable technologies and the associated explosion of data that blur distinctions between public and private information and raise questions about privacy and surveillance.

Taylor, T. L. (2009). *Play between worlds: Exploring online game culture*. MIT Press.

There is a large literature on digital gaming as an industry and a leisure practice I touch on this in the chapter, but for those interested in the study of gaming in particular the work of T.L. Taylor, is a good starting point. Her books include *Play between worlds: Exploring online game culture, Raising the stakes: E-Sports and the professionalization of computer gaming, and Watch me play: Twitch and the rise of game live streaming.*

7

PRIVACY AND SURVEILLANCE

As technologies have embedded themselves in our everyday lives they create new possibilities for communicating and accessing information while simultaneously presenting new challenges for managing, negotiating and protecting privacy (Palen & Dourish, 2003). Chapters 3 and 4 introduced the concept of social surveillance, a set of practices through which surveillance of and between individuals is digitised and normalised through social media (Marwick, 2012). For Marwick, this is a domestication of surveillance practices that exist in mundane day-to-day interactions, that flow through social relationships and that take place between individuals. Our use of social media has normalised this kind of surveillance and the logic of social media platforms is one of sharing and the exchange of information. As we have seen in earlier chapters, this culture of disclosure has given rise to concerns about what has been defined as social privacy: privacy from our social networks and our need and desire to control access to our personal information and to manage and curate our online presence and visibility (boyd & Marwick, 2011).

In 2010, Facebook founder Mark Zuckerberg famously said that privacy is no longer a social norm:

> People have really gotten comfortable not only sharing more information and different kinds, but more openly and with more people. That social norm is just something that has evolved over time. (Cavoukian, 2010)

Nine years later, following a wave of privacy scandals and criticism about how the company use and share data, Zuckerberg announced a refocusing of the company claiming, at F8 (the social network's annual developer conference) that the future was private (Nieva, 2019). Both positions reflect changing norms, expectations and understandings of privacy and exemplify what has been defined as the privacy paradox (Barth & de Jong, 2017).

The paradox is that we are willing to disclose personal information online while at the same time being concerned about invasions of our privacy (Barnes, 2006; Norberg et al., 2007; Sujon, 2018; Young & Quan-Haase, 2013). We use social media to connect and express ourselves and in doing so actively disclose and make public a range of personal information. This activity is contrary to our concerns about how data generated by our online habits is being used. This paradox is unsurprising, we are willing to trade personal information and data for the convenience and connectivity that digital media technologies afford. This is not a naïve undertaking and we employ a range of conscious strategies to navigate privacy concerns, including restricting and manipulating privacy settings, deleting content and creating distinct tiers or groups of friends to enable varying levels of social privacy (Young & Quan-Haase, 2013).

This chapter on privacy shifts the focus from social privacy to institutional privacy: privacy from algorithms, social media platforms, governments and other unknown third parties that want to access and use our data (Raynes-Goldie, 2010). Chapter 6 introduced the concept of datafication in the context of wearable technologies. The concept of datafication is increasingly central when understanding digital culture and institutional privacy. Datafication is the consequence of the digitisation of our lives and the data trails that these activities generate pose a profound challenge to privacy. Using two examples, the surveillance of students and learning analytics and the domestication of surveillance devices in the home, this chapter explores the relationship between datafication, privacy and surveillance.

As you read this chapter, I encourage you to think about the following questions:

* What is the difference between social and institutional privacy?
* Where does user privacy begin and end?
* What counts as invasion of privacy in a digital context?
* Who gets to decide what is and isn't private?
* How can we understand digitally mediated surveillance?

DEFINING PRIVACY

Privacy is recognised as a basic human right in contemporary democracies and the principle of privacy is enshrined in Article 12 of the Universal Declaration of Human Rights (United Nations General Assembly, 1948) and in Article 8 of the Human Rights Act (1998) (Sujon, 2018). Definitions of privacy, however, are complex and contested. Privacy is multifaceted and dynamic and our expectations and experiences of privacy are bound to cultural, political, economic and technological change (Blatterer et al., 2010). The concept of privacy spans a range of different understandings, from privacy as an economic commodity, a psychological feeling, a legal and political right and a philosophical idea of control (Lutz & Ranzini, 2017).

> privacy is a sweeping concept, encompassing (among other things) freedom of thought, control over one's body, solitude in one's home, control over personal information, freedom from surveillance, protection of one's reputation, and protection from searches and interrogations. (Solove, 2008)

At its most basic, privacy is about control and the degree to which we feel that we have control over what in our lives is public and private. The meaning of privacy is socially constructed and socially negotiated. Privacy is fluid and profoundly shaped by context. For example, nudity that is appropriate in your bedroom would be experienced very differently in another social context or setting. Privacy can be relational (controlling privacy in relation to other people and spaces around us) or informational (controlling the collection and storage of personal data) (Holvast, 2007). Privacy relates to our ability to limit and restrict access to our personal data and to control and manage access to our information (Tavani, 2008). In other words, privacy is about how we regulate the flow of information about us, how we can exercise control over that information, how we ensure others use this information responsibly and how we limit the ways this data can be used (Solove, 2010).

Finn et al. (2013) provide a typology of seven types of privacy: privacy of the person (the right to keep bodily functions, genetics and biometrics private); privacy of behaviour and action (the right to participate in private and public life without being monitored or controlled with regards to sensitive issues around sexual preferences and habits, political activities or religious practices); privacy of communication (privacy from interception or recording of communications); privacy of data and image (the ability to control our personal data and its use); privacy of thoughts and feelings (a right not to share thoughts or feelings or to have our thoughts or feeling revealed); privacy of location and space (the right to move in public or semi-public spaces without being identified, tracked or monitored); and privacy of association (the right to associate with whomever we wish, without being monitored) (Finn et al., 2013).

The emergence of new digital technologies introduces new and unforeseen facets of privacy that impact these seven privacy types. Using the examples of full body scanners, RFID-enabled travel documents (like e-passports and travel cards), surveillance drones and biometrics Finn at al. (2013) argue that digital technologies monitor, reconstruct and infer our behaviours and actions with different technologies posing different risks across the different types of privacy they defined. This is made more complicated by the inherently heterogeneous and multidimensional nature of privacy and the proliferation of technologies impacting various types of privacy (privacy types which themselves may be emergent).

In digital environments, privacy is networked, dynamic and complex, shifting from definitions of privacy that emphasise control and restricted access, to definitions that see multiple and overlapping versions of networked privacy (Lutz & Ranzini, 2017; Sujon, 2018). As we have seen in the context of social privacy, social media has profoundly changed how we understand privacy with debates polarised between conceiving of privacy as a dead relic or, conversely, as deeply important in an increasingly digitised landscape.

Those who argue that privacy is dead point to our sharing on social media as indicative that we have abandoned any sense of or desire for individual privacy (Madden, 2012). In contrast, those who argue that we still care deeply about our privacy point to the ways in which our ability to manage and navigate privacy and data sharing settings is hampered by technology companies who stand to gain from our sharing of data (Madden, 2012).

A brief caveat, and to revisit a point made repeatedly in this book, this is not to suggest that our social media technologies and habits are novel. The relationship between technology and privacy dates back to the 1890s when Warren and Brandeis in their *Harvard Law Review* essay 'The Right to Privacy' discuss how newspaper photography threatened to invade private life (Finn et al., 2013):

> Instantaneous photographs and newspaper enterprise have invaded the sacred precincts of private and domestic life; and numerous mechanical devices threaten to make good the prediction that 'what is whispered in the closet shall be proclaimed from the house-tops.' (Warren & Brandeis, 1890:195)

As technologies have continued to develop, conceptualisations of privacy have developed alongside them. Social media is simply the latest articulation of practices that have evolved for centuries (Friesen, 2017): from wiretaps, lie detector machines and video surveillance, to biometric identification, chip/smart cards, GPS and a range of ambient technologies and digital data mining tools (Holvast, 2007). Ambient technologies include things like the digital wearables discussed in Chapter 6. They are tiny often mobile devices that are embedded in many objects such as cars, appliances or consumer goods. They monitor and react to our data and behaviour; for example, the smart fridge reordering goods that are low in stock or the ability to view and interact with someone at our door while we are out by using a smart video doorbell. The key issue with the digital data trails we leave behind us is that managing and maintaining our privacy is increasingly difficult and complex.

PRIVACY AND SURVEILLANCE

Privacy exists inextricably with and in opposition to surveillance (Fuchs, 2014b). Derived from the French word *surveiller*, meaning to watch from above, surveillance typically refers to an activity that enables a nation state, or capitalist formations like corporations, to manage a population (Ogura, 2006). Surveillance is nothing new. From Bentham's panopticon to Orwell's dystopian *1984* vision of Big Brother watching us, the concept of pervasive monitoring by a central authority has an extensive and well-theorised history.

Bentham's panopticon has been a widely used metaphor for surveillance. Designed as a utopian project by 18th-century English philosopher and social theorist Jeremy Betham, the panopticon is an institutional prison building created as a means of social control. The design of a central tower surrounded by a circular ring of prison cells meant that large numbers of prisoners could be monitored by the fewest number of guards possible. The design created an illusion of constant surveillance. The guards could potentially watch prisoners at all times, an invisible, omnipotent omnipresence leaving prisoners constantly visible and vulnerable to surveillance (Galič et al., 2017).

The design of the panopticon was employed by Foucault in his writing on power and surveillance (Foucoult, 1975). Foucault used the panopticon as a symbol of social control that he extended beyond the institution of the prison into everyday life. Offering an architectural theory of surveillance Foucault argued that as citizens we internalise surveillance. The internalising of authority and collective expectations manifests in self-surveillance, thus rendering the actual act of watching unnecessary (Galič et al., 2017). Drawing on Foucault's (1975) concept of surveillance as a form of disciplinary power we can understand surveillance as information gathering based on control, manipulation and dominance (Fuchs, 2014b). This conception of surveillance is asymmetrical with individuals in a position of subordination to their surveillors (Marwick, 2012).

Post-panopticon theorising

There has been a wealth of literature that has drawn parallels with Bentham's panopticon as a system of surveillance that also applies to social media, as well as alternative theoretical frameworks attempting to conceptualise surveillance in modern Western societies (Barnes, 2006; Katz & Rice, 2002). Shifting from ideas about surveillance as governance to control, Deleuze and Guattari (1988) map new socio-technical landscapes and rather than focusing on architecture or space to understand surveillance they emphasise flows of power. Surveillance no longer needs physical spaces or architectural structures, rather it operates by 'not confining the subjects from outside but passing through the spaces and subjects' (Basturk, 2017).

The post-panopticon theorising of Deleuze and Guattari notes the advance in technological capabilities and tools for surveillance and the ways in which these have become part of our daily lives. We are living in a society dominated by what has been defined as dataveillance or datafication. Our human behaviours are traced through the digital footprints and data flows that we leave behind us as we engage with ubiquitous digital technologies. New capacities of dataveillance extend the concept of surveillance. Surveillance through data is increasingly the norm, less about power through a visible, tangible or physical force and instead a more abstract and embedded part of our cultural and social relations (Basturk, 2017; Galič et al., 2017).

Haggerty (2006) warns against the tendency in surveillance studies to assume that this proliferation of surveillance is wholly negative, pointing to the potential of institutional surveillance to contribute to a range of human endeavours around public health, education and environmental issues. However, concerns about the implications of dataveillance on privacy and surveillance are well founded when we consider the value of our data to corporations, advertisers, marketers and governments in the context of a digital data economy dominated by propriety platforms and commercial interests.

Haggerty and Ericson (2000) also move beyond the panopticon arguing that contemporary surveillance fundamentally differs from past surveillance. Using the concept of 'surveillant assemblage' they argue that post-panoptic surveillance represents a transition from a disciplinary society to a control society. A surveillant assemblage highlights how digital technologies have enabled the convergence and integration of previously discrete systems of surveillance, combining practices and technologies and integrating them into a larger whole:

> This assemblage operates by abstracting human bodies from their territorial settings and separating them into a series of discrete flows. These flows are then reassembled into distinct 'data doubles' which can be scrutinized and targeted for intervention. In the process, we are witnessing a rhizomatic levelling of the hierarchy of surveillance, such that groups which were previously exempt from routine surveillance are now increasingly being monitored. (Haggerty & Ericson, 2000:606)

This notion of data doubles speaks to the ways in which digital data increasingly spreads and expands beyond simply governance and control, to security, profit and entertainment. New populations are targeted for surveillance and are monitored with new and intensified technological possibilities (Galič et al., 2017). This is a growth and expansion of surveillance described by Deleuze and Guattari as rhizomatic (referencing the rhizome, a creeping underground plant capable of producing the shoot and root systems of a new plant, growing extensions through interconnected roots) (Deleuze & Guattari, 1988). Rhizomatic surveillance is constitutive of modern capitalism (Fuchs, 2014b), as citizens become consumers to be controlled rather than subjects to be disciplined. Surveillance is employed to monitor and construct consumer profiles and to understand their interests, tastes and behaviours. The resulting data doubles have real impacts on us as individuals, with corporations using them to make decisions about what places, information and resources we can access; for example, reduced insurance costs or beneficial mortgage rates based on our credit ratings and consumer habits.

The concept of mass surveillance emerged following the 9/11 attacks in New York and the subsequent US government surveillance and listening initiatives (Ribeiro-Navarrete et al., 2021). Surveillance tools to track data became a new normal, couched in narratives of helping authorities to predict and prevent a range of events, from terrorist attacks to traffic jams. Mass surveillance has morphed into a corporate desire for data about our tastes and preferences and surveillance has proliferated into spheres of consumption, entertainment, health promotion, education and governance. As such, surveillance does not function with a coherent or singular purpose (Galič et al., 2017). For example, the Cambridge Analytica scandal in the 2010s, in which Facebook provided the data firm Cambridge Analytica with unauthorised access to the personally identifiable information of more than 87 million users (Isaak & Hanna, 2018), raised questions about how data can be collected in a digitally connected society (Ribeiro-Navarrete et al., 2021). Subsequent revelations that social networking data, combined with socio-demographic data, could be used to shape the voting intentions of millions of voters by predicting the way users think, act, and behave has changed our understandings of the relationship between democracies and large technology companies.

Our data doubles are increasingly part of a diverse range of databases and flows of data, subject to heterogeneous malleable, fluid and unstable surveillant assemblages and rooted in the privacy paradox of modern capitalism:

> On the one hand modernity advances the ideas of a right to privacy, but on the other hand it must continuously advance surveillance that threatens to undermine privacy rights. An antagonism between privacy ideals and surveillance is therefore constitutive of capitalism. (Fuchs, 2014b:160)

This view of surveillance as a dominant and overarching feature of capitalist society forms the basis of what has been defined as a new form of information or surveillance capitalism.

Surveillance capitalism

Zuboff argues that surveillance capitalism is a new kind of social and political relation that aims to predict and modify human behaviour in order to produce revenue and market control (Zuboff, 2015). Surveillance capitalism links surveillance as a practice of power and knowledge to capitalism as an economic system (Zuboff, 2019). The logic of surveillance capitalism is grounded in 'big data' where our personal data is the commodity for sale. The capture and processing of this data relies on mass surveillance of the internet by companies that want to find out our likes, dislikes, consumer preferences and purchases. Big data includes data from computer-mediated economic transactions, institutional and trans-institutional systems, data from sensors in objects, bodies and places, data from government and corporation databases, data from private and public surveillance cameras (like Google Street View and Google Earth) as well as data from our individual day-to-day interactions with and through digital technologies. The ubiquity of this digital data has the potential to 'feed on' and shape every aspect of human life (Zuboff, 2019)

Focusing particularly on Google and Facebook as exemplars of surveillance capitalism, Zuboff argues that their practices of accumulating and extracting data have been largely obscured, made visible only through a range of conflicts around contested data collection techniques including bypassing privacy settings, retention of search data and tracking of smartphone location data (Zuboff, 2015). The concentration of privacy rights among these corporations has profound implications not just for privacy but for democracy:

> Surveillance capitalists have skillfully exploited a lag in social evolution as the rapid development of their abilities to surveil for profit outrun public understanding and the eventual development of law and regulation that it produces. In result, privacy rights, once accumulated and asserted, can then be invoked as legitimation for maintaining the obscurity of surveillance operations. (Zuboff, 2015)

Knowability and visibility is highly asymmetrical and held in the hand of a small number of corporations (Cinnamon, 2017). An accompanying lack of regulation means that we know little of the range and type of data companies like Google, Amazon, Facebook and Apple hold about us or about how our data is stored, shared, instrumentalised and monetised. We share our data because surveillance capitalism places us in a global network of platforms and tools that many of us perceive as essential for participating in the world. Take Amazon and the convenience of surveillance as a service, as Swisher (2020) in the *New York Times* suggests:

> This enormous idea has been at the heart of Mr. Bezos's dream for a long time: to suck up the data from willing participants and give them back exactly what they want, for a price. This may be perhaps the most perfect signal-to-noise ratio ever collected. Health info, entertainment likes and dislikes, and purchase data offer a panoply of insights.
>
> Am I upset? Send the ice cream and antidepressants! Happy? Send the champagne and music! Am I sleepless? Perhaps some warm milk and a weighted blanket — only $39.99 on Amazon and delivered today. (Swisher, 2020)

Zuboff argues that creating this social dependency on digital technologies is central to contemporary surveillance. Amazon collects vast amounts of data about our consumer behaviour, our purchases, wishlists, reviews, searches and page clicks. This data facilitates the predictive algorithms that make their service feel more seamless and personal (West, 2019). Despite the fact that they sell this data to third parties in agreements that are, at best, opaque, we still are drawn to this surveillance as service as it produces a 'psychic numbing that inures people to the realities of being tracked, parsed, mined, and modified – or disposes them to rationalize the situation in resigned cynicism' (Zuboff, 2019:25).

Privacy and social inequality

While more diffuse models of surveillance shift away from panoptical models of a unidirectional gaze this is not to suggest that surveillance doesn't continue to play an important role in social exclusion and inequality. Contemporary politics of surveillance result in differentials in who is able to exploit surveillance potentials and these differences map closely on to traditional social cleavages. Privacy becomes another marker of privilege and power while minority groups face increased and disproportionate exposure to surveillance (Haggerty, 2006).

Research has noted the discrepancy between the data rich (corporations and institutions that that can generate or purchase and store large datasets) and the data poor (those excluded from access to the data, expertise, and processing power) (Andrejevic, 2014; boyd & Crawford, 2011). In the case of personal data,

Cinnamon (2017) argues that we are divided into three data classes: those who create data, those who collect data, and those who can analyse data. This is not to suggest that big data is inherently digital, rather that the contemporary concept of big data distinguishes our ability to store, process, automate, correlate and identify patterns in data as opposed to simply searching and querying large databases (Andrejevic, 2014).

This has important societal consequences as we are increasingly subjected to surveillance and automated classification, what Andrejevic (2014) calls an emergent social sorting. Social sorting is not a new phenomenon, but digital technologies can identify previously invisible and unanticipated patterns in data that are used to make decisions that shape us as groups and individuals. These decisions and predictions impact health care, policing, urban planning, financial planning, job screening and educational admissions. Using the example of algorithms and the rental housing market, Cinnamon highlights the ways in which algorithmic processes can avoid illegal discrimination on the basis of race or socio-demographic characteristics by profiling vulnerable groups and building in socio-cultural discrimination:

> algorithms can be designed that intentionally avoid advertising on social media platforms to users from deemed undesirable backgrounds or statuses, which can be inferred from analysis of their Web activities, such as their 'likes' on Facebook. (Cinnamon, 2017:616)

The operation of largely invisible personal data scores have important and unequal impacts on our lives; our ability to secure a loan, a mortgage or affordable insurance for example, with profiling algorithms posing a risk to open, democratic society (Tene & Polonetsky, 2013). This creates new kinds of inequality and a discussion of these will be the focus on the final concluding chapter.

Using the concept of marginalising surveillance, Monahan (Hoy, 2018) argues that surveillance is unequal with different surveillance systems disproportionately targeting ethnic minority groups, women and those on lower incomes. This discrimination may take the form of mandatory surveillance of low-paid employees in the form of keystroke-tracking software and time- or location-tracking tools or the intense surveillance of particular locations populated by minority groups. This surveillance acts to regulate but also to reinforce the identities, alienation and conditions of marginality faced by these groups and individuals:

> Automated control depends predominantly upon algorithmic surveillance systems, which take empirical phenomena—translated into data—as their raw material, ranging from commercial purchases to mobility flows

to crime rates to insurance claims to personal identifiers. Spaces, activities, people, and systems are then managed through automated analysis of data and socio-technical intervention...exclusionary politics are encoded in their design, enforced by bureaucratic structures of technical experts, and propagated through the application of such systems to social settings. (Monahan, 2010: 98–99)

Importantly, these surveillance tools and the inequalities they engender are difficult to resist and critique as the algorithms on which they are based are largely opaque, rendering invisible their latent discriminatory functions. These inequalities also challenge the emancipatory potentials of the internet 'by proposing the superiority of a post-explanatory pragmatics (available only to the few) to the forms of comprehension that digital media were supposed to make more accessible to the many' (Andrejevic, 2014: 1675).

The key question we need to ask is privacy for whom? If we concieve of privacy as the ability of dominant groups in society to keep wealth and power secret from the public then privacy is fundamentally unequal. If, however, privacy can function for the majority of the public by protecting them and their data from dominant interests, this acknowledges that privacy rights need to be differentiated according to the power and status differentials and moves towards what Fuchs defines as a concept of socialist privacy (2014b: 190).

The final section of this chapter turns to two specific examples that explore some of the issues of institutional privacy and surveillance introduced in the discussion so far. The first uses an example close to home (with the assumption that the primary readers of this book are students) focusing on the field of Higher Education and learning analytics. The second looks at the domestication of surveillance by looking at digital devices in the home and the commodification and connection of familial domestic spaces with corporate networks.

PRIVACY AND LEARNING ANALYTICS

As with other spheres of life, engaging in learning leaves behind a trail of data. Students registering with university systems, visiting the library, submitting assignments and using their Virtual Learning Environments (VLEs) generate a wealth of digital data points. The use of student data has always been used to inform policy and pedagogy (Prinsloo and Slade, 2016), but the growth of online learning and an increase in digital student data has led to the rise of learning analytics. Learning analytics and data-driven decision making are now part of the structure and organisation of Higher Education Institutions (Beetham et al., 2022) intended to help them understand and optimise students' learning experience (Heath, 2021; Jones et al., 2020).

Learning analytics refer to the measurement, collection, analysis and reporting of data relating to student activities and the contexts in which their learning takes place (Sclater et al., 2016; Willis et al., 2016). Data about students is collected in order to monitor and understand retention, to allocate resources for support and to help institutions understand and predict factors that may influence, enhance, or impede student learning (Jones et al., 2020). This data comes primarily from the VLEs which students use to access timetables, course information and learning materials. VLEs are also spaces in which students interact with each other, participate in learning activities, submit assessments and monitor their progress. Data also comes from university systems that contain information about students' prior qualifications, socio-economic status, ethnic group, learning adjustments and funding sources as well as their course selections and grades obtained. Learning analytics provide data on all aspects of the student experience, accessible to a range of stakeholders, including university administrators, academics and support staff.

Proponents of learning analytics point to the ability to identify and address issues of concern and enhance the student experience. For example, learning analytics can be used to understand attrition rates and progression issues. Data from students' prior qualifications can be aggregated with data on progress and attainment in order to identify and provide timely support and feedback for students who may be struggling or at risk of withdrawing (Beetham et al., 2022; Sclater et al., 2016).

Altruistic understandings of learning analytics emphasise their pedagogical benefits, but issues of student privacy have often been side-lined in these discussions. Prinsloo and Slade (2016) argue that anecdotal evidence suggests that students are largely unaware or unconcerned that their institutions collects data about them. They have little understanding of what is done with their data, or of how data collection practices could harm them (Jones et al., 2020; Prinsloo & Slade, 2016). This anecdotal evidence is certainly supported by my own experience. In my undergraduate teaching I show students (redacted and anonymised) data that I am able to see using our VLE and associated universty systems. I can view aggregated and individual data showing the days of the week and the times of day when students login to the VLE and the content they view. I could, if I chose, access their individual profiles to view the personal information and data that the university holds about them. This activity is usually met with, at best, feelings of discomfort (countering narratives that young people, raised in a world of ubiquitous digital media, are blasé about their privacy) when attention is drawn to their rather mundane but very detailed digital data trails.

The aim here is not to evaluate the efficacy or purpose of learning analytics, but to highlight them as a form of surveillance. Technologies of student surveillance include VLEs, student record-keeping systems, plagarism detection and remote proctoring software which provide data 'solutions' (Beetham et al., 2022). These solutions are proprietorial platforms from EdTech companies with business models based on data harvesting that may be at odds with the logic of Higher Education as a space of critical enquiry, open debate, transparency and trust:

> Even if the broadly benevolent purposes of monitoring learning analytics were fully realised...the rendering of students into collections of needs and behaviours that can be serviced through a variety of responses from the 'system' can reinforce a deficit model of learning, rather than viewing students as members of a learning community in which trust is, at least, desirable. (Beetham et al., 2022: 20)

In the context of wider debates about dataveillance in society, the growing body of research around learning analytics highlights the relative absence of discussions about student privacy and surveillance and an understanding of what student privacy is in the context of learning analytics is far from clear (Beetham et al., 2022; Kruse & Pongsajapan, 2012; Prinsloo & Slade, 2016).

Learning analytics and the pandemic

The issue of student data is particularly salient in the context of the COVID-19 pandemic. The rapid move to online learning changed the relationship between commercial educational technology providers and educational institutions. Edtech companies increased the deployment of data analytics in HE emphasising 'personalised learning' and 'data driven decision-making'. This shift raises important questions about student privacy and digital surveillance (Prinsloo et al., 2021).

During the pandemic lockdowns studying at home was made possible via a range of digital technologies and institutions made use of digital tools to deliver and monitor teaching and learning. The rapid transition to remote learning meant that there was little time to restructure courses and provide alternative models of learning and assessment. Assessments that were designed to take place in person had to be delivered remotely, challenging ideas of academic integrity (Balash et al., 2021). The problem of how to assess students remotely led many universities to adopt digital exam supervision platforms such as Examity, Respondus and ProctorU (traditionally used in online distance learning contexts). These tools use a variety of technologies to target academic cheating or dishonesty:

browser extensions that track computer activity and lock down web browsers; automatic monitoring in the form of eye tracking; connecting students' microphones and webcams to remote proctors paid to watch students take assessments (Balash et al., 2021; Harwell, 2020). As well as 'live' human proctors, online proctoring software also employs AI, facial recognition and algorithmically driven procedures 'designed to seamlessly authenticate students' identity and recognise their in-test (mis)behaviour' (Selwyn et al., 2023).

In addition to increasing student anxiety about assessment, use of these tools gives universities and Edtech companies access to students' home environments as well as to their biometric data. This raises important questions about privacy (Halaweh, 2021) and displays a lack of trust for students that, in turn, undermines students' trust in their educators and institutions. During the pandemic concerns about 'surveillance pedagogy' were echoed in the media and in student protests with headlines emphasising the surveillance creep of Edtech solutions: *'"Unfair surveillance"? Online exam software sparks global student revolt'* (Asher-Schapiro, 2020); *'Cheating-detection companies made millions during the pandemic. Now students are fighting back.'* (Chin, 2020). However, online proctoring appears set to become a normal part of post-pandemic Higher Education, mirroring the long-standing paradox of 'convenience versus control' that leads us to accept everyday surveillance technologies and practices (Selwyn et al., 2023).

This is particularly concerning when we consider inequalities in access to the internet, highlighted by the pandemic, that are gendered, raced and geopolitical. Learning analytics, intended to support, may have the opposite outcome by becoming pathogenic and exacerbating or generating new vulnerabilities and inequalities rather than ameliorating them (Prinsloo & Slade, 2016).

> Tools that use eye tracking can flag students who fail to keep their eyes on the webcam or screen, even if the reason is autism or disability rather than cheating. In the all-seeing eye of the remote proctor, all students become potential cheaters. Equity is also not a consideration for online proctoring. Some platforms use discriminatory facial recognition technologies that work poorly with darker skin, forcing students to sit for exams with bright lights shining in their faces in order to be recognized by AI. Others force students to verify their identity via government-issued ID, potentially outing trans or undocumented learners. (Stewart, 2020)

The technologies that enabled our lives to continue during pandemic lockdowns are not politically neutral. Their incorporation into a new post-pandemic 'normal' has the potential to heighten surveillance and control creep which will not be experienced equally or evenly (Maalsen & Dowling, 2020). Surveillance creates visibilty and the potential harms of these technologies to students and faculty are felt most by those who are marginalised, disadvantaged by inequality, caring responsibilities or inadequate equipment (Beetham et al., 2022). Amid discussions about analytics we need to be critical of the assumed objectivity and neutrality of data and to acknowledge the potential for discrimination inherent in the process of sharing and gathering data (Heath, 2021; Prinsloo & Slade, 2016). Quantifying students in terms of the number of logins, time spent on tasks or the number of clicks or downloads they make and combining these with socio-demographic characteristics (age, gender, race, and/or disability) may inadvertently amplify the vulnerability of some students (Prinsloo & Slade, 2016).

The second example I draw in a discussion of privacy and data relates to surveillance capitalism in the home and the framing of privacy as a personal decision based on a trade-off between convinience and surveillance.

DIGITAL DEVICES AND INTIMATE SPACES

Science fiction and popular culture abounds with examples of smart computers, from 'HAL 9000 and the Starship Enterprise's computer to Marvin the Paranoid Android and KITT the car' (Hoy, 2018) and the realisation of this science fiction dream of interacting with our computers is increasingly a reality. In 2021, Amazon launched the Astro as part of its 'Day 1' beta program aiming to bring innovative ideas to the market. Described by Amazon as a consumer robot that will become part of your home and life the Astro is a camera equipped robot on wheels with sensors and onboard AI:

> Keep home closer with Astro, the household robot for home monitoring, with Alexa. When you're away, use the Astro app to see a live view of your home, check in on specific rooms and viewpoints, and get activity alerts. When you're home, Astro can follow you from room to room playing your favorite music, podcasts or shows, and find you to deliver calls, reminders, alarms, and timers set with Alexa. (https://www.amazon.com/Introducing-Amazon-Astro/dp/B078NSDFSB)

The functionality of Astro is reliant on enormous amounts of personal data, raising concerns about dystopian levels of surveillance capitalism in the home (Laura, 2022). While there is currently no confirmed release date for the Astro, contemporary consumer-led voice interfaces are now widely available and are increasingly being incorporated into our day-to-day activities and routines in the domestic setting of the household. Internet-connected software that runs on smartphones or purpose-built speakers like Amazon's Echo, Google Home with

Google Assistant and Apple's Siri can respond to many commands and questions. As well as providing information on news, weather and traffic and answering a range of other queries these devices can play media requested by a user, send, receive and read messages, play games, set reminders and timers and interact with and control a range of connected smart devices (for example smart thermostats, locks and lightbulbs) via voice control (Hoy, 2018). Pridmore and Mols (2020) define this as the 'platformisation of the household' that they argue is shifting our everyday experiences with technology and changing patterns of human–computer interaction. Given the reliance of these devices on data they raise significant concerns about privacy and data protection.

Amazon, Alexa and the boundaries of privacy

Privacy is a major concern with voice assistant devices, which, by definition, are required to be always listening in order to respond to their wake word (for example 'Hey Google' or 'Alexa'). The domestication of these devices challenges understandings of privacy, blurring the lines between public/private and the boundaries of the household. The concept of domestication of technology comes from the work of Silverstone and Haddon (2016) which explores social and cultural processes around adoption and non-adoption of ICTs in the home and in society more broadly.

New media technologies have a long history of challenging and reshaping privacy in the home but the ubiquitous nature of smart technologies and the Internet of Things (a broad concept referring to consumer goods and everyday objects being combined with internet connectivity and sensors allowing these devices and objects to generate, store and collect data) mean that devices like the Echo place consumers in the position of trading privacy for convenience and functionality. This choice is problematic because as users we are disempowered by our lack of knowledge of the technical systems that we engage with. These systems are largely black boxed, we have little understanding of their internal workings, the algorithms they rely on or how we might be able to circumvent the privacy policies of their parent companies.

As digital technologies are placed in the domestic sphere the issue of privacy has been subject to much debate. Security researchers highlight vulnerabilities while users question what data is being recorded and how it will be collected, used and stored (Lau et al., 2018). We choose convenience with different levels of deliberation and with varying level of resignation towards technology's progressive intrusiveness (Lau et al., 2018):

> technological development and its requisite pervasive data collection are slowly chipping away at people's agency regarding their privacy...users

adopting new technologies, especially those that may be privacy-invasive, should not be misconstrued as a sign of people accepting and endorsing privacy-invasive data practices; rather, it might be evidence of their struggle to balance the benefits of using new technologies and being forced to give up their privacy bit by bit. (Lau et al., 2018:102:19)

Devices like the Echo are designed to improve through increased use, adapting to users' habits and speech patterns and learning through AI and deep-learning algorithms, increasing ease of use and accuracy (Pridmore & Mols, 2020). I experience this almost daily in my own home with Alexa, used most frequently by my husband, who has set the request 'make it dark' to turn off our downstairs lighting. Less familiar with my patterns of speech the response I frequently get from Alexa when asking the same thing is a track of dogs barking as she mistakes my 'dark' for 'bark'. Anecdotes aside, this ability to learn amplifies debates about privacy and surveillance issues. It exemplifies Zuboff's concept of surveillance capitalism, through the commodification and connection of familial domestic spaces with corporate networks (Pridmore & Mols, 2020).

Always on 'listening' devices are eavesmining (a portmanteau merging the meanings of eavesdropping and data mining) platforms and processes (Neville, 2020). In a case study of the Amazon Echo and Alexa conditions of use Neville argues that the privacy and surveillance implications of these devices are intensified in a domestic sphere. Amazon End User Agreements (EUA) are challenging to understand and appear to be designed to encourage users to skip over or skim read them, discouraging any meaningful understanding of surveillance and privacy implications (Neville, 2020). The onus is on us as users to keep ourselves updated about any changes to the EUAs without prompts from Amazon. This framing of privacy assumes that we are aware of the trade-off we are making between convenience and surveillance and assumes that our acquiescence to these terms is a willing acceptance (Andrejevic, 2014). However, lack of knowledge about the technical and legal details of EUAs, a perceived lack of options or alternatives and an assumption that our acceptance has no discernible negative impacts is not the same as our informed consent.

For example, Neville (2020) cites the 2019 Amazon privacy scandal, in which Amazon admitted that they employed people to listen to voice input data from customers. In order to improve Alexa's response to commands employees listen to voice recordings which are then transcribed before being fed back into the software in order to fill gaps in Alexa's understanding of speech. While privacy settings give users the option of disabling this use of their voice recordings, Neville argues that the scandal highlighted users' lack of understanding of their privacy control options and of their realistic ability to opt out, particularly in the context of ever changing and updating terms of service and use.

Smart devices in homes accelerate and amplify the capabilities of digital surveillance because they are not simply isolated individual devices but are connected to a range of systems and digital flows (Maalsen & Sadowski, 2019):

> The devices are more than agents that are actively sensing, recording, analysing, and responding. They are also agents that represent the interests of their makers, communicate with them via the internet, invite them (and maybe their friends) into our homes, and enrol the smart home into a growing network of infrastructure and institutions. Every device and platform installed in the home enlarges the network and multiplies the connections. (Maalsen & Sadowski, 2019:120)

The implications of these connection of flows are multiple. Using the example of insurance providers, Maalsen and Sadowski (2019) highlight the ways in which smart homes, at the same time as providing convenience, comfort and fun, also open up their inhabitants to new kinds of dataveillance. They argue that insurance companies have a business model of providing devices at a subsidised rate in exchange for access to the data they generate and record. This data can then be used to regulate or punish actions and behaviours that are percieved by insurers as 'risky'. Maalsen and Sadowski cite the examples of procrastinating on home maintenance, watching too much TV or eating unhealthy food as behaviours monitored by smart devices in the home that may be sanctioned by increased premiums. Inequities are embedded into these forms of surveillance. Technologies and platforms reproduce structures of racialised and gendered power (Rottinghaus, 2021) with more privileged users being given discounts on digital devices in exchange for access to their data, while more vulnerable users may simply be coerced into giving up their data in exchange for necessary insurance cover (Maalsen & Sadowski, 2019). This integrates our private domestic habits into the information networks of global capitalism, opening up the private space of the home up to new forms of data surevillance.

Similarly, the Amazon Ring, the 'smart' video doorbell camera, highlights the way in which companies like Amazon use surveillance not only as part of their platform logic but also as a service to consumers (West, 2019). Products like the Ring doorbell, with a built-in camera triggered by motion, enables consumers to conduct surveillance on their own home and surrounding areas by recording video and audio. The video doorbell is marketed as a tool for homeowers to see who or what is on their doorstep without answering the door or being at home. Users can watch live video footage or store footage. Promising increased safety and reduced theft, the Ring enables its owners to post videos of suspicious activity and share information and video footage with other people.

The Ring has come under scrutiny, not only from within Amazon where Max Eliaser, an Amazon software engineer, is quoted as saying that it is 'simply not compatible with a free society' (Bridges, 2021), but also from critics highlighting its partnerships with law enforcement agencies (Morris, 2021). Footage from Ring can be uploaded to the Amazon Neighbors app enabling users to get real-time crime and safety alerts from neighbours and local law enforcement:

> Neighbors is a security solution that every community member, regardless of whether or not they own a Ring device, can use. When communities work with one another, safer neighborhoods become a reality – it's as simple as that. The Neighbors app enables community members – and, in some cases, law enforcement – to work together in order to reduce crime. (Ring website https://en-uk.ring.com/blogs/alwayshome/how-ring-s-neighbors-creates-safer-more-connected-communities)

This extends corporate surveillance further into private spaces creating an infrastructure of domestic surveillance with few limitations on how content can be used, stored and shared. Importantly, this kind of surveillance perpetuates and reinforces the bias of users and those policing residential space. There are obvious race, gender and class-based inequities that may be exacerbated wherever the device and app are used (Bridges, 2021; West, 2019):

> The concerns of activists and scholars have been compounded by developments in facial recognition technology and other forms of machine learning that could be conceivably applied to Ring recorded content and live feeds. Facial recognition technology has been denounced by AI researchers and civil rights groups for its racial and gendered biases. Although Ring doesn't currently use facial recognition in its cameras, Amazon has sold this technology to police in the past. (Bridges, 2021)

Technologies like the Ring and its accompanying app reconfigure our private spaces and entangle us with digital platforms services in ways that may be unintended or unanticipated leaving us open to new forms of surveillance capitalism 'evolving into data and computation authoritarianism, one cool service at a time' (Tufekci, 2017).

The use of this kind of data, the domestication of institutional privacy and the problematic and complex EUAs they rely on need to be reconfigured, demanding increased platform responsibility rather than emphasising the need for individuals to manage and be responsible for their own privacy rights in an increasingly complex digital landscape (Sujon, 2018).

DATA PRIVACY AND DIGITAL RESEARCH ETHICS

This chapter has focused on the ways in which we manage, negotiate and protect privacy in the context of a domestication of surveillance practices and of changing norms, expectations and understandings of privacy. In reflecting on these issues methodologically a concern closely related to issues of privacy is that of the ethical challenges that face social researchers wishing to conduct research in and of online spaces.

All social research involves ethical decision making, shaping the choices we can make in the pursuit of knowledge as we ensure that the rights and sensibilities of human subjects are protected (Bulmer, 2001). We face ethical decisions when we formulate our research questions, when we make decisions about how and who we sample, when we negotiate access to data and/or respondents and when we gather, analyse and disseminate that data (Ali & Kelly, 2004).

Ethical issues are particularly salient when things go wrong (Tiidenberg, 2018). A history of research ethics has critiqued ethical breaches. One famous example is Milgram's controversial obedience studies in the 1960s. The participants (both administering and receiving shocks) in the study were subjected to significant psychological and emotional distress raising serious questions about the ethics of using human subjects in psychological research. At Yale University, Stanley Milgram carried out a series of experiments studying the effect of authority on obedience (Blass, 1999; Miller et al., 1995). In the studies an authority figure ordered research participants to deliver what they believed were dangerous electrical shocks to another person. The participants were given the role of 'teacher' giving shocks to 'students' (who were part of the research team) when they gave incorrect answers or when they refused to answer or became agitated. His findings showed that 65% of the participants in the study delivered what they believed to be the maximum shock. The participants in the study were subjected to significant psychological and emotional distress raising serious questions about the ethics of using human subjects in psychological research.

Similarly, Laud Humphreys' controversial covert 'Tea room trade' research used covert methods of observation to study homosexual sex in public toilets in the 1960s. Acting as a voyeur Humphreys systematically observed sexual activities and recorded the licence plate numbers of a sample of tea room participants that he later tracked down and interviewed. His research prompted heated debates over research ethics and highlighted a range of ethical issues that remain ongoing challenges for social researchers (Babbie, 2004).

In the context of digital research, the potential for ethical abuse and the perceived ease with which this abuse can occur online has been a longstanding feature of academic debate:

> The ease of covert observation, the occasional blurry distinction between
> public and private venues, and the difficulty of obtaining informed consent

of subjects make cyber-research particularly vulnerable to ethical breaches. (Thomas, 1996: 108)

We can chart a more recent history of ethical mistakes in digital contexts including the 2008 'Tastes, Ties, and Time' study where a group of researchers publicly released data collected from the Facebook accounts of an entire cohort of college students. Despite their attempts to delete or encode all identifying information 'conceptual gaps in the researchers' understanding of the privacy risks related to their project' meant that the identity of the dataset as Harvard University was quickly established and the privacy of student data compromised (Zimmer, 2020).

Similarly, the 2014 Facebook 'emotional contagion' study created ethical controversy when it manipulated Facebook's news feed seeking to prove that emotional states can be transferred in online environments (in other words if people perceive others as posting negatively would they post more negatively and vice versa) leading people to experience the same emotions without their awareness (Kramer et al., 2014). The research, a collaboration between Facebook and academic researchers at Cornell, did not seek consent from participants (Hunter & Evans, 2016) and was ethically controversial in its covert manipulation (Jouhki et al., 2016) and in exploiting users' inability to determine how information is presented to others on the platform (Selinger & Hartzog, 2016).

Contemporary research ethics have developed from philosophical debates about ethics as a moral philosophy of human action. But ethics and ethical practices are temporal, contextual, evolving and often contested. There is no ethical absolute given the complexity of human action (Ali & Kelly, 2004). When this complexity is matched with rapidly evolving digital research objects, settings and tools, ethical decision making in digital contexts can pose challenging questions and nebulous grey areas (Tiidenberg, 2018). This is compounded by the challenge of navigating ethical guidelines and requirements laid out by disciplinary bodies (for example, the British Sociological Association Statement of Ethical Practice and their Ethical Guidelines for Digital Research, the Association of Internet Researchers, AoIR, Ethical Guidelines), funding bodies (for example, the Economic and Social Research Council framework for research ethics) and the legal terms of use and service of digital apps and platforms.

Beyond these guidelines and requirements there are issues around operationalising key ethical concepts like privacy and confidentiality, informed consent and anonymity. This is particularly the case in networked publics where our data is replicable, searchable, scalable and highly visible (boyd, 2010). For Tiidenberg, these affordances of persistence, replicability, scalability and searchability come with methodological ambiguities 'of whether, what for, when, and for how long these processes should be observed, collected, and preserved for the sake of research' (2018: 470).

The ideal of informed consent

Informed consent places a responsibility on the researcher to explain, in appropriate detail, and in terms meaningful to participants, what the research is about, who is undertaking and financing it, why it is being undertaken and how it is to be distributed, in order that a participant can make a decision about taking part.

Informed consent can be problematic in all forms of research and processes of fieldwork involve complex interactions that are not easily reduced to a consent form. But the concept of informed consent can pose a particular challenge to ethical research methodology in the online field. The transient and ephemeral nature of many digital environments, often with large and fluctuating populations of disembodied online participants, may be difficult or impossible to obtain (Markham & Buchanan, 2017).

For example, in online spaces with hundreds of participants posting each day maintaining informed consent would require continual and regular posts which explained the research and requested the consent of other participants. This kind of message would disrupt the natural flow of the interaction and significantly alter the nature of the environment to the extent that what we are trying to research and understand is transformed or rendered invisible. Some have argued that an alternative solution to posting regular announcements of research and requests for informed consent is the use of a 'signature' at the end of each posting; however, to condense an ethically appropriate description of any research is problematic. More importantly, to assume informed consent from this solution would be premature as this transfers the responsibility of reading the message onto the participants, thereby 'exonerating' the researcher from ethical responsibility.

The ideal notion of informed consent must be balanced with practicality and the degree to which the ideal can be implemented without jeopardising the validity of the research. The Association of Internet Researchers Ethics Working Committee guidelines advocate a case-based approach that is sensitive to the research context(s), mindful of ethical pluralism and cross-cultural awareness and conscious of the need to do no harm (Franzke et al., 2020).

Public and private spaces and data

The importance of applying ethical principles inductively rather than universally extends to debates around what digital spaces and interactions can be public or private. The concept of informed consent becomes problematic when online spaces are conceived of as public, and therefore accessible to social research, with content posted there seen as unproblematically publicly available (Tiidenberg, 2018). As discussed in Chapter 4, the implications of participating in networked publics mean that the potential for visibility and context collapse online requires ethical attention to how we and our potential participants define the public sphere. Definitions of public and private spaces may blur in participants' minds and change across temporal and social contexts. Just because someone uses publicly available online tools does not mean they assume that these tools are 'mechanisms for the storage, transmission, and retrieval of comments' of their data (Walther, 2002).

Being 'in public' is not consent to being researched and participants may understand and perceive their imagined audiences in unanticipated ways. Markham and Buchanan (2015) argue that reflecting on the 'distance' between individuals and their data is a helpful way to try and understand ethics and privacy. The concept of distance takes into account the distance between researcher and participant and between the data and whoever created the content of that data (Markham & Buchanan, 2015; H. Nissenbaum, 2010; Tiidenberg, 2018):

> The smaller the distance, the more careful we need to be. Distance is considered to be smaller between a small sample of identifiable status updates and the people who posted them, than it is, for example, between the people who have tweeted and a large sample of automatically scraped, aggregated tweets. (Tiidenberg, 2018: 472)

The decision to define something online as private or public therefore raises important methodological and ethical questions about how we can approach its study. While there are no ethical absolutes, a range of scholars have advocated for contextual understandings that acknowledge, in their decision making, fluid and emerging understandings of privacy and of the sensitivity and vulnerability of people and data online (Markham & Buchanan, 2015; Nissenbaum, 2010; Tiidenberg, 2018).

Anonymity and confidentiality online

Confidentiality and anonymity are related but distinct concepts in ethical social research, integral to an understanding of an individual's right to privacy (Wiles et al., 2008). Given the nature of social research as something to be reported and shared as new knowledge it is something of a misnomer to claim that research is confidential. Rather, researchers need to acknowledge the extent to which they can promise confidentiality and detail the ways in which they will use anonymity as a means with which to make these claims (Snyder, 2002). Assurances can be made about how data will be confidentially managed, stored and accessed as well as how it will be separated from identifiable individuals with anonymity used to protect the identity of participants when research is disseminated (Wiles et al., 2008).

In a social world saturated with ubiquitous and freely available information Markham and Buchanan argue that the Sisyphean task of preserving confidentiality and anonymity has shifted as we recognise that the sheer volume of data we generate and access may make promises of anonymity rather empty:

> The flood of personal data being created by individuals' devices (e.g. geolocation, physical data, online trackers) combined with big data collection tools creates increasingly complicated criteria for ethically conducting internet research. As of yet, there is no consensus on the best way to interact with personally identifiable information. (Markham & Buchanan, 2015: 204)

Debates about how and when to remove identifiable data, how and if researchers can use internet pseudonyms and the degree to which participants may wish to reject anonymity and exert ownership over their data reflect this lack of consensus. There is an increasing understanding that digital traceability may shift conventional ethical understandings of confidentiality and anonymity as concepts (Tiidenberg, 2018).

Given these complexities it is perhaps unsurprising that many of the ethical grey areas remain unresolved and hotly debated. For social researchers grappling with these questions there are often no simple answers or clear guidelines. Rather, ethical decision making and careful reflection throughout the research process is required in order to navigate ethical decisions. These ethical decisions must take account of the diverse range of human activity across different online contexts and reflect on how this activity interacts with the affordances and structures of different digital platforms and spaces. These contextual decisions must then be grounded in moral principles that maximise benefits of research, minimise possible harms and protect human dignity.

CONCLUSION

This chapter has explored institutional privacy and the relationship between datafication, privacy and surveillance. Key ideas in this chapter can be summarised as followed:

- In digital society, privacy is networked, dynamic and complex with debates polarised between visions of privacy as 'dead' or no longer relevant or, conversely, as profoundly important.
- The technological capabilities and tools of surveillance have become part of our daily lives as we engage with ubiquitous and mundane digital technologies. Surveillance through data is increasingly the norm with surveillance assemblages integrating a range of monitoring practices and technologies.
- Our data doubles are embedded in diverse flows of data, forming new social and political relations, characterised by highly asymmetrical relationships of knowability and visibility.
- Surveillance plays an important role in social exclusion and inequality with privacy becoming another marker of privilege and power as marginalising practices of surveillance exacerbate divisions between the data rich and the data poor.
- Institutional surveillance is also domesticated through, for example, learning analytics and the commodification of domestic spaces.
- In the context of surveillance and privacy, ethically responsible research in the pursuit of knowledge is vital for understanding public and private spaces and data.

Further reading

Zuboff, S. (2019). *The age of surveillance capitalism: The fight for a human future at the new frontier of power: Barack Obama's books of 2019*. Profile books.

The chapter introduced Zuboff's influential concept of surveillance capitalism and for students seeking to explore this in more depth the primary text is a fascinating but challenging read. Try reading it in conjunction with Chapter 6 (Facebook and WhatsApp: Surveillance in the Age of Fake News) in Fuchs, C. (2021). *Social media: A critical introduction*. Sage, for a more accessible overview.

Fuchs, C., Boersma, K., & Albrechtslund, A. (Eds.) (2012). *Internet and surveillance: The challenges of Web 2.0 and social media* (Vol. 16). New York: Routledge.

For a broader discussion of privacy in the context of web 2.0 this collection brings together theoretical discussion about the nature of internet surveillance with a range of empirical case studies exploring consumer data collection, self-disclosure on social networking sites and the nature of privacy in an internet age. In particular, Chapter 4, *Key features of social media surveillance* relates to the ideas discussed in this chapter.

Dodel, M. (2023). Inequalities and privacy in the context of social media. In *The Routledge handbook of privacy and social media* (pp. 204-214). Routledge.

I argued in the chapter that as we are increasingly subjected to surveillance the resultant digital data has important but unequal impacts on our lives. Linking the socio-economic inequalities and privacy in the context of social media this chapter provides a clear introduction to micro and macro impacts of privacy as a cause of socio-economic disparities.

Brause, S. R., & Blank, G. (2023). 'There are some things that I would never ask Alexa' - privacy work, contextual integrity, and smart speaker assistants. *Information, Communication and Society*, pp. 1-16.

The chapter discussed the domestication of digital devices into domestic spaces and this article examines how users perceive privacy with smart speaker assistants in their homes. Drawing on qualitative interviews the authors argue that users engage in privacy work and develop privacy rationales and reasoning to manage and protect their privacy from devices voluntarily brought into the home.

Townsend, L., & Wallace, C. (2016). Social media research: A guide to ethics. *University of Aberdeen*, *1*(16).

There is a wealth of literature around ethics and digital research and a good introduction to key issues can be found in this guide that was the result of an ESRC (Economic and Social Research Council) project 'Social Media, Privacy and Risk: Towards More Ethical Research Methodologies'. The Association of Internet Researchers ethical guidelines are also a valuable point of reference *Internet Research: Ethical Guidelines 3.0 Association of Internet Researchers* available online: https://aoir.org/reports/ethics3.pdf

8

CONCLUSION: OPPORTUNITIES, INEQUALITIES AND DIVISIONS

The chapters in this book have demonstrated the value and importance that digital technologies have in our lives. They enable us to connect and form communities unbounded by geographic restrictions, they give us spaces in which to foster and maintain friendships and relationships, to express our identities and have a global voice, to create and engage with new cultural forms and to participate in new kinds of politics, citizenship and play.

Much of this discussion has highlighted the technologically deterministic optimism or pessimism that has characterised visions of technological change and its effects on society. These polarised debates can be appealing and powerful. They speak to our desires to seek new solutions to complex global problems or to find some outlet to blame for our fears and concerns about the future. While digital technologies and internet connectivity were hailed by some as the 'great equaliser' (Lindgren, 2021a) we can see a rather more mundane reality where digital technologies have become imbued with human baggage:

> As the internet has become something used by the majority of the population, that population has brought with it all of the habits, inclinations and prejudices which are endemic to society as a whole. As a result, much of this early optimism that the internet would radically change our culture

in some sort of knowledge revolution has begun to fade in the light of
the realisation that our culture has perhaps transformed the internet more
than vice versa. (Miller, 2011:67)

In trying to temper an optimist's enthusiasm for the value of digital technologies
with a sociologist's sensitivity to the socio-technical complexities that underpin
the ways in which we experience technology, this chapter will conclude the book
by exploring the injustices and inequalities that are created and exacerbated by
digital technologies.

Bringing together the ideas that have been discussed throughout the book,
the chapter begins by exploring the concept of what has been called the digital divide and outlines the multiple inequalities that shape access to and use of
digital technologies. The chapter then explores some of the social, cultural and
economic advantages of digital connectivity and the ways that these are experienced unequally between individuals from different socio-economic and cultural
backgrounds.

With the understanding that digital inequalities can reinforce and exacerbate
existing inequalities in society the chapter then considers the ways in which digital divide(s) played out during the pandemic when, for many, digital technologies
became a lifeline of connectivity. The chapter concludes by focusing on critical
algorithm studies that have identified new digital cleavages found in the digital
traces that we leave behind online and discusses the unequal consequences of our
data trails and how these may contribute to existing markers of inequality.

THE DIGITAL DIVIDE(S)

The term 'Digital Divide' has many competing definitions but broadly can be
understood as a division between people who have access to and can use digital
media and those who do not (van Dijk, 2020). Early definitions of the digital divide
(from the late 1990s to early 2000s) emphasised access to digital technologies as
the defining feature of inequality. Access to a computer and an internet connection was unevenly spread, largely replicating existing global divisions between the
poorest counties of the world and the former colonial powers of the West. As adoption of digital technologies increased among young, affluent, well-educated and
employed people of majority ethnic backgrounds there was an assumption among
policy makers and academic researchers that adoption and use would trickle down
from these early adopters through market forces (van Dijk, 2020).

More recent understandings of the digital divide have moved beyond characterising digital inequalities as simply related to physical access to technologies.
Increasingly, the the digital divide is recognised not to be a cleavage between the

'haves' and the 'have-nots' as two distinct and clearly separated social categories. These broader conceptualisations of digital inequalities recognise that physical access (the first level of digital divide), unless accompanied by the skills, knowledge and support required for its effective use (a second level of digital divide), does not constitute *access* as we might traditionally understand it.

Together, the first and second level divides create a third level of inequality in differential outcomes experienced when using digital technologies (Hargittai, 2001; Helsper, 2021). These three levels of division have been recognised as profoundly social, economic, cultural and political *and* technical (Selwyn, 2004; van Dijk, 2020).

DEFINING ACCESS

Understanding the various ways in which we can define access is central to more nuanced conceptualisations of digital inequality. Helsper distinguishes three aspects of access. First, infrastructure. In order to be online there needs to be an infrastructure of connectivity in place where you live. This connectivity needs to be reliable, high quality and ubiquitous providing you with the freedom and autonomy to move between home, work, school and places of leisure while staying connected. Second, in order to benefit from this infrastructure and connectivity you must have a device that can access the internet and, finally, the skills to use it to access and engage with content and services (Helsper, 2021: 54).

On a global scale, digital infrastructure is largely better in countries with higher GDPs. In Europe, the USA and China larger proportions of the populations are connected compared with Africa, Latin America and South East Asia. While mobile devices were once seen as tools that may help overcome challenges of infrastructure and increase digital inclusion there is little evidence that they have enabled an 'economic leapfrogging' that has reduced digital inequality (Helsper, 2021: 57). Global inequalities are also accompanied by inequalities within countries, with unequal distribution of access between urban and rural locations and between different groups in society (Gerli & Whalley, 2021; Lappalainen & Rosenberg, 2022).

WHY DIGITAL DIVIDES MATTER: OUTCOMES OF DIGITAL EXCLUSION

The ubiquity of digital technologies and the ways in which they have become embedded and everyday makes access matter: it is increasingly difficult to participate in many aspects of contemporary society without using digital technologies:

> The centrality of the internet in many areas of social economic and political activity is tantamount to marginality for those without or with only limited access to the internet as well as for those unable to use it effectively. [This] adds a fundamental cleavage to existing sources of inequality and social exclusion…that appears to increase the gap between the promise of the information age and its bleak reality for many people around the world. (Castells, 2002:248)

Digital inequalities also matter as they map on to and reinforce social inequalities that have a long and embedded history. The people already most marginalised in society are the least likely to benefit from the growing number of online tools and services that do not have offline counterparts with many organisations, including governments, working on the assumption that internet access is near universal (Watts, 2020).

In the UK, there is evidence to suggest there are high levels of internet use and access with data from the 2022 Ofcom Adults' Media Use and Attitudes report finding that 99% of 16–34-year-olds, 97% of 35–54-year-olds, 96% of 55–64-year-olds and 73% of those over 65 use the internet at home. Conversely 6% of households have no access to the internet with these households likely to be the most financially vulnerable (Ofcom, 2022).

The data appears to paint a reasonably equitable picture, certainly in terms of first level digital access, but there is digital poverty within these statistics that questions the assumption of universality even in a country where internet penetration is high. Digital poverty, defined by the Digital Poverty Alliance[1] as 'the inability to interact with the online world fully, when, where, and how an individual needs to' relates to Helsper's (2021) conceptualisation of access. Digitally poor households and individuals include those who are fully offline and excluded as a result of a lack of devices or infrastructure for connectivity. But digital poverty also includes those who are online but are unable to access the benefits of their connectivity because of a lack of skills, education or other forms of social and cultural capital.

The UK Digital Poverty Alliance identify five determinants of digital poverty beyond structural determinants of socio-economic position and circumstantial determinants of living conditions, employment stability and health and family circumstance:

1   Device and connectivity: related to issues of affordability, data and infrastructure.
2   Access: related to accessibility, availability and user-centred design.
3   Capability: related to skills, education and understanding.
4   Motivation: related to awareness and convenience.
5   Support: related to technical and educational networks of help.

The Alliance argues that these determinants shape inequalities and digital poverty and are a result of multiple, compounding and intersectional forms of inequality.

The tangible outcomes of digital inequalities focus on divisions within societies where internet access is widely diffused in the population. Patterns of access to, and use of, digital technologies range from a highly technologically literate information elite with easy access to connectivity, to those who are digitally excluded or illiterate, with the majority of the population somewhere between these two extremes (van Dijk, 2020). For example, the 2022 Ofcom Adults' Media Use and Attitudes report found that 29% of UK internet users could be considered 'narrow users', only ever engaged in very a limited type of online activity, ranging from e-mail to using social media sites to online shopping[2].

Overwhelmingly, education and income are reliable predictors of digital inclusion. They afford greater access to connectivity and enable better skills for evaluating and engaging with online content. Conversely, those with lower levels of education have lower levels of digital literacy and are less likely to use the internet in ways that are economically beneficial to them (Helsper & van Deursen, 2017). Internet users who have more digital literacy skills, who have access to more resources and who have more social and economic capital benefit most from their digital engagement. A scenario in which the digitally rich get richer and the poor get poorer.

Support networks are an important part of being digitally included and form a type of social capital (Bourdieu, 2018) that is key to participation in society. Social indicators shape the type of access and support networks that people have available to them in getting online and effectively using the internet (Helsper & van Deursen, 2017). In a digital society this social capital enables us to seek solutions from formal helpdesks or online resources, to ask for help from more technically literate friends or colleagues, or to seek support from our informal networks of friends and family (as anyone who has spent an afternoon patiently trying to explain some aspect of computer use to a parent or grandparent will have experienced).

For Helsper and van Deursen (2017), differences in access to these kinds of support networks form another layer of digital inequality with those most isolated (the unemployed, disabled, retired, or housewives/husbands) having more problems with using the internet and more problems getting support even when it is available through formal and informal networks. They argue that this creates an even larger digital 'gap' between those who do and do not need support, reinforcing the point that digital connectivity is more beneficial for those with a higher social status.

The type of device used to access the internet also has implications for digital inequalities. Developing the concept of a mobile internet underclass Napoli and Obar (2014) argue that accessing the internet via a mobile device is a second-class form of access compared to non-mobile internet use. This second-class access offers 'lower levels of functionality and content availability; operates on less open and flexible platforms; and contributes to diminished levels of user engagement, content creation, and information seeking' (2014: 323). The differences in experience between mobile and PC internet access can, they argue, reinforce and exacerbate existing inequities in digital skill sets and participation. An underclass of mobile users has important implications for global inequalities as the main way new internet users are getting online (and these new users are more likely to be those already disadvantaged by being from lower income groups and/or less developed economies) is via mobile devices (Napoli & Obar, 2014).

INEQUALITIES AND OUTCOMES OF DIGITAL ENGAGEMENT

In research based in the Netherlands, van Deursen and Helpser (2015) studied offline outcomes in economic, social, political, institutional and educational fields of activity then related these outcomes to individuals' digital engagement. They argue that internet usage contributes to a range of offline outcomes across several life realms.

> Common economic outcomes achieved relate to commerce, such as gaining price advantages. Social gains facilitated by internet use include increased contact with family and friends and the creation of new friendships online that continue offline. Furthermore, the internet facilitates institutional engagement by providing access to up-to-date public information. Striking is the fact that over a quarter of the respondents claimed to live healthier due to online information. (van Deursen & Helsper, 2015:45)

The emphasis on outcomes in this conceptualisation of the digital divide largely focus on the positive economic, social and cultural benefits of digital media access. Highspeed digital infrastructures are vital for national and individual participation in a global digital economy with evidence suggesting countries and individuals with lower access to ICT face economic disadvantage (Helsper, 2021).

Positive economic outcomes relate to schooling, e-commerce and income, with digital media an embedded necessity in many public services and in many aspects of our daily working lives (van Dijk, 2020). Job searches and applications are increasingly online, use of ICTs in education is widespread and the use of the internet to shop and bank affords savings and access to offers and deals not available offline. In this economic sphere young people, men and those employed and with higher education or income levels have statistically significant digital advantages (van Deursen & Helsper, 2018; van Dijk, 2020).

As discussed in Chapters 2, 3 and 4, socially, digital technologies afford us ways to connect with networks of family and friends, avoid isolation and combat loneliness. They enable us to join community groups, seek out others with shared interests and meet and date partners. This enhancement of our social capital is not the sole preserve of younger generations or 'digital natives', as is often assumed to be the case. While we can identify some generational digital divides, smartphones in particular connect older generations with grandchildren and family as they actively incorporate digital tools in their lives (Caliandro et al., 2021). Social inequalities remain, however, and their impacts are felt unequally between individuals from different socio-economic backgrounds (van Deursen et al., 2017).

Cultural use of the internet is also shaped by patterns of digital inequality. There is a tendency to assume that spaces of content creation create a more level playing field for cultural participation, particularly among those from minority ethnic groups (Literat, 2016). However, as I argued in Chapter 5, while many of us spend a substantial amount of time on social media a much smaller percentage are engaged and creative in participatory ways. This again highlights inequalities in participation, excluding those who do not have the digital opportunities or literacies to benefit from participation (Lussier et al., 2010; Porlezza, 2019). Beyond access and digital literacies, however, are more deeply felt cultural inequalities that assume a meritocracy of creativity and choice rather than recognising fundamental structural divisions and power inequalities in who gets to be visible online:

> Content creation – online and offline – is about the representation of ideologies, norms, values, and lifestyles, or embodied cultural capital learned through socialisation…if only certain people create content, the world is represented in ways that reflect how they see the world. (Helsper, 2021: 149)

Across economic, social and cultural axes of inequality we can identify general trends. People with higher levels of education, those in employment and younger generations benefit more from the internet than older people, those not in employment and those with lower levels of education. These digital inequalities reinforce and exacerbate inequalities for those less advantaged creating a new dimension of social segmentation that maps onto traditional economic, cultural and social inequalities:

> Some people and some social classes benefit more and earlier from the outcomes of digital media use than others. Relative inequality matters in a network

society where some are able to take greater advantage of resources via relationships than others. In terms of absolute inequality, digital media use may reflect and reinforce existing social inequality when the positive outcomes are reached only by some in society. Absolute inequality matters too in an information society when some cannot find vital information necessary to live and work. When the use of digital media becomes absolutely essential, those without access or elementary digital skills will be excluded. (van Dijk, 2020:125)

Social exclusion is multi-dimensional, and it is important to be mindful of the complex intersectionality of inequalities between and across different socio-economic and socio-cultural groups. These are not sufficiently explained by a single socio-economic or socio-cultural characteristic and are potentially complicated further by unequal access to and use of digital technologies (Helsper, 2021; Zheng & Walsham, 2021). A focus on intersectionality and overlapping issues of gender, class, ethnicity, education and geography may be a more helpful lens for understanding the complex ways that digital technologies interact with the multiple systems of power an individual is positioned within (Zheng & Walsham, 2021).

DIGITAL DIVIDES AND THE PANDEMIC

Issues around digital divides and access to the internet were brought to the fore during the COVID-19 pandemic and lockdowns. We became 'digital by default' (Livingston, 2020) and being online was, for many, almost compulsory. Crisis-driven digital transformations during the pandemic meant that hybrid working, online learning and digital health provision became the norm and we used technologies to access digitised versions of face-to-face services and to connect with family and friends (Allmann, 2022; Lai & Widmar, 2021).

A variety of digital tools and applications were used to sustain community networks and personal relationships online, facilitating communication and shared leisure through instant messaging apps, social media and video conferencing (discussed in Chapter 6). TikTok and participatory culture thrived as a space of user-generated content during lockdowns (discussed in Chapter 5) while also becoming a space for healthcare professionals and governments to share guidelines and information (Chen et al., 2021).

Educational inequalities

For those without access a vital lockdown lifeline was unavailable. Even for households with access connectivity was often still problematic. Multiple devices and multiple users within a household created competing demands for the connectivity speeds required to effectively participate in school, work or leisure (Lai & Widmar, 2021). Infrastructure and bandwidth constraints created inequalities as internet access was negotiated in the home with concerns around education and childhood inequalities particularly acute. In the UK during lockdown schools were closed to all children except for children of key workers and specific vulnerable groups. For all other children provision was moved online. Concerns about children in households with limited access to technology focused on the potential for deepening gaps in attainment and social mobility as lockdowns continued.

A research brief from the Sutton Trust reported some stark differences in educational provision and take up across the sector. 23% of pupils were reported to be taking part in live and recorded lessons online every day with pupils from middle-class homes more likely to participate than their working-class counterparts. In the private sector, 51% of primary and 57% of secondary students participated in online lessons every day, twice as likely as those in state schools (Cullinane & Montacute, 2021). In terms of access, in the most deprived schools in the UK teachers reported that over a third of their pupils would not have adequate access to an electronic device for learning, compared to 2% in more affluent state schools. Given this limited access to internet-enabled devices and the pivot to learning delivered largely online, the potential learning gap was compounded by the fact that children from the poorest households were likely to have benefitted the most from online content when schools were closed (Coleman, 2021).

Outside of the UK comparable patterns of inequality also emerged. Research in Malaysia highlighted the existence of a pronounced digital divide among students particularly in rural areas, with limited availability of digital devices at home motivating students to take part-time employment in order to attend online classes (Surianshah, 2021). Similarly, research on remote learning for children in Nigeria found students' access to learning opportunities correlated to their socio-economic status. During COVID, the closure of schools affected 39,440,016 primary and secondary school learners across Nigeria, exacerbating existing inequalities in education. Children whose parents or carers paid for private school had better access to learning resources and lockdown remote learning provision than students in government schools. Inequalities in access to ICT-based learning intensified existing disparities in learning outcomes along socio-economic and geographic (urban-rural) lines (Azubuike et al., 2021).

In Nigeria more than half the population is not online (with an internet penetration of 42%) and already disadvantaged populations have limited access to electricity and technological infrastructure, exacerbating educational and digital inequalities. During lockdown this inequality was compounded by a lack of social and cultural capital around digital skills and competencies with parents from the most disadvantaged backgrounds feeling unable to support their children with remote learning (Azubuike et al., 2021). These kinds of findings have been replicated across India, Pakistan, Bangladesh, Nepal and Afghanistan (Mathrani et al., 2022), highlighting the need to understand the ways in which inequalities and digital divides were exacerbated during the global health crisis and continue the legacy of inequality into the 'new normal'.

Health inequalities

Digital inequalities and divisions arising from the pandemic were not limited to education. Access to technology has emerged as a fundamental social determinant of access to healthcare (Eruchalu et al., 2021). Mirroring research findings about education inequalities, healthcare inequalities in the lockdown shift to telemedicine (health provision, information and monitoring that is delivered by technology) disproportionately affected those from minority ethnic groups, those on low incomes and other vulnerable populations. Socio-economic factors and structural disadvantage were reinforced by the digital divide and during the pandemic this worsened health access disparities (Clare, 2021).

The importance of social determinants of health have long been recognised. Defined by the World Health Organization as the non-medical factors that influence health outcomes these determinants have an important influence on health inequities. Those in lower socio-economic positions face poorer health outcomes. Income, education, employment, housing and social inclusion are among the social determinants recognised to impact health equity in positive and negative ways with access to digital technologies now another potential social cleavage. In the context of the pandemic this divide meant that those who did not have first and second level access to digital technology were excluded from a range of services, activities and resources to support their physical and mental health needs during the pandemic (Spanakis et al., 2021).

Concerns over mental health during the pandemic were particularly acute. Isolation, uncertainty and stress created social trauma as we faced rapid, unexpected and often radical changes in our lives (Frąckowiak-Sochańska, 2020). With social interactions disrupted, digital exclusion and an inability to draw on online resources for social support or leisure exposed those vulnerable to an even greater risk of loneliness and mental health challenges (Spanakis et al., 2021).

These kinds of digital exclusion become particularly problematic when the digital practices employed during lockdown become normalised post pandemic. For non-digitally engaged people this presents a continuation of inequalities that may embed the health and social inequalities they already experience (Spanakis et al., 2021).

DIGITAL INFRASTRUCTURE AND NEW KINDS OF DIGITAL DIVIDES

Inequalities also emerge from the technical infrastructures that make up digital technologies. A new kind of digital divide exists in the form of the profound impact our digitally traceable behaviours and online presence can have on our lives (Gran et al., 2021; Micheli et al., 2018).

As I discussed in Chapters 6 and 7, in an increasingly digitised world data traces and the impact they have are important as our digital traces are shaped and sorted in practices associated with surveillance capitalism (Zuboff, 2019). This sorting is unevenly distributed and extends understandings of digital inequalities to include the unequal consequences of our data trails and the ways in which these may contribute to existing markers of inequality (Lutz, 2019).

Algorithms have become a central feature of the infrastructure of the internet and are increasingly a part of many aspects of everyday life (Gran et al., 2021; Raub, 2018). An algorithm is a mathematical construct that is implemented in construction of a technology and configured for a specific task or tasks (Mittelstadt et al., 2016).

Algorithms use personal data, including digital data, to automate decision making. In the context of computing an algorithm is a set of instructions, created by data engineers, mathematicians and programmers that tell a computer how to accomplish a task or make a decision. Decision-making tasks use models generated by algorithms to attempt to predict or estimate a relevant outcome (Beigang, 2022). Algorithms are about making something happen and are designed to execute and bring about a desired outcome according to certain needs. They make decisions about the best action to take in a given situation or about how best to interpret data based on complex rules that often rely on computational power that is beyond human comprehension (Mittelstadt et al., 2016). In doing so, they mediate the ways online communication and information is located, retrieved, filtered and presented (Willson, 2017).

Algorithms influence the content we see online and play a key role in how we consume the internet. They act as recommender systems helping us to decide what to watch next on Netflix or what to listen to on Spotify (Hallinan & Striphas, 2016). They personalise Google search results and curate the content we see on our social media feeds (Bucher, 2017). Beyond these seemingly banal applications algorithms are also used in social credit scoring, public administration, social services, healthcare and governance (Micheli et al., 2018). They play a pervasive role in our lives and an emerging field of critical algorithm studies has emphasised the need to understand in more detail how they mediate our online and offline experiences (Beer, 2017; Willson, 2017).

Algorithms work within larger systems of data and, importantly, they are not neutral. They are woven into our social worlds and their design and implementation is a product of political, technical, cultural and social interactions (Beer, 2017; Willson, 2017). This social embeddedness means that we need to think critically about how algorithms shape how people are treated and judged, how they open or close opportunities, and how these decisions and outcomes may be unfair. When the data they rely on are skewed as a result of bias or a lack of awareness of consequence the outcomes can promulgate and perpetuate existing divisions (Raub, 2018).

The impact of algorithms is less visible than other markers of inequality and digital division but still affect peoples' lives in fundamental and fundamentally unequal ways (Gran et al., 2021). Algorithms have been used to make decisions about policing and justice, about employment, school admissions, health and insurance and social services and have been demonstrated to reproduce and exacerbate social inequalities (Eubanks, 2018; Noble, 2018; O'Neil, 2017).

Algorithms, inequalities and justice

In an article entitled 'Machine bias: there's software used across the country to predict future criminals. And it's biased against blacks', Angwin et al. (2016) present an analysis of a tool called COMPAS (Correctional Offender Management Profiling for Alternative Sanctions) produced by Northpointe software. COMPAS is a tool that uses algorithms to assess a criminal defendant's likelihood of becoming a recidivist (a term that describes criminals who re-offend). Tools like COMPAS are widely used in the USA with the aim of removing human bias in key decision-making points in the justice system. They are used to predict which defendants were likely to commit new crimes and in doing so aim to create a fairer criminal justice system and reduce rates of incarceration (Angwin et al., 2016).

The research of Angwin et al. set out to examine the accuracy of the COMPAS recidivism algorithm and to test whether it was biased against certain groups. They found that the tool correctly predicted an offender's recidivism 61% of the time but that White and Black defendants were treated differently. Black offenders were more likely to be predicted as higher risk and were almost twice as likely to be misclassified as higher risk compared to White offenders (45% vs. 23%). Conversely, White offenders were more likely to be misclassified as lower risk with Black offenders 45% more likely to be assigned higher risk scores and significantly more likely to be misclassified as being a higher risk of violent recidivism (Angwin et al., 2016).

Similar discriminatory algorithmic practices have been found in policing. O'Neil (2017) argues that algorithms as 'Weapons of Maths Destruction' create feedback loops that perpetuate inequalities. Also looking at recidivism models she argues that if, for example, the algorithm looks at data about a person's first encounter with law enforcement then it is likely that Black people will be modelled as having encountered problems earlier than White people. This is a result of well-documented systemic racism in policing practices, such as stop and frisk, where Black people are five times[3] as likely to be stopped without just cause than their White counterparts.

Racial profiling and targeting may itself be the result of predictive policing tools that use location-based algorithms to predict where crimes are likely to occur on the basis of data about places, events and crime rates as well as data about the socio-demographic features of the location, a proxy that also disproportionally targets young Black men.

These kinds of structural biases may be baked into code when an algorithm is trained on data that does not adequately represent a population or when data is optimised to prioritise certain kinds of decisions (Yarger et al., 2019). Bias is embedded in the design of algorithms where the consequences of their design are not considered in broader social contexts. But the consequences, as we have seen in the examples above, can be life changing, and as complex data models are increasingly applied to personal aspects of our lives the danger is that inequality and discrimination will be reinforced (Yarger et al., 2019).

Algorithms, inequalities and health

Algorithms can also profoundly affect health outcomes. In the USA, healthcare systems use commercial algorithms to guide health decisions. Their promise is in improving healthcare delivery with machine learning predicted to become integral in fields that demand close scrutiny of images, like radiology and anatomical pathology, and to help reduce existing inequalities in care if algorithms can overcome known biases in diagnosis and treatment (Char et al., 2018). The use of big data in healthcare also aims to generate new insights about health and disease and new understandings from what is defined as 'precision medicine' (Ferryman and Pitcan, 2018).

However, like in the field of justice, there is evidence to suggest that the use of big data and of algorithmic modelling is reproducing gender and race inequalities (Chouldechova & Roth, 2018; Obermeyer et al., 2019). These inequalities exist both across and within nations and are reflected in medical outcomes.

In their work on algorithms and race, Obermeyer et al. (2019) argue that algorithms trained on data reflect structural inequalities. So, for example, using mortality or readmission rates to measure the performance of a hospital penalises hospitals that serve poor and/or non-White populations. They also found that

Black patients assigned the same level of risk by an algorithm are sicker than White patients and algorithms used to identify patients for special medical treatment systemically underdiagnosed Black people:

> The bias arises because the algorithm predicts health care costs rather than illness, but unequal access to care means that we spend less money caring for Black patients than for White patients. Thus, despite health care cost appearing to be an effective proxy for health by some measures of predictive accuracy, large racial biases arise. (Obermeyer et al., 2019:1)

Algorithmic biases in health reflect the structural bias of the data they use to model decision making. They also reflect a bias in outcomes, where neoliberal models of health place responsibility on individuals for their own health and well-being and populations who have lower levels of health literacy or who live in areas with fewer resources are marginalised (Ferryman & Pitcan, 2018).

This has important implications for access to healthcare with algorithm-based appointment scheduling systems making Black patients wait longer than White patients. The algorithm uses data based on previous appointment no-shows to make decisions about scheduling and this data systematics overrepresents Black patients as they are overrepresented in lower socio-economic groups. Lower socio-economic groups are more likely to be unable to attend scheduled appointments due to limited transportation, lack of health insurance and inconsistent employment, and so are systematically disadvantaged (Samorani & Blount, 2020). This structural inequality may compound health issues and inequalities as the patients least able to afford to wait are left longer before being seen and as a result may experience more negative health outcomes.

Algorithms, inequalities and employment

Using the example of employment processes, Mann and O'Neil (2016) demonstrate how the hiring decisions of human resource managers are increasingly data driven. The use of AI and algorithms in automating hiring provides a great deal of efficiency in weeding out unsuitable candidates. As well as gains in efficiency the use of AI aims to address human prejudice around a candidate's ethnicity, disability, age, class, educational background, social networks, or gender. Their goal is also to tackle a long history of human bias and discrimination, well documented and prevalent in hiring practices (Raghavan et al., 2020).

By removing personally identifying information that may be a source of unconscious bias, by using chat to screen potential candidates for roles, by analysing candidates' diction, tone, and facial movements in video job interviews or by testing job adverts for gender-neutral language likely to attract the most diverse applicant pools, the use of AI attempts to encode the values of equity of opportunity (Raub, 2018). The emphasis is on 'de-biasing' the dataset that algorithms use, and mitigating human prejudice in recruitment by using principles of design justice (Stinson, 2022).

While these tools have the potential to foster more equality their goals and efficiencies come at a cost. The algorithms that automated decisions rely on reflect the bias of their human designers and the outcomes are not free from mistakes and misinterpretations. Applicants may be excluded unfairly based on their socio-cultural-economic characteristics, as the algorithm mimics flawed human decision making rather than, as purported, mitigating human bias (Mann & O'Neil, 2016). The use of AI in hiring can lead to unequal access to employment opportunities and, as has already been established, employment status is a resilient indicator of digital inclusion.

Algorithmic diversity and neutrality

An overarching issue and inequality faced in the context of AI and debates about fairness is the lack of diversity in tech and the inability of tech companies to recruit and retain a diverse staff cohort (Raub, 2018; Yarger et al., 2019). White men occupy the most powerful and well-paying positions in tech, an industry with a reputation for a masculine culture and persistent inequalities around gender (Mickey, 2022). People of colour are also largely excluded from leadership roles, limiting their capacity to shape the development and design of new technologies (Alegria, 2020).

In order to foster more equality, IT professionals historically under-represented in the field (women and people of colour, particularly people of color professionals) need to be recruited to diversify the AI landscape. The homogenous nature of the industry results in a homogenous worldview that emerges in the algorithms that shape in hiring decisions (Raub, 2018):

> If diverse people across racial, ethnic, gender, sexual identities, and socio-economic backgrounds are absent from the IT workforce that is designing and developing AI systems, how well will the software foster inclusion and equity? How will these systems engage with and support these populations if their voices are not present to raise questions, illuminate blind spots, and check implicit assumptions? (Byrne, 2018)[4]

This emphasis reflects the need to understand the ways in which our technologies are socially shaped, in their design, implementation and use. Without this diversification the bias is unchallenged, sustained and replicated.

A recognition of their social nature helps to undermine arguments that rely on the illusion of algorithmic neutrality. Stinson (2022) cites the 2020 controversy in the UK around algorithmically calculated A-levels scores that were used to award grades 'more fairly' in the light of the extreme disruption that a cohort of students had experienced around exams as a result of the pandemic. She argues that initial government responses pointed to 'the algorithm' as a neutral decision-maker, ignoring the statistical weaknesses of the data employed and the failure to recognise the complexity of the 'average student' as modelled by the algorithm.

Similar defences of algorithmic neutrality abound with Stinson citing examples of algorithms that have been defended against concerns about inequality and injustice; from Apple's rejection of the complaint that its credit card was systematically giving men higher credit limits than women despite identical or better credit scores, to the algorithm at Stanford Hospital that prioritised non front-line administrative workers for COVID vaccinations over medical staff working in COVID wards (Stinson, 2022).

Algorithms, inequalities and searching

The lack of algorithmic diversity also plays out in shaping how we experience and view content online. Search platforms and social media sites use algorithms that reflect the dominant social, cultural, political and commercial discourses of those spaces and tools. Like the algorithms that shape it, the information we encounter is not neutral and objective, and inequality is recapitulated in internet search algorithms (Cotter & Reisdorf, 2020).

This is complicated by the fact that algorithms are largely 'black boxed'. Platforms and corporations keep the functioning of their algorithms secret, and their outputs and outcomes are not transparent (Pasquale, 2015). Even if they were, the complexity of the variables and the computation techniques they employ may render them largely opaque anyway (Cotter & Reisdorf, 2020; Pasquale, 2015). Our awareness of how algorithms function and our understandings of them are limited, but our interactions with them are routine and part of many everyday practices, searching the web being a seemingly mundane but illuminating example.

Internet search engines like Google are used ubiquitously to gather information but, despite the promise of AI and objectivity, systemic biases in society are replicated in search engine functionality and their algorithmic output (Vlasceanu & Amodio, 2022). In the same way that algorithms have discriminated in justice, health and hiring decisions, patterns of discrimination are also evident in search engines.

As the quantity of information available to us online expands exponentially we use search engines like Google in order to manage and sort that information.

In turn, system designers use algorithms to make decisions about what information is shown to whom (Kay et al., 2015). As this chapter has detailed, algorithms mirror existing inequalities and prejudice and so the search results returned to us from Google represent the world in indexed and sorted ways. This sorting is significant as we tend to rely on the order and ranking in which search findings are returned to us and take these as proxies for quality and relevance (Kammerer & Gerjets, 2012).

In a digital landscape where users are information rich and attention poor, search engines act as digital gatekeepers, directing and filtering us to particular content (Hargittai, 2000). This creates what has been defined as a filter bubble (Pariser, 2011), removing us from serendipitous encounters with random and unexpected content and instead enclosing us in information loops where we are only shown content that we have previously expressed an interest in. We become ringfenced in information environments that shield us from encounters with radically different content and we instead consume information that is easy, comfortable and reassuring in an echo chamber that amplifies confirmation bias.

Auto complete me...

Google's personalisation algorithm builds a profile of the sort of person using a particular machine, based on their location, the browser they are using and the ways in which they search, in order to return preferred content to them when they search the web (Pariser, 2011). This means that different people using the same search terms on Google can have different results returned. As I argue above, this creates a search system that feeds us the kind of content we prefer and encourages us to consume information that aligns with our world view rather than challenging us to think critically about a range of ideas.

Bias is also inherent in Google's page ranking and auto-complete search algorithms. Page ranking algorithms mean pages with multiple links to them are privileged in the search results and are one way in which information from the web is sorted and prioritised for us. Page ranking is used in combination with auto-completion algorithms to predict what is being searched for as we start to type into the search bar. We are then offered suggestions of what we might be looking for (try typing 'why do I...' or 'how do I...' into Google and see what your predicted search terms are).

The search queries we enter show us a series of responses that are ordered accordingly to what the algorithm thinks is most relevant to us. They also function to cast a vote 'vouching for the popularity of the search string' (Baker & Potts, 2013). They indicate what searches are trending but can draw our attention to suggestions that were not planned for and yield predictions which perpetuate and reinforce existing prejudices (Al-Abbas et al., 2020).

Baker and Potts' (2013) research on the auto-complete search algorithm offered by Google has highlighted the way it produces suggested terms that are racist, sexist or homophobic when prompted to auto complete questions containing identity words related to gender, ethnicity and sexuality. Baker and Potts studied how different religious, gender, sexual and ethnic groups were stereotyped in ways relating to physical, behavioural and sexual attributes in Google's predictive text: 'do Asians sweat more', 'why do black people have big lips', 'why do gay guys have a weird voice' (Baker & Potts, 2013). They argue that search strings perpetuated negative stereotypes about vulnerable social groups and that the algorithm-driven search strings offer 'a window into the collective Internet consciousness, and what this window reveals is not an attractive scene' (Baker & Potts, 2013).

Research on gender inequalities in internet search algorithms finds similar discriminatory outputs. Kay et al. (2015) looked at gender-segregated career stereotypes studying how genders are represented in image search results for occupations. They found both stereotyped exaggeration and systematic under-representation of women and argue that the prevalence and characteristics of these kinds of search results can reinforce prejudices and stereotypes particularly as people tend to rely on search engines' selection and ordering of results as signs of quality and relevance (Kay et al., 2015).

The AI tools that are now part of our digital landscape are contributing to a cycle of inequality in which existing bias and prejudice is recapitulated by algorithms. In turn, these algorithms are guiding the kinds of decisions I have outlined in this chapter around justice, health and employment (and many more) that reinforce and remake existing stereotypes and inequalities; reifying hegemonic ideals via the information they choose to serve and prioritise (Cotter & Reisdorf, 2020; O'Neil, 2017; Vlasceanu & Amodio, 2022).

Algorithmic knowledge and digital inequality

The extent to which we are aware of these algorithmic interventions creates another layer of digital division based on an uneven distribution of data and knowledge. That these processes are largely invisible and we are largely unaware of them means that algorithm 'knowledge gaps' (Cotter & Reisdorf, 2020) are creating new layers of inequality.

Without knowing how algorithms are working we lack a sense of the bigger picture that may help us assess the merit of information we seek out online, rendering us unknowingly reliant on them. Inequalities then come from differentials in the skills to question and critique algorithmically driven representations of reality and knowledge with some more likely to 'unwittingly internalize the normative discourses inscribed in algorithmic outputs' (Cotter & Reisdorf, 2020). Unsurprisingly, given what this chapter has outlined so far, those with higher socio-economic status are more likely to have the digital capital and skills to navigate algorithmic knowledge as knowledge disparities map closely onto structural inequalities (Cotter & Reisdorf, 2020).

As we become increasingly reliant on digital technologies and tools the kinds of divisions and inequalities outlined in this chapter have real and meaningful social, cultural, political and economic consequences. Are we in danger of sacrificing too much for a convenient and personalised digital experience and of (more or less) unwittingly reproducing the hierarchies, power relations and structural inequalities that are so damaging to our social world?

> With an algorithmic infrastructure that automatically amplifies existing patterns through machine-learning mechanisms, there is a greater risk of reinforcing whatever democratic deficit existed in the first place, weakening the condition for an informed public and democratic participation...demographic digital divides raise the question of *who* gets to make informed decisions about how to navigate the digital infrastructure conditioning information flow and public participation today. (Gran et al., 2021:1792)

In her book *Algorithms of oppression* Noble (2018) argues that inequality, particularly racism and sexism, are part of the architecture and language of technology. The sociological study of digital culture takes seriously her point that it is not of social benefit to organise the web in ways that solidify the kinds of inequalities this chapter has discussed.

It is vital that the sociological study of digital culture contributes to efforts to understand and ameliorate the social divisions that emerge from a data-driven social world. Without this the pleasures, friendships and communities, the entertainment, play and wealth of knowledge and opportunities available to us through our engagement with digital technologies start to look and feel very uncomfortable.

The sociological study of technology, and the mutual dependencies of society and technology in contemporary society, forces us to think about what the future of our global digital society *can* and *should* be. With that in mind I conclude the book as it began by asking chat GPT what it thinks the future of digital society is.

Sociology should heed its prescient warning that it is important that we remain critical and aware of the implications new and emerging technologies may have on our lives.

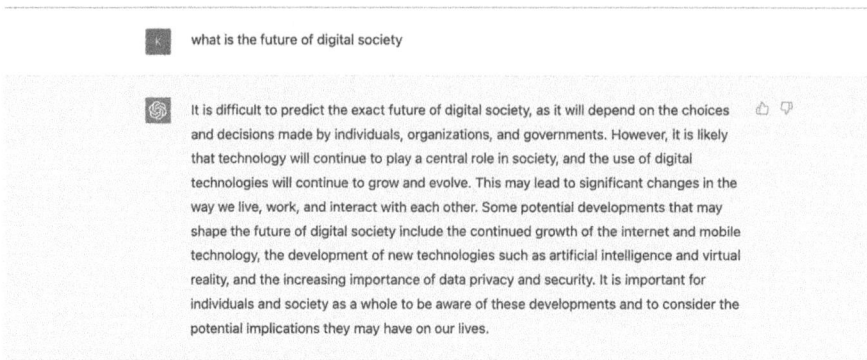

Figure 8.1 Screenshot from ChatGPT interaction December 10th 2022.

CONCLUSIONS

This concluding chapter has reflected on some of the social, cultural and economic advantages of digital connectivity and the ways that these advantages are experienced unequally between individuals from different socio-economic backgrounds. Key ideas in this chapter can be summarised as followed:

- The term 'digital divide' initially referred to a division between those who have access to digital technologies and those who do not. More nuanced understandings have been developed that recognised that access is not the sole axis of division and research has identified three levels of divide related to access to technology, the ability to effectively use technology and the differential outcomes experienced from use.
- Digital inequalities map onto existing inequalities with digital poverty compounding multiple and intersectional forms of inequality, an issue made highly visible during the pandemic when many resources became digital by default.
- Inequalities also emerge from technical infrastructures as our digital traces are sorted with unequal consequences in practices of surveillance capitalism. The algorithms that shape our technical infrastructures perpetuate and compound inequalities and social divisions with bias baked into the tools that structure and shape our daily lives.

— **Further reading** —

Lutz, C. (2019). Digital inequalities in the age of artificial intelligence and big data. *Human Behaviour and Emerging Technologies*, *1*(2), pp. 141-148.

This article presents a concise and accessible overview of literature on digital inequalities at the first, second and third level of digital divides.

Arora, P. (2019). *The next billion users: Digital life beyond the West*. Harvard University Press.

An excellent book that traces patterns of internet usage in India, China, South Africa, Brazil and the Middle East. Arora focuses on the digital lives of people in the Global South examining how users engage with digital media and manage their privacy and data management online. Her book covers a range of themes that connect with chapters throughout this book – digital leisure, mediated friendships and identities, consumption and inequality – emphasising the need to move beyond understandings of the global poor as primarily using digital tools for socio-economic mobility.

Zajko, M. (2022). Artificial intelligence, algorithms, and social inequality: Sociological contributions to contemporary debates. *Sociology Compass*, *16*(3), p .e12962.

Gerdon, F., Bach, R.L., Kern, C., & Kreuter, F. (2022). Social impacts of algorithmic decision-making: A research agenda for the social sciences. *Big Data and Society*, *9*(1), p. 20539517221089305.

Davis, J. L., Williams, A., & Yang, M. W. (2021). Algorithmic reparation. *Big Data and Society*, *8*(2), p. 20539517211044808.

These three articles tackle the issue of algorithmic inequality. They argue that Artificial intelligence (AI) and algorithmic systems may reinforce social inequality and existing hierarchies, perpetuating bias and unjust discrimination. They highlight the need for socially responsible algorithmic decision making and the role of the social sciences in effecting change and algorithmic reparation given the impacts of these systems.

NOTES

1. https://digitalpovertyalliance.org
2. https://digitalpovertyalliance.org/uk-digital-poverty-evidence-review-2022/ introduction-myths-and-shifts/
3. https://www.technologyreview.com/2020/07/17/1005396/predictive-policing-algorithms-racist-dismantled-machine-learning-bias-criminal-justice/
4. https://www.fastcompany.com/40536485/now-is-the-time-to-act-to-stop-bias-in-ai

References

Abercrombie, N., & Longhurst, B. J. (1998). *Audiences: A sociological theory of performance and imagination*. Sage.

Abidin, C. (2014). # In $ tagLam: Instagram as a repository of taste, a burgeoning marketplace, a war of eyeballs. In *Mobile media making in an age of smartphones* (pp. 119–128). Springer.

Abidin, C. (2016a). 'Aren't these just young, rich women doing vain things online?': Influencer selfies as subversive frivolity. *Social Media and Society*, *2*(2). p.2056305116641342.

Abidin, C. (2016b). Visibility labour: Engaging with influencers' fashion brands and# OOTD advertorial campaigns on Instagram. *Media International Australia*, *161*(1), 86–100.

Abidin, C., Lee, J., Barbetta, T., & Miao, W. S. (2021). Influencers and COVID-19: Reviewing key issues in press coverage across Australia, China, Japan, and South Korea. *Media International Australia*, *178*(1), 114–135.

Abidin, C. (2021). From "networked publics" to "refracted publics": A companion framework for researching "below the radar" studies. *Social Media+ Society*, *7*(1), 2056305120984458.

Agger, B. (2012). Oversharing: Presentations of self in the internet age. In *Oversharing: Presentations of Self in the Internet Age*. Routledge

Al-Abbas, L. S., Haider, A. S., & Hussein, R. F. (2020). Google autocomplete search algorithms and the Arabs' perspectives on gender: A case study of Google Egypt. *GEMA Online® Journal of Language Studies*, *20*(4), 95–112.

Albury, K. (2015). Selfies, sexts, and sneaky hats: Young people's understandings of gendered practices of self-representation. *International Journal of Communication*, *9*(1), 1734–1745.

Alegria, S. N. (2020). What do we mean by broadening participation? Race, inequality, and diversity in tech work. *Sociology Compass*, *14*(6), e12793.

Alex, H. (2019). *Revealed: How TikTok censors videos that do not please Beijing*. The Guardian. https://www.theguardian.com/technology/2019/sep/25/revealed-how-tiktok-censors-videos-that-do-not-please-beijing

Alfalqi, K., & Bellaiche, M. (2021). IoT-based disaster detection model using social networks and machine learning. *2021 4th International Conference on Artificial Intelligence and Big Data, ICAIBD 2021*, 92–97. https://doi.org/10.1109/ICAIBD51990.2021.9458964

Ali, S., & Kelly, M. (2004). Ethics and social research. *Researching Society and Culture*, *2*, 116–127.

Alkiviadou, N. (2019). Hate speech on social media networks: towards a regulatory framework?. *Information & Communications Technology Law*, *28*(1), 19–35.

Allaby, M., & Shannon, C. S. (2020). 'I just want to keep in touch': Adolescents' experiences with leisure-related smartphone use. *Journal of Leisure Research*, *51*(3), 245–263.

Allmann, K. (2022). *UK digital poverty evidence review 2022*. Digital Poverty Alliance.

Amanatidis, D., Mylona, I., Kamenidou, I. E., Mamalis, S., & Stavrianea, A. (2021). Mining textual and imagery Instagram data during the COVID-19 pandemic. *Applied Sciences*, *11*(9), 4281.

Amit, V. (2000). Introduction. In V. Amit (Ed.), *Constructing the field*. Routledge.

Amit, V. (2003). Introduction: Constructing the field. In *Constructing the field* (pp. 9–26). Routledge.

Anderdal Bakken, S. (2022). App-based textual interviews: Interacting with younger generations in a digitalized social reality. *International Journal of Social Research Methodology*, 1–14.

Anderson, B. (1991). Imagined communities: Reflections on the origins and spread of nationalism. *Revue Médicale Suisse*, *6*, 1–7. https://doi.org/10.1017/CBO9781107415324.004

Anderson, K. E. (2020). Getting acquainted with social networks and apps: It is time to talk about TikTok. *Library Hi Tech News*.

Andreassen, R., Petersen, M. N., Harrison, K., & Raun, T. (2017). *Mediated intimacies: Connectivities, relationalities and proximities*. Routledge.

Andrejevic, M. (2010). Social network exploitation. In Z. Papacharissi (Ed.), *A networked self* (pp. 90–110). Routledge.

Andrejevic, M. (2014). Big data, big questions| the big data divide. *International Journal of Communication*, *8*, 17.

Angwin, J., Larson, J., Mattu, S., & Kirchner, L. (2016). Machine bias: There's software used across the country to predict future criminals. And it's biased against blacks. *ProPublica*.

Apperley, T. H., & Gray, K. L. (2020). *Digital divides and structural inequalities*. New York: Routledge.

Archibald, M. M., Ambagtsheer, R. C., Casey, M. G., & Lawless, M. (2019). Using zoom videoconferencing for qualitative data collection: Perceptions and experiences of researchers and participants. *International Journal of Qualitative Methods*, *18*, 1609406919874596.

Are, C. (2020). How Instagram's algorithm is censoring women and vulnerable users but helping online abusers. *Feminist media studies*, *20*(5), 741–744.

Armentor-Cota, J. (2011). Multiple perspectives on the influence of gender in online interactions. *Sociology Compass*, *5*(1), 23–36.

Armstrong, A., & Hagel, J. I. (2000). The real value of online communities. In *Knowledge and Communities* (pp. 85–98). Lesser, E., Fontaine, M. and Slusher, J., 2009. *Knowledge and communities*. Routledge.

Arthur, T. O. (2021). #Catchmeinashithole: Black travel influencers and the contestation of racialized place myths. *Howard Journal of Communications, 32*(4), 382–393.

Asenas, J. J., & Hubble, B. (2018). Trolling free speech rallies: social media practices and the (un) democratic spectacle of dissent. *Taboo: The Journal of Culture and Education, 17*(2), 6.

Asher-Schapiro, A. (2020). *FEATURE-'Unfair surveillance'? Online exam software sparks global student revolt | Reuters.* Reuters Technology, Media and Telecommunications. https://www.reuters.com/article/global-tech-education-idUSL8N2HP5DS

Atkinson, P. and Hammersley, M. (1998). Ethnography and participant observation. *Strategies of Qualitative Inquiry.* Thousand Oaks: Sage, pp.248–261.

Attwood, F., Hakim, J., & Winch, A. (2017). Mediated intimacies: Bodies, technologies and relationships. *Journal of Gender Studies, 26*(3), 249–253.

Avgitidou, A. (2003). Performances of the self. *Digital Creativity, 14*(3), 131–138.

Avram, G. (2014). Turning spaces into places–weaving the digital double. In *Workshop on Making Places: Visualization, Interaction and Experience in Urban Space, in NordiCHI* (Vol. 14).

Azubuike, O. B., Adegboye, O., & Quadri, H. (2021). Who gets to learn in a pandemic? Exploring the digital divide in remote learning during the COVID-19 pandemic in Nigeria. *International Journal of Educational Research Open, 2,* 100022.

Babbie, E. (2004). Laud Humphreys and research ethics. *International journal of sociology and social policy, 24*(3/4/5), 12–19.

Bainotti, L., Caliandro, A., & Gandini, A. (2021). From archive cultures to ephemeral content, and back: Studying Instagram Stories with digital methods. *New Media & Society, 23*(12), 3656–3676.

Baker, A. J. (2009). Mick or Keith: Blended identity of online rock fans. *Identity in the Information Society, 2*(1), 7–21.

Baker, P., & Potts, A. (2013). 'Why do white people have thin lips?', Google and the perpetuation of stereotypes via auto-complete search forms. *Critical Discourse Studies, 10*(2), 187–204.

Baker, S. A., & Walsh, M. J. (2018). 'Good Morning Fitfam': Top posts, hashtags and gender display on Instagram. *New media & society, 20*(12), 4553–4570.

Balash, D. G., Kim, D., Shaibekova, D., Fainchtein, R. A., Sherr, M., & Aviv, A. J. (2021). Examining the examiners: Students' privacy and security perceptions of online proctoring services. *Seventeenth Symposium on Usable Privacy and Security (SOUPS 2021)*, 633–652.

Barbe, D., Neuburger, L., & Pennington-Gray, L. (2020). Follow us on Instagram! Understanding the driving force behind following travel accounts on Instagram. *E-Review of Tourism Research, 17*(4).

Barnes, S. B. (2006). A privacy paradox: Social networking in the United States. *First Monday.* https://doi.org/10.5210/fm.v11i9.1394

Barth, S., & De Jong, M. D. (2017). The privacy paradox–Investigating discrepancies between expressed privacy concerns and actual online behavior–A systematic literature review. *Telematics and informatics, 34*(7), 1038–1058.

Basch, C. H., Hillyer, G. C., & Jaime, C. (2022). COVID-19 on TikTok: harnessing an emerging social media platform to convey important public health messages. *International journal of adolescent medicine and health, 34*(5), 367–369.

Basturk, E. (2017). A brief analyse on post panoptic surveillance: Deleuze & Guattarian approach. *International Journal of Social Sciences, 6*(2), 1–17.

Bau Baudrillard, J. (1994). *Simulacra and simulation.* University of Michigan press.

Baudrillard, J. (2007). The ecstasy of communication. In *Stardom and celebrity: A reader* (pp. 53–60). https://doi.org/10.4135/9781446269534.n7

Bauman, Z. (2001). *Community: Seeking safety in an insecure world.* Polity.

Bauman, Z. (2013). *Liquid love: On the frailty of human bonds.* John Wiley & Sons.

Bayer, J. B., Ellison, N. B., Schoenebeck, S. Y., & Falk, E. B. (2016). Sharing the small moments: ephemeral social interaction on Snapchat. *Information, communication & society, 19*(7), 956–977.

Baym, N.K. (1997). Interpreting soap operas and creating community: Inside an electronic fan culture. Culture of the Internet, pp.103–120.

Baym, N. K. (1998). The emergence of on-line community. cybersociety, 2(0), 35–68.

Baym, N. K. (2000). *Tune in, log on: Soaps, fandom, and online community* (Vol. 3). Sage.

Baym, N. K. (2015). *Personal connections in the digital age.* John Wiley & Sons.

BBC (2021). *Facebook, Whatsapp and Instagram back after outage—BBC News.* https://www.bbc.co.uk/news/technology-58793174

Beer, D. (2017). The social power of algorithms. *Information, Communication & Society, 20*(1), 1–13.

Beer, D., & Burrows, R. (2010). Consumption, prosumption and participatory web cultures: An introduction. *Journal of consumer culture, 10*(1), 3–12.

Beetham, H., Collier, A., Czerniewicz, L., Lamb, B., Li, Y., Ross, J., Scott A.M & Wilson, A. (2022). Surveillance practices, risks and responses in the post pandemic university. *Digital Culture and Education, 14*(1), 16–37.

Beigang, F. (2022). On the advantages of distinguishing between predictive and allocative fairness in algorithmic decision-making. *Minds and Machines,* 1–28.

Bell, C. and Newby, H. (2012). *Sociology of community: A collection of readings.* Routledge.

Bell, G. (2006). The age of the thumb: A cultural reading of mobile technologies from Asia. *Knowledge, Technology & Policy, 19*(2), 41–57.

Bennett, S., Maton, K., & Kervin, L. (2008). The 'digital natives' debate: A critical review of the evidence. *British Journal of Educational Technology, 39*(5), 775–786.

Beranuy, M., Oberst, U., Carbonell, X., & Chamarro, A. (2009). Problematic internet and mobile phone use and clinical symptoms in college students: The role of emotional intelligence. *Computers in Human Behavior, 25*(5), 1182–1187.

Berriman, L., & Thomson, R. (2015). Spectacles of intimacy? Mapping the moral landscape of teenage social media. *Journal of Youth Studies, 18*(5), 583–597.

Berry, D. M. (2011). The computational turn: Thinking about the digital humanities. *Culture Machine, 12.*

Blackwell, C., Birnholtz, J., & Abbott, C. (2015). Seeing and being seen: Co-situation and impression formation using Grindr, a location-aware gay dating app. *New Media and Society, 17*(7), 1117–1136.

Blanchard, A., & Horan, T. (1998). Virtual communities and social capital. *Social Science Computer Review, 16*(3), 293–307.

Blanco, A. V. (2015). The transformation of leisure in the digital age. *Social Media and Social Movements: The Transformation of Communication Patterns, 165.*

Blass, T. (1999). *Obedience to authority: Current perspectives on the Milgram paradigm.* Routledge

Blatterer, H. (2010). Social networking, privacy, and the pursuit of visibility. In H. Blatterer, P. Johnson, & M. R. Markus (Eds.), *Modern Privacy: Shifting Boundaries, New Forms.* Springer.

Boase, J. (2008). Personal networks and the personal communication system. *Information, Communication & Society, 11*(4), 490–508.

Boase, J., & Humphreys, L. (2018). Mobile methods: Explorations, innovations, and reflections. *Mobile Media & Communication, 6*(2), pp. 153–162.

Bobkowski, P., & Smith, J. (2013). Social media divide: Characteristics of emerging adults who do not use social network websites. *Media, Culture & Society, 35*(6), 771–781.

Boellstorff, T., Nardi, B., Pearce, C., & Taylor, T. L. (2012). *Ethnography and virtual worlds.* Princeton University Press.

Boepple, L., & Thompson, J. K. (2016). A content analytic comparison of fitspiration and thinspiration websites. *International Journal of Eating Disorders, 49*(1), 98–101.

Boler, M. (2007). Hypes, hopes and actualities: new digital Cartesianism and bodies in cyberspace. *New media & society, 9*(1), 139–168.

Boon, S., & Pentney, B. (2015). Virtual lactivism: Breastfeeding selfies and the performance of motherhood. *International Journal of Communication, 9*(1), 1759–1772.

Boswell, W. R., & Olson-Buchanan, J. B. (2007). The use of communication technologies after hours: The role of work attitudes and work-life conflict. *Journal of Management, 33*(4), 592–610.

Bourdieu, P. (1986). The forms of capital. *Education: Culture, Economy, and Society,* 46–58. https://doi.org/10.1002/9780470755679.ch15

Bourdieu, P. (2018). Distinction a social critique of the judgement of taste. In *Inequality Classic Readings in Race, Class, and Gender* (pp. 287–318). Routledge.

Bowater, D. (2013). The beer glass that only stands upright when balanced on your phone. *The Telegraph.* https://www.telegraph.co.uk/news/worldnews/south-america/brazil/10113715/The-beer-glass-that-only-stands-upright-when-balanced-on-your-phone.html

Boyd, J. (2002). In community we trust: Online security communication at eBay. *Journal of Computer-Mediated Communication, 7*(3).

boyd, d. (2006). Friends, friendsters, and top 8: Writing community into being on social network sites. First monday.

boyd, d. (2010). Social Network Sites as Networked Publics: Affordances, Dynamics, and Implications. In *Networked Self: Identity, Community, and Culture on Social Network Sites* (pp. 39–58). https://doi.org/10.1162/dmal.9780262524834.119

boyd, d. (2015). Social media: A phenomenon to be analyzed. *Social Media+ Society, 1*(1), 2056305115580148.

boyd, d. & Crawford, K. (2012). Critical questions for big data: Provocations for a cultural, technological, and scholarly phenomenon. *Information, Communication & Society, 15*(5), 662–679.

boyd, d. & Marwick, A. E. (2011). Social privacy in networked publics: Teens' attitudes, practices, and strategies. *A Decade in Internet Time: Symposium on the Dynamics of the Internet and Society*.

Brajša-Žganec, A., Merkaš, M., & Šverko, I. (2011). Quality of life and leisure activities: How do leisure activities contribute to subjective well-being? *Social Indicators Research, 102*(1), 81–91.

Bridges, L. (2021). Amazon's Ring is the largest civilian surveillance network the US has ever seen. *The Guardian*. https://www.theguardian.com/commentisfree/2021/may/18/amazon-ring-largest-civilian-surveillance-network-us

Brock, A. (2012). From the blackhand side: Twitter as a cultural conversation. *Journal of Broadcasting and Electronic Media, 56*(4), 529–549. https://doi.org/10.1080/08838151.2012.732147

Brock A. (2020). *Distributed Blackness: African American Cybercultures* (Vol. 9). NYU Press.

Broom, A. (2005). The eMale: Prostate cancer, masculinity and online support as a challenge to medical expertise. *Journal of Sociology, 41*(1), 87–104. https://doi.org/10.1177/1440783305050965

Brown, K. M., Dilley, R., & Marshall, K. (2008). Using a head-mounted video camera to understand social worlds and experiences. *Sociological Research Online, 13*(6), 31–40.

Brubaker, R. (2020). Digital hyperconnectivity and the self. *Theory and Society, 49*(5), 771–801. https://doi.org/10.1007/S11186-020-09405-1

Bruns, A. (2008). Blogs, Wikipedia, Second Life, and beyond: From production to produsage (Vol. 45). Peter Lang.

Bryce, J. (2001). The technological transformation of leisure. *Social Science Computer Review, 19*(1), 7–16.

Bucher, T. (2013). The friendship assemblage: Investigating programmed sociality on Facebook. *Television & New Media, 14*(6), 479–493.

Bucher, T. (2017). The algorithmic imaginary: Exploring the ordinary affects of Facebook algorithms. *Information, Communication & Society, 20*(1), 30–44.

Bull, M. (2000). *Sounding out the city: Personal stereos and the management of everyday life*. Berg.

Bull, M. (2015). *Sound moves: iPod culture and urban experience*. Routledge.

Bullingham, L., & Vasconcelos, A. C. (2013). 'The presentation of self in the online world': Goffman and the study of online identities. *Journal of information science, 39*(1), 101–112.

Bulmer, M. (2001). The ethics of social research. *Researching Social Life, 3*, 45–57.

Burgess, J. (2012). The iPhone moment, the Apple brand, and the creative consumer: From 'hackability and usability' to cultural generativity. In *Studying mobile media* (pp. 36–50). Routledge.

Burns, A. (2015). Self(ie)-discipline: Social regulation as enacted through the discussion of photographic practice. *International Journal of Communication, 9*(1), 1716–1733.

Buyukozturk, B. (2022). Reproducing the gaming gender hierarchy. *Symbolic Interaction, 45*(1), 27–49.

Caldwell, L. L. (2012). Are we there yet? Finite curves and E-leisure. *Loisir et Société/ Society and Leisure, 35*(1), 21–29.

Caliandro, A., Garavaglia, E., Sturiale, V., & Di Leva, A. (2021). Older people and smartphone practices in everyday life: An inquire on digital sociality of Italian older users. *The Communication Review*, *24*(1), 47–78.

Cameron, A. (2019). No more games: An intersectional approach to geek masculinity and marginalization in video gaming culture. *A Journal of Communication, Culture & Technology*, 18.

Carrotte, E. R., Prichard, I., & Lim, M. S. C. (2017). "Fitspiration" on social media: A content analysis of gendered images. *Journal of medical Internet research*, *19*(3), e95.

Carstensen, T. (2009). Gender trouble in Web 2.0: Gender relations in social network sites, wikis and weblogs. *International Journal of Gender, Science and Technology*, *1*, 1–23.

Carter, S., Green, J., & Speed, E. (2018). Digital technologies and the biomedicalisation of everyday activities: The case of walking and cycling. *Sociology Compass*, *12*(4), e12572.

Cassell, J., & Jenkins, H. (2000). *From Barbie® to Mortal Kombat: Gender and Computer Games*. MIT Press.

Castells, M. (1996). *Rise of the network society: The information age: Economy, society and culture*. Blackwell Publishers, Inc..

Castells, M. (2000). Toward a sociology of the network society. *Contemporary Sociology*, *25*(9), 693–699.

Castells, M. (2002). *The Internet galaxy: Reflections on the Internet, business, and society*. Oxford University Press on Demand.

Castells, M. (2010). The rise of the network society. In *Massachusetts: Blackwell Publishing: Vol. I*. https://doi.org/10.2307/1252090

Cavagnuolo, M., Capozza, V., & Matrella, A. (2022). The walkthrough method: State of the art, innovative aspects, and application fields. *Handbook of Research on Advanced Research Methodologies for a Digital Society*, 461–486.

Cavender, E, (2021, December 31). TikTok cried "make Instagram casual," and now users are having second thoughts: https://sea.mashable.com/life/18806/tiktok-cried-make-instagram-casual-and-now-users-are-having-second-thoughts

Cavoukian, A. (2010). *Opinion: Privacy is still a social norm—The Globe and Mail*. https://www.theglobeandmail.com/opinion/privacy-is-still-a-social-norm/article1209523/

Ceci, L. (2022). *U.S. TikTok users by age 2021*. Statista. https://www.statista.com/statistics/1095186/tiktok-us-users-age/

Cha, M., Kwak, H., Rodriguez, P., Ahnt, Y. Y., & Moon, S. (2007). I tube, you tube, everybody tubes: Analyzing the world's largest user generated content video system. *Proceedings of the ACM SIGCOMM Internet Measurement Conference, IMC*, 1–14. https://doi.org/10.1145/1298306.1298309

Chalfen, R. (2014). 'Your panopticon or mine?' Incorporating wearable technology's Glass and GoPro into visual social science. *Visual Studies*, *29*(3), 299–310.

Chambers, D. (2013). *Social media and personal relationships: Online intimacies and networked friendship*. Springer.

Chambers, D. (2017). Networked intimacy: Algorithmic friendship and scalable sociality. *European Journal of Communication*, *32*(1), 26–36.

Chambers, D. (2023). 'A huge social experiment': Postdigital social connectivity under lockdown conditions. In T. Sikka Longstaff, & Walls, S. (Eds.), *Disrupted Knowledge* (pp. 34–54). Brill.

Char, D. S., Shah, N. H., & Magnus, D. (2018). Implementing machine learning in health care—Addressing ethical challenges. *The New England Journal of Medicine, 378*(11), 981.

Chaudhry, I. (2016). 'Not so black and white' discussions of race on Twitter in the Aftermath of# Ferguson and the shooting death of Mike Brown. *Cultural Studies? Critical Methodologies, 16*(3), 296–304.

Chen, Q., Min, C., Zhang, W., Ma, X., & Evans, R. (2021). Factors driving citizen engagement with government TikTok accounts during the COVID-19 pandemic: Model development and analysis. *Journal of Medical Internet Research, 23*(2), e21463.

Chesak, J. (2021). *How Social Media Is Taking Away from Your Friendships.* Healthline. https://www.healthline.com/health/how-social-media-is-ruining-relationships#1

Chin, M. (2020). Exam anxiety: How remote test-proctoring is creeping students out. *The Verge.* https://www.theverge.com/2020/4/29/21232777/examity-remote-test-proctoring-online-class-education

Chiu, A. (2019). Poppy super bloom leaves Lake Elsinore, California overrun with tourists, declaring safety crisis. *The Washinton Post.* https://www.washingtonpost.com/nation/2019/03/18/poppy-apocalypse-small-california-city-overrun-by-thousands-tourists-declares-public-safety-crisis/

Cho, I., Kaplanidou, K., & Sato, S. (2021). Gamified wearable fitness tracker for physical activity: A comprehensive literature review. *Sustainability (Switzerland), 13*(13).

Choi, Y., & Dattilo, J. (2017). Connections between media technology and leisure: Insights from Aristotle and Heidegger. *Annals of Leisure Research, 20*(2), 152–168.

Chotpitayasunondh, V., & Douglas, K. M. (2016). How 'phubbing' becomes the norm: The antecedents and consequences of snubbing via smartphone. *Computers in Human Behavior, 63*, 9–18.

Chouldechova, A., & Roth, A. (2018). The frontiers of fairness in machine learning. *ArXiv Preprint ArXiv:1810.08810.*

Chua, T. H. H., & Chang, L. (2016). Follow me and like my beautiful selfies: Singapore teenage girls' engagement in self-presentation and peer comparison on social media. *Computers in Human Behavior, 55*, 190–197.

Cinnamon, J. (2017). Social injustice in surveillance capitalism. *Surveillance & Society, 15*(5), 609–625.

Clare, C. A. (2021). Telehealth and the digital divide as a social determinant of health during the COVID-19 pandemic. *Network Modeling Analysis in Health Informatics and Bioinformatics, 10*(1), 26.

Clark, L. S. (2013). *The parent app: Understanding families in the digital age.* Oxford University Press.

Cohen, S. (1972). Folk devils and moral panics: The creation of the mods and rockers. *London, England.*

Coleman, J. S. (1988). Social capital in the creation of human capital. *American Journal of Sociology, 94*, 95–120.

Coleman, V. (2021). Digital divide in UK education during COVID-19 pandemic: Literature review. Research Report. *Cambridge Assessment.*

Condis, M. (2015). No homosexuals in Star Wars? BioWare,'gamer' identity, and the politics of privilege in a convergence culture. *Convergence, 21*(2), 198–212.

Constantinides, E., & Fountain, S. J. (2008). Web 2.0: Conceptual foundations and marketing issues. *Journal of Direct, Data and Digital Marketing Practice, 9*(3), 231–244.

Cooley, C. H. (1902). *Human nature and the social order.* Transaction Publishers.

Cost, B. (2020). *Coronavirus spawns viral TikTok dance about washing your hands.* https://nypost.com/2020/03/04/coronavirus-spawns-viral-tiktok-dance-about-washing-your-hands/

Cotter, K., & Reisdorf, B. C. (2020). Algorithmic knowledge gaps: A new horizon of (digital) inequality. *International Journal of Communication, 14*, 21.

Couldry, N. (2011). More sociology, more culture, more politics: Or, a modest proposal for 'convergence' studies. *Cultural Studies, 25*(4–5), 487–501.

Coward-Gibbs, M. (2021). Why don't we play pandemic? Analog gaming communities in lockdown. *Leisure Sciences, 43*(1–2), 78–84.

Craig, L. (2020). Coronavirus, domestic labour and care: Gendered roles locked down. *Journal of Sociology, 56*(4), 684–692.

Crawford, K., Lingel, J., & Karppi, T. (2015). Our metrics, ourselves: A hundred years of self-tracking from the weight scale to the wrist wearable device. *European Journal of Cultural Studies, 18*(5), 479–496.

Cresswell, T. (2014). *Place: An introduction.* John Wiley & Sons.

Crow, G. (2018). *What are community studies?* Bloomsbury Publishing.

Cullinane, C., & Montacute, R. (2020). COVID-19 and social mobility impact brief# 1: School closures. *The Sutton Trust.*

Czitrom, D. J. (1982). *Media and the American mind: From Morse to McLuhan.* University of North Carolina Press.

Danet, B. (1998). Text as mask: Gender, play, and performance. In S. G. Jones (Ed.), *Cybersociety 2.0: Revisiting computer-mediated community and technology (Vol. 2).* (pp. 129–158.). Sage.

Daniels, J. (2018). The algorithmic rise of the 'alt-right'. *Contexts, 17*(1), 60–65.

Daniels, J., & Gregory, K. (2016). *Digital sociologies.* Policy Press.

Darr, C.R. and Doss, E.F. (2022). The fake one is the real one: Finstas, authenticity, and context collapse in teen friend groups. *Journal of Computer-Mediated Communication, 27*(4), p.zmac009.

Datareportal. (2023). The Latest Instagram Statistics: Everything You Need to Know—DataReportal – Global Digital Insights. In *Kepios.*

David, G., & Cambre, C. (2016). Screened intimacies: Tinder and the swipe logic. *Social media+ society, 2*(2), 2056305116641976.

Davis, J. L., & Jurgenson, N. (2014). Context collapse: Theorizing context collusions and collisions. *Information, Communication & Society, 17*(4), 476–485.

Day, B. H. (2020). The value of greenspace under pandemic lockdown. *Environmental and Resource Economics, 76*(4), 1161–1185.

de Guzman, A. B., Mesana, J. C. B., Manuel, M. E., Arcega, K. C. A., Yumang, R. L. T., & Miranda, K. N. V. (2022). Examining intergenerational family members' creative activities during COVID-19 lockdown via manifest content analysis of YouTube and TikTok videos. *Educational Gerontology*, 1–14.

de Souza e Silva, A., & Frith, J. (2010). Locative mobile social networks: Mapping communication and location in urban spaces. *Mobilities*, 5(4), 485–505.

Deakin, H., & Wakefield, K. (2014). Skype interviewing: Reflections of two PhD researchers. *Qualitative Research*, 14(5), 603–616.

Dekker, R., Engbersen, G., Klaver, J., & Vonk, H. (2018). Smart refugees: How Syrian asylum migrants use social media information in migration decision-making. *Social Media+ Society*, 4(1), 2056305118764439.

Deleuze, G. (1992). Postscript on the societies of control. *October, 59*, 3–7.

Deleuze, G., & Guattari, F. (1988). *A thousand plateaus: Capitalism and schizophrenia.* Bloomsbury Publishing.

Delwiche, A., & Henderson, J. J. (2012). Introduction: What is participatory culture? In *The participatory cultures handbook* (pp. 21–27). Routledge.

Dewey, C. (2014). The only guide to Gamergate you will ever need to read. *The Washington Post, 14.*

DeWinter, J., Kocurek, C. A., & Nichols, R. (2014). Taylorism 2.0: Gamification, scientific management and the capitalist appropriation of play. *Journal of Gaming & Virtual Worlds*, 6(2), 109–127.

Dixon, S. (2023). *User-generated internet content per minute 2022 | Statista.* Statista. https://www.statista.com/statistics/195140/new-user-generated-content-uploaded-by-users-per-minute/

Djuraskovic, O. (2022, December 26). *47 Blogging Statistics (2022): How Many Blogs Are There?* First Site Guide. https://firstsiteguide.com/blogging-stats/

Döring, N., Reif, A., & Poeschl, S. (2016). How gender-stereotypical are selfies? A content analysis and comparison with magazine adverts. *Computers in Human Behavior, 55*, 955–962.

Du Gay, P., Hall, S., Janes, L., Madsen, A.K., Mackay, H. and Negus, K. (2013). *Doing cultural studies: The story of the Sony Walkman.* Sage.

Duffy, A. (2019). If I say you're authentic, then you're authentic: Power and privilege revealed in travel blogs. *Tourist Studies*, 19(4), 569–584.

Duffy, B. E., & Chan, N. K. (2019). 'You never really know who's looking': Imagined surveillance across social media platforms. *New Media and Society*, 21(1), 119–138.

Duguay, S. (2016). Lesbian, gay, bisexual, trans, and queer visibility through selfies: Comparing platform mediators across Ruby Rose's Instagram and Vine presence. *Social Media+ Society*, 2(2), 2056305116641975.

Duguay, S. (2017). Dressing up Tinderella: Interrogating authenticity claims on the mobile dating app Tinder. *Information, Communication & Society*, 20(3), 351–367.

Dunford, J. (2020). In lockdown, I went on a surfing and yoga retreat – via Zoom | Learning holidays. *The Guardian.* https://www.theguardian.com/travel/2020/apr/25/lockdown-learning-surfing-and-yoga-virtual-retreat-holiday?CMP=Share_AndroidApp_Messenger

Duru, A. (2018). Wearable cameras, in-visible breasts: intimate spatialities of feminist research with wearable camcorders in Istanbul. Gender, Place & Culture, 25(7), 939–954.

Dyer, H. T. (2020). The role of technology in shaping student identity during transitions to University. *Mediated identities in the futures of place: emerging practices and spatial cultures*, 97–113.

Dyer-Witheford, N., & de Peuter, G. (2021). Postscript: Gaming while empire burns. *Games and Culture, 16*(3), 371–380.

Edwards, R., & Holland, J. (2020). Reviewing challenges and the future for qualitative interviewing. *International Journal of Social Research Methodology, 23*(5), 581–592.

Ellison, N. B., Steinfield, C., & Lampe, C. (2007). The benefits of Facebook "friends:" Social capital and college students' use of online social network sites. *Journal of computer-mediated communication, 12*(4), 1143–1168.

Erturan-Ogut, E., & Demirhan, G. (2020). Leisure activities in Turkey during stay-at-home time. *World Leisure Journal, 62*(4), 349–351.

Eruchalu, C. N., Pichardo, M. S., Bharadwaj, M., Rodriguez, C. B., Rodriguez, J. A., Bergmark, R. W., Bates, D. W., & Ortega, G. (2021). The expanding digital divide: Digital health access inequities during the COVID-19 pandemic in New York City. *Journal of Urban Health, 98*(2), 183–186.

Eubanks, V. (2018). *Automating inequality: How high-tech tools profile, police, and punish the poor*. St. Martin's Press.

Evans, K. (2013). Re-thinking community in the digital age?. In *Digital sociology: Critical perspectives* (pp. 79–94). London: Palgrave Macmillan UK.

Evans, L. (2015). *Locative social media: Place in the digital age*. Springer

Farquhar, L. K., & Meeds, R. (2007). Types of fantasy sports users and their motivations. *Journal of computer-mediated communication, 12*(4), 1208–1228.

Femenia-Serra, F., Gretzel, U., & Alzua-Sorzabal, A. (2022). Instagram travel influencers in# quarantine: Communicative practices and roles during COVID-19. *Tourism Management, 89*, 104454.

Fernback, J. (1999). There is a there there: Notes toward a definition of cybercommunity. *Doing Internet research: Critical issues and methods for examining the Net*, 203–220.

Ferryman, K., & Pitcan, M. (2018). *Fairness in precision medicine*. Data & Society Research Institute https://apo.org.au/node/134536

Fine, G. A., & Stryker, S. (1982). Symbolic interactionism: A social structural version. In *Contemporary Sociology, 11*(1), p. 26.

Finn, R. L., Wright, D., & Friedewald, M. (2013). Seven Types of privacy. European Data Protection Coming of Age. *Fraunhofer Institute for Systems and Innovation Research*, 1–26.

Fischer, C. S. (1994). *America calling: A social history of the telephone to 1940*. Univ of California Press.

Fischer, C. S. (2011). Still connected. *Family and Friends in America Since 1970*, 167.

Fiske, J. (1987). *Television culture*. Methuen & Co Ltd.

Fotopoulou, A., & O'Riordan, K. (2016). Health Sociology Review Training to self-care: Fitness tracking, biopedagogy and the healthy consumer. *Health Sociology Review, 26*(1), 54–68.

Foucoult, M. (1975). *Discipline and punish*. A. Sheridan, Tr., Paris, FR, Gallimard.

Fox, R. (1995). Newstrack. *Communications of the ACM, 38*(8), 11–12.

Frąckowiak-Sochańska, M. (2020). Mental health in the pandemic times. *Society Register, 4*(3), 67–78.

Franzke, A. S., Bechmann, A., Zimmer, M., & Ess, C. (2020). The Association of Internet Researchers. *Internet Research: Ethical Guidelines, 3*(0).

Freelon, D., McIlwain, C. D., & Clark, M. D. (2017). Beyond the hashtags: #Ferguson, #Blacklivesmatter, and the online struggle for offline justice. *SSRN Electronic Journal*. https://doi.org/10.2139/ssrn.2747066

Friesen, N. (2017). Confessional technologies of the self: From Seneca to social media. *First Monday*.

Frith, J. (2018). *Smartphones as locative media*. John Wiley & Sons.

Fuchs, C. (2014a). Digital prosumption labour on social media in the context of the capitalist regime of time. *Time & Society, 23*(1), 97–123.

Fuchs, C. (2014b). *Social Media: A Critical Introduction*. Sage

Furlong, A. (2008). The Japanese hikikomori phenomenon: acute social withdrawal among young people. *The sociological review, 56*(2), 309–325.

Furlong, M. S. (1989). An electronic community for older adults: The SeniorNet Network. *Journal of Communication, 39*(3), 145–153.

Galič, M., Timan, T., & Koops, B. J. (2017). Bentham, Deleuze and beyond: An overview of surveillance theories from the panopticon to participation. *Philosophy and Technology, 30*(1), 9–37.

Gammon, K. (2019). #Superbloom or #poppynightmare? Selfie chaos forces canyon closure. *The Guardian*. https://www.theguardian.com/environment/2019/mar/18/super-bloom-lake-elsinore-poppies-flowers

Gammon, S., & Ramshaw, G. (2021). Distancing from the present: Nostalgia and leisure in lockdown. *Leisure Sciences, 43*(1–2), 131–137.

Gandy, O. H. (2021). The panoptic sort: A political economy of personal information. Oxford University Press.

Ganesh, B. (2020). Weaponizing white thymos: Flows of rage in the online audiences of the alt-right. *Cultural Studies, 34*(6), 892–924.

Gans, H. (1982). The urban villagers. *The Free Press*.

Garfinkel, H. (1967). Ethnomethodology. *Englewood Cliffs*.

Gauntlett, D. (2013). *Making is connecting*. John Wiley & Sons.

Georgakopoulou, A. (2016). From narrating the self to posting self(ies): A small stories approach to selfies. *Open Linguistics, 2*(1), 300–316.

Georgakopoulou, A. (2017). Small stories research: A narrative paradigm for the analysis of social media. In *The SAGE Handbook of Social Media Research Methods*, pp 266–281.

Gerli, P., & Whalley, J. (2021). Fibre to the countryside: A comparison of public and community initiatives tackling the rural digital divide in the UK. *Telecommunications Policy, 45*(10), 102222.

Georgakopoulou, A. (2022). Co-opting small stories on social media: A narrative analysis of the directive of authenticity. Poetics Today, 43(2), 265–286.

Gershon, I. (2020). The Breakup 2.1: The ten-year update. *The Information Society, 36*(5), 279–289.

Ghaznavi, J., & Taylor, L. D. (2015). Bones, body parts, and sex appeal: An analysis of# thinspiration images on popular social media. *Body Image, 14,* 54–61.

Giddens, A. (1991). Modernity and self-identity: Self and society in the late modern age. In *Modernity and self-identity*.

Gill, R. (2012). Media, empowerment and the 'sexualization of culture' debates. *Sex Roles, 66*(11–12), 736–745.

Ginsburg, P. S. M. (2000). Virtual communities of transaction: The role of personalization in electronic commerce. *Electronic Markets, 10*(1), 45–55.

Giorgi, G. (2022). Methodological directions for the study of memes. In *Handbook of Research on Advanced Research Methodologies for a Digital Society* (pp. 627–663). IGI Global.

Goe, W. R. and Noonan, S. (2007). The sociology of community. In *21st century sociology: A reference handbook* (pp. 455–464.). Sage

Goffman, E. (1959). The presentation of self in everyday life. Doubleday.

Goffman, E. (1964). The neglected situation. *American Anthropologist, 66*(6_Part 2), pp.133–136.

Goffman, E. (1974). *Frame analysis: An essay on the organization of experience.* Harvard University Press.

Goffman, E. (1979). *Gender advertisments.* Harper and Row.

Goggin, G. and Hjorth, L. (2009). Waiting to participate Introduction. *Communication, Politics & Culture, 42*(2), 1.

Gordon, E., & de Souza e Silva, A. (2011). *Net locality: Why location matters in a networked world.* John Wiley & Sons.

Goulden, M., Tolmie, P., Mortier, R., Lodge, T., Pietilainen, A. K., & Teixeira, R. (2018). Living with interpersonal data: Observability and accountability in the age of pervasive ICT. *New Media and Society, 20*(4), 1580–1599.

Gran, A.-B., Booth, P., & Bucher, T. (2021). To be or not to be algorithm aware: A question of a new digital divide? *Information, Communication & Society, 24*(12), 1779–1796.

Gray, K. L. (2017). 'They're just too urban': Black gamers streaming on Twitch. *Digital Sociologies, 1,* 355–368.

Green, C. (2020). Embodied childhood nature experiences through sensory tours. *Research handbook on childhood nature: Assemblages of childhood and nature research,* pp 879–899.

Greer, B. (2008). *Knitting for good!: A guide to creating personal, social, and political change stitch by stitch.* Shambhala Publications.

Grieve, R. (2017). Unpacking the characteristics of Snapchat users: A preliminary investigation and an agenda for future research. *Computers in Human Behavior, 74,* 130–138.

Griffiths, M. (2000). Does internet and computer 'addiction' exist? Some case study evidence. *CyberPsychology & Behavior, 3*(2), 211–218.

Grindstaff, L., & Torres Valencia, G. (2021). The filtered self: selfies and gendered media production. *Information, Communication & Society, 24*(5), 733–750.

Griswold, C. (1980). Style and philosophy. *Monist, 63*, 530–546.

Grossman, L. (2006). You–yes, you–are TIME's Person of the Year, *Time, 25 December 2006*. Accessed.

Guiora, A., & Park, E. A. (2017). Hate speech on social media. *Philosophia, 45*, 957–971.

Gurchiek, K. (2018). *Phone Zombies Create Problems at Work.* SHRM. https://www.shrm.org/hr-today/news/hr-news/pages/phone-zombies-create-problems-at-work.aspx

Habuchi, I. (2005). Accelerating reflexivity. In *In* M, Ito, M, Matsuda and D, Okabe *Personal, portable, pedestrian: Mobile phones in Japanese life.* MIT Press.

Haggerty, K. D. (2006). Tear down the walls: On demolishing the panopticon. In *Theorizing surveillance* (pp. 37–59). Willan.

Haggerty, K. D., & Ericson, R. V. (2000). The surveillant assemblage. *The British Journal of Sociology, 51*(4), 605–622.

Haimson, O.L., Brubaker, J.R., Dombrowski, L. and Hayes, G.R. (2016, May). Digital footprints and changing networks during online identity transitions. In Proceedings of the 2016 CHI Conference on Human Factors in Computing Systems (pp. 2895–2907).

Halaweh, M. (2021). Are universities using the right assessment tools during the pandemic and crisis times? *Higher Learning Research Communications, 11*, 1–9.

Halegoua, G., & Polson, E. (2021). Exploring 'digital placemaking'. *Convergence: The International Journal of Research into New Media Technologies, 27*(3), 573–578.

Hall, S. (1973). Encoding/decoding in the television discourse (working paper 7). CCCS stencilled occasional papers. from http://www.birmingham.ac.uk/Documents/collegeartslaw/history/cccs/stencilled-occasional-papers/1to8and11to24and38to48/SOP07.pdf

Hallinan, B., & Striphas, T. (2016). Recommended for you: The Netflix Prize and the production of algorithmic culture. *New Media & Society, 18*(1), 117–137.

Hand, M. (2017). Visuality in social media: Researching images, circulations and practices. In *The SAGE Handbook of Social Media Research Methods*, pp. 217–231.

Hanifan, L. J. (1916). The rural school community center. *Annals of the American Academy of Political and Social Science, 67*(0), 130–138.

Hannell, B. (2021). Muslim girlhood, skam fandom, and DIY citizenship. *Girlhood Studies, 14*(2), 46–62.

Hammersley, M. and Atkinson, P. (2019). *Ethnography: Principles in practice.* Routledge.

Haraway, D. (1991). A cyborg manifesto: Science, technology and socialist-femenism in the late twentiety century. In *Simians, Cyborgs and Women: The Reinvention of Nature* (pp. 149–181). Routledge

Hardey, M. (2007). The city in the age of web 2.0 a new synergistic relationship between place and people. *Information Communication and Society, 10*(6), 867–884.

Hargittai, E. (2000). Open portals or closed gates? Channeling content on the World Wide Web. *Poetics, 27*(4), 233–253.

Hargittai, E. (2001). Second-level digital divide: Mapping differences in people's online skills. *arXiv preprint cs/0109068.*

Harwell, D. (2020). Cheating-detection companies made millions during the pandemic. Now students are fighting back. In *Ethics of Data and Analytics* (pp. 410–417). Auerbach Publications.

Harwell, D., & Romm, T. (2019). Hong Kong protests: Chinese-owned TikTok censoring demonstrations online, says research. *Sydney Morning Herald.* https://www.smh.com.au/world/asia/don-t-look-for-the-hong-kong-protests-on-tiktok-you-won-t-find-them-on-platform-20190917-p52s08.html

Haubursin, C. (October 31ˢᵗ 2018). How geotagged photos harm nature. *Vox.* https://www.vox.com/the-goods/2018/10/31/18047386/geotagged-instagram-nature-harm

Hayes, M. (2022). Social media and inspiring physical activity during COVID-19 and beyond. *Managing Sport and Leisure, 27*(1–2), 14–21.

Haythornthwaite, C. (2005). Social networks and Internet connectivity effects. *Information, Community & Society, 8*(2), 125–147.

Heath, M. K. (2021). Buried treasure or ill-gotten spoils: The ethics of data mining and learning analytics in online instruction. *Educational Technology Research and Development, 69*(1), 331–334.

Helsper, E. (2021). The digital disconnect: The social causes and consequences of digital inequalities. *The Digital Disconnect,* 1–232.

Helsper, E. J., & van Deursen, A. J. A. M. (2017). Do the rich get digitally richer? Quantity and quality of support for digital engagement. *Information, Communication & Society, 20*(5), 700–714.

Hemingway, J. L. (1996). Emancipating leisure: The recovery of freedom in leisure. *Journal of Leisure Research, 28*(1), 27–43.

Herring, S. C., Scheidt, L. A., Wright, E., & Bonus, S. (2005). Weblogs as a bridging genre. *Information Technology & People, 18*(2), 142–171

Hidy, K., & McDonald, M. S. (2013). Risky business: The legal implications of social media's increasing role in employment decisons. Available at SSRN 3188753.

Highfield, T., & Leaver, T. (2016). Instagrammatics and digital methods: Studying visual social media, from selfies and GIFs to memes and emoji. *Communication research and practice, 2*(1), 47–62.

Hiley, C. (2021). *UK mobile phone statistics 2023—Mobiles facts and stats report.* https://www.uswitch.com/mobiles/studies/mobile-statistics/

Hillery, G. (1955). Definitions of community: Areas of agreement. *Rural Sociology, 20*(2), 111–123.

Hiltz, S. R., & Turoff, M. (1993). Superconnectivity: Computers, communication, and social organization. In *The network nation: Human communication via computer* (pp. 455–514). MIT Press

Hine, C. (2000). *Virtual Ethnography.* Sage.

Hine, C. (2015). *Ethnography for the internet: Embedded, embodied and everyday*. Taylor and Francis.

Hinton, S. and Hjorth, L. (2013). *Understanding social media*. Sage.

Hitler's 'Downfall' Parodies | Know Your Meme. (n.d.). Retrieved 18 April 2023, from https://knowyourmeme.com/memes/hitlers-downfall-parodies#photos

Hjorth, L. (2008). Being real in the mobile reel: A case study on convergent mobile media as domesticated new media in Seoul, South Korea. *Convergence, 14*(1), 91–104.

Hjorth, L. (2012). iPersonal: A case study of the politics of the personal. In *Studying Mobile Media* (pp. 190–212). Routledge.

Hjorth, L. (2018). Ambient and soft play: Play, labour and the digital in everyday life. *European Journal of Cultural Studies, 21*(1), 3–12.

Hjorth, L., & Richardson, I. (2016). Mobile games and ambient play. Social, casual and mobile games: The changing gaming landscape, 105–116.

Hobbs, M., Owen, S., & Gerber, L. (2017). Liquid love? Dating apps, sex, relationships and the digital transformation of intimacy. *Journal of Sociology, 53*(2), 271–284.

Hobsbawm, J. (2018). *Fully connected: Surviving and thriving in an age of overload*. Bloomsbury Publishing.

Hogan, B. (2010). The presentation of self in the age of social media: Distinguishing performances and exhibitions online. *Bulletin of Science, Technology & Society, 30*(6), 377–386.

Holvast, J. (2007). History of privacy. In *The history of information security* (pp. 737–769). Elsevier.

Hooton, C. (2014, November 11). Woman 'finds herself' in South-east Asia with a little help from Photoshop to satirise Facebook bragging. *The Independent*. https://www.independent.co.uk/travel/news-and-advice/woman-finds-herself-in-southeast-asia-with-a-little-help-from-photoshop-to-satirise-facebook-bragging-9726396.html

Hoy, M. B. (2018). Alexa, Siri, Cortana, and more: An Introduction to voice assistants. *Medical Reference Services Quarterly, 37*(1), 81–88.

Huang, X. and Vitak, J. (2022). "Finsta gets all my bad pictures": Instagram Users' Self-Presentation Across Finsta and Rinsta Accounts. Proceedings of the ACM on Human-Computer Interaction, 6(CSCW1), pp.1–25.

Hugentobler, L. (2022). The Instagram interview: Talking to people about travel experiences across online and offline spaces. *Media and Communication, 10*(3).

Humphreys, L. (2016). Involvement shield or social catalyst: Thoughts on sociospatial practice of Pokémon GO. *Mobile Media & Communication, 5*(1), 15–19.

Humphreys, L., & Liao, T. (2013). Foursquare and the parochialization of public space. *First Monday*. https://doi.org/10.5210/FM.V18I11.4966

Hunnicutt, B. K. (2006). The history of western leisure. *A Handbook of Leisure Studies*, 55–74.

Hunt, E. (2015, November 3). Essena O'Neill quits Instagram claiming social media 'is not real life'. *The Guardian*.

Hunter, D., & Evans, N. (2016). Facebook emotional contagion experiment controversy. *Research Ethics, 12*(1), 2–3.

Illouz, E. (2007). *Cold intimacies: The making of emotional capitalism*. Polity.

Isaak, J., & Hanna, M. J. (2018). User data privacy: Facebook, Cambridge Analytica, and privacy protection. *Computer, 51*(8), 56–59.

Jacobsen, M. (2010). Goffman through the looking glass: From 'classical' to contemporary Goffman. In *The contemporary Goffman*. (pp. 1–50). Routledge.

Jakubowicz, A. (2017). Alt_Right white lite: Trolling, hate speech and cyber racism on social media. *Cosmopolitan Civil Societies, 9*(3), 41–60.

Jamieson, L. (2011). Intimacy as a concept: Explaining social change in the context of globalisation or another form of ethnocentricism?: *Sociological Research Online, 16*(4), 15.

Jamieson, L., (2013) Personal relationships, intimacy and the self in a mediated and global digital age. In Digital sociology: Critical perspectives (pp. 13–33). London: Palgrave Macmillan UK.

Jandrić, P. (2020). Postdigital research in the time of Covid-19. *Postdigital Science and Education, 2*(2), 233–238.

Jean Kenix, L. (2009). Blogs as alternative. *Journal of Computer-Mediated Communication, 14*(4), 790–822.

Jenkins, H. (1992). Textual poachers: Television fans & participatory culture. Routledge.

Jenkins, H. (2006). Confronting the challenges of participatory culture: Media education for the 21st century. An occasional paper on digital media and learning. *John D. and Catherine T. MacArthur Foundation*.

Jenkins, H. (2009). *Confronting the challenges of participatory culture: Media education for the 21st century* (p. 145). The MIT press.

Jenkins, H. (2014). Rethinking convergence/culture. *Cultural Studies, 28*(2), 267–297.

Jenkins, H., Ford, S., & Green, J. (2013). Spreadable media: Creating value and meaning in a networked culture. In *Spreadable media: Creating value and meaning in a networked culture*. New York University Press.

Jenkins, Henry. (2006). *Convergence culture: Where old and new media collide*. New York University.

Jenkins R. (2010). The 21-century interaction order. In M. H. Jacobsen (Ed.), *The contemporary Goffman*. (pp. 157–174.). Routledge.

Johnston, K., Tanner, M., Lalla, N., & Kawalski, D. (2013). Social capital: the benefit of Facebook 'friends'. *Behaviour & Information Technology, 32*(1), 24–36.

Jones, A. (2006). *Self image: Technology, representation, and the contemporary subject*. Routledge.

Jones, K. M. L., Asher, A., Goben, A., Perry, M. R., Salo, D., Briney, K. A., & Robertshaw, M. B. (2020). 'We're being tracked at all times': Student perspectives of their privacy in relation to learning analytics in higher education. *Journal of the Association for Information Science and Technology, 71*(9), 1044–1059.

Jones, S. (1997). Virtual culture: Identity and communication in cybersociety. In *Virtual culture: Identity and communication in cybersociety* (p. 262). https://doi.org/10.1080/15564886.2011.607402

Jong, S. T., & Drummond, M. J. (2016). Exploring online fitness culture and young females. *Leisure Studies, 35*(6), 758–770.

Jouhki, J., Lauk, E., Penttinen, M., Sormanen, N., & Uskali, T. (2016). Facebook's emotional contagion experiment as a challenge to research ethics. *Media and Communication, 4*(4).

Kahn, S. (2015). *7 Ways Technology Is Killing Your Relationship | Thought Catalog*. Thought Catalogue. https://thoughtcatalog.com/samira-khan/2015/02/7-ways-technology-is-killing-your-relationship/

Kale, S. (2020). How coronavirus helped TikTok find its voice | TikTok | *The Guardian*. https://www.theguardian.com/technology/2020/apr/26/how-coronavirus-helped-tiktok-find-its-voice

Kammerer, Y., & Gerjets, P. (2012). How search engine users evaluate and select Web search results: The impact of the search engine interface on credibility assessments. In *Web search engine research*. Emerald Group Publishing Limited.

Kang, M.E. (1997). The portrayal of women's images in magazine advertisements: Goffman's gender analysis revisited. *Sex roles, 37*, pp.979–996.

Kang, J., & Wei, L. (2020). Let me be at my funniest: Instagram users' motivations for using Finsta (aka, fake Instagram). The Social Science Journal, 57(1), 58–71.

Katz, J., Aakhus, M., & Gergen, K. J. (2002). Perpetual Contact: Mobile Communication, Private Talk, Public Performance. In *Mobile communication, private talk, public*. Cambridge University Press.

Katz, J. E., & Rice, R. E. (2002). *Social consequences of Internet use: Access, involvement, and interaction*. MIT Press.

Katz, J. E., Rice, R. E., & Aspden, P. (2001). The Internet, 1995–2000: Access, civic involvement, and social interaction. *American Behavioral Scientist, 45*(3), 405–419.

Kaufmann, K. (2018). Navigating a new life: Syrian refugees and their smartphones in Vienna. *Information, Communication & Society, 21*(6), 882–898.

Kaufmann, K. (2020). Mobile methods: Doing migration research with the help of smartphones. In *The Sage Handbook of Media and Migration* (pp. 167–179).

Kaufmann, K., & Peil, C. (2020). The mobile instant messaging interview (MIMI): Using WhatsApp to enhance self-reporting and explore media usage in situ. *Mobile Media & Communication, 8*(2), 229–246.

Kaufmann, K., Peil, C., & Bork-Hüffer, T. (2021). Producing in situ data from a distance with mobile instant messaging interviews (MIMIs): Examples From the COVID-19 pandemic. *International Journal of Qualitative Methods, 20*, 16094069211029696.

Kay, M., Matuszek, C., & Munson, S. A. (2015). Unequal representation and gender stereotypes in image search results for occupations. *Proceedings of the 33rd Annual ACM Conference on Human Factors in Computing Systems*, 3819–3828.

Kendall, L. (1999). Recontextualizing "cyberspace": Methodological considerations for on-line research. *Doing Internet research: Critical issues and methods for examining the Net, 2455*, 57–74.

Kendall, L. (2002). *Hanging out in the virtual pub: Masculinities and relationships online*. University of California Press.

Kendall, T. (2021). From Binge-Watching to Binge-Scrolling: TikTok and the Rhythms of# LockdownLife. *Film Quarterly, 75*(1), 41–46.

Kennedy, M. (2020). 'If the rise of the TikTok dance and e-girl aesthetic has taught us anything, it's that teenage girls rule the internet right now': TikTok celebrity, girls and the Coronavirus crisis. *European Journal of Cultural Studies, 23*(6), 1069–1076.

Kil, N., Kim, J., Park, J., & Lee, C. (2021). Leisure boredom, leisure challenge, smartphone use, and emotional distress among US college students: Are they interrelated? *Leisure Studies, 40*(6), 779–792.

King, S. A. (1994). Analysis of electronic support groups for recovering addicts. *Interpersonal Computing and Technology, 2*(3), 47–56.

Kling, R. (1996). Social relationships in electronic forums: Hangouts, salons, workplaces and communities. In Kling, R (ed) *Computerization and Controversy: Value Conflicts and Social Morgan Kauffman.*

Klug, D. (2020). "It took me almost 30 minutes to practice this". Performance and Production Practices in Dance Challenge Videos on TikTok. *arXiv preprint arXiv:2008.13040.*

Komito, L. (1998). The net as a foraging society: Flexible communities. *Information Society, 14*(2), 97–106.

Koro-Ljungberg, M., Cirell, A. M., Gong, B., & Tesar, M. (2017). The importance of small form:'Minor' data and 'BIG' neoliberalism. In *Qualitative inquiry in neoliberal times* (pp. 59–72). Routledge.

Kozinets, R. V. (2019). *Netnography: The essential guide to qualitative social media research.* Sage.

Kramer, A. D. I., Guillory, J. E., & Hancock, J. T. (2014). Experimental evidence of massive-scale emotional contagion through social networks. *Proceedings of the National Academy of Sciences, 111*(24), 8788–8790.

Krotz, F. (2008). Media connectivity: Concepts, conditions, and consequences. *Network, Connectivity and Flow. Conceptualising Contemporary Communications,* 13–31.

Kruse, A., & Pongsajapan, R. (2012). Student-centered learning analytics. *CNDLS Thought Papers, 1*(9), 98–112.

Kücklich, J. (2005). *FCJ-025 precarious playbour: Modders and the digital games industry.* The Fibreculture Journal,(5)

Kunert, J. (2021). The footy girls of Tumblr: How women found their niche in the online football fandom. *Communication & Sport, 9*(2), 243–263.

Kuykendall, L., Boemerman, L., & Zhu, Z. (2018). The importance of leisure for subjective well-being. *Handbook of Well-Being.* DEF Publishers.

Labayen, M. F., & Gutierrez, I. (2021). Digital placemaking as survival tactics: Sub-Saharan migrants' videos at the Moroccan–Spanish border. *Convergence, 27*(3), 664–678.

Lai, J., & Widmar, N. O. (2021). Revisiting the digital divide in the COVID-19 era. *Applied Economic Perspectives and Policy, 43*(1), 458–464.

Lambert, A. (2016). Intimacy and social capital on Facebook: Beyond the psychological perspective. *New Media & Society, 18*(11), 2559–2575.

Lanford, M., Tierney, W. G., & Lincoln, Y. (2019). The art of life history: Novel approaches, future directions. *Qualitative Inquiry, 25*(5), 459–463.

Lappalainen, A., & Rosenberg, C. (2022). Can 5G fixed broadband bridge the rural digital divide? *IEEE Communications Standards Magazine, 6*(2), 79–84.

Lash, S. (2002). *Critique of information.* Sage.

Latzko-Toth, G., Bonneau, C., & Millette, M. (2017). Small data, thick data: Thickening strategies for trace-based social media research. *The SAGE Handbook of Social Media Research Methods*, 199–214.

Lau, J., Zimmerman, B., & Schaub, F. (2018). Alexa, are you listening? Privacy perceptions, concerns and privacy-seeking behaviors with smart speakers. *Proceedings of the ACM on human-computer interaction*, 2(CSCW), 1–31.

Laura, H. (2022). *Amazon's Astro raises questions about privacy in the home.* CNET.

Lavery Irelyne. (2022, December 10). *ChatGPT: Everything to know about the viral, 'groundbreaking' AI bot—National | Globalnews.ca.* https://globalnews.ca/news/9339517/chatgpt-artificial-intelligence/

Law, S. (2017). Improvements to Horseshoe Bend get underway. *Lake Powell Chronical.* https://lakepowellchronicle.com/article/improvements-to-horseshoe-bend-get-underway

Lawrence, L. (2022). Conducting cross-cultural qualitative interviews with mainland Chinese participants during COVID: Lessons from the field. *Qualitative Research*, 22(1), 154–165.

Leadbeater, C. (2009). *We-think.* Profile books.

Leaver, T. (2017). Intimate surveillance: Normalizing parental monitoring and mediation of infants online. *Social Media+ Society*, 3(2), 2056305117707192.

Leaver, T., Highfield, T., & Abidin, C. (2020). *Instagram: Visual social media cultures.* John Wiley & Sons.

Lego, Valerie. (2018). 'Phubbing': Why 'phone snubbing is bad for mental health'. *USA Today.* https://eu.usatoday.com/story/tech/news/2018/04/24/phubbing-phone-snubbing-mental-health/546124002/

Lehman, E. T. (2021). "Washing hands, reaching out"–Popular music, digital leisure and touch during the COVID-19 pandemic. *Leisure Sciences*, 43(1–2), 273–279.

Lepp, A., Barkley, J. E., & Karpinski, A. C. (2014). The relationship between cell phone use, academic performance, anxiety, and satisfaction with life in college students. *Computers in Human Behavior*, 31(1), 343–350.

Lessig, L. (2008). *Remix: Making art and commerce thrive in the hybrid economy.* Penguin.

Levinson, P. (2004). *Cellphone: The story of the world's most mobile medium and how it has transformed everything!* Macmillan.

Li, C. (2010). Groundswell. Winning in a world transformed by social technologies. *Strategic Direction.*

Light, B., Burgess, J., & Duguay, S. (2016). The walkthrough method: An approach to the study of apps: *New Media & Society*, 20(3), 881–900.

Lin, J. H., Peng, W., Kim, M., Kim, S. Y., & LaRose, R. (2012). Social networking and adjustments among international students. *New media & society*, 14(3), 421–440.

Lin, R., Levordashka, A., & Utz, S. (2016). Ambient intimacy on Twitter. *Cyberpsychology.* https://doi.org/10.5817/CP2016-1-6

Lincoln, S., & Robards, B. (2014). Being strategic and taking control: Bedrooms, social network sites and the narratives of growing up. *New Media and Society*, 18(6), 927–943.

Lindgren, S. (2017). *Digital media and society*. Sage.

Lindgren, S. (2021a). *Digital media and society*. Sage.

Lindgren, S. (2021b). *The day the internet died. The story of the inception of the....* Medium. Com/@simonlindgren. https://medium.com/@simonlindgren/the-day-the-internet-died-a1884a002a22

Ling, R., & Yttri, B. (2005). *Control, emancipation and status: The mobile telephone in the teen's parental and peer group control relationships* [Electronic Version]. Retrieved April 18, 2008.

Lingel, J. (2013). The digital remains: Social media and practices of online grief. *Information Society, 29*(3), 190–195.

Literat, I. (2016). Interrogating participation across disciplinary boundaries: Lessons from political philosophy, cultural studies, art, and education. *New Media & Society, 18*(8), 1787–1803.

Litt, E., & Hargittai, E. (2016). The imagined audience on social network sites. *Social Media+ Society, 2*(1), 2056305116633482.

Livingston, S. (2020). *Digital by default: The new normal of family life under COVID-19*. LSE Blogs. https://blogs.lse.ac.uk/medialse/2020/05/21/digital-by-default-the-new-normal-of-family-life-under-covid-19/

Livingstone, S., & Brake, D. R. (2010). On the rapid rise of social networking sites: New findings and policy implications. *Children & society, 24*(1), 75–83.

Livingstone, S., & Sefton-Green, J. (2016). *The class: Living and learning in the digital age* (Vol. 1). NYU Press.

Lock, S. (2022). What is AI chatbot phenomenon ChatGPT and could it replace humans? | Artificial intelligence (AI.) *The Guardian*. https://www.theguardian.com/technology/2022/dec/05/what-is-ai-chatbot-phenomenon-chatgpt-and-could-it-replace-humans

Lomborg, S., & Bechmann, A. (2014). Using APIs for data collection on social media. *The Information Society, 30*(4), 256–265.

Lupton, D. (2014). *Digital sociology*. Routledge.

Lupton, D. (2016). Foreword: lively devices, lively data and lively leisure studies. *Leisure Studies, 35*(6), 709–711.

Lury, C. (2013). *Prosthetic culture*. Routledge.

Lussier, J. T., Raeder, T., & Chawla, N. V. (2010). Digging up the dirt on user generated content consumption. *COMAD*, 155.

Lutz, C. (2019). Digital inequalities in the age of artificial intelligence and big data. *Human Behavior and Emerging Technologies, 1*(2), 141–148.

Lutz, C., & Ranzini, G. (2017). Where dating meets data: Investigating social and institutional privacy concerns on Tinder. *Social Media+ Society, 3*(1), 2056305117697735.

Luyt, B. (2003). Digital divide: Civic engagement, information poverty, and the internet worldwide. *Social Science Computer Review, 21*(1), 120–123. https://doi.org/10.1177/0894439302238974

Maalsen, S., & Dowling, R. (2020). Covid-19 and the accelerating smart home. *Big Data & Society, 7*(2), 2053951720938073.

Maalsen, S., & Sadowski, J. (2019). The smart home on FIRE: Amplifying and accelerating domestic surveillance. *Surveillance & Society, 17*(1/2), 118–124.

Macionis, J. J. (1978). The search for community in modern society: An interpretation. *Qualitative Sociology, 1*(2), 130–143.

Madden, M. (2012). Privacy management on social media sites. *Pew Internet Report, 24*, 1–20.

Maddox, J. L. (2018). Fear and selfie-loathing in America: Identifying the interstices of othering, iconoclasm, and the selfie. *Journal of Popular Culture, 51*(1), 26–49.

Malema, M. J., Achmat, G., Smithdorf, G. E., Andrews, B., Schippers, R., Onagbiye, S., & Malema, M. P. (2021). Online sports and e-gaming as means to promote leisure activity amidst COVID-19 pandemic. *International Leisure Review, 10*(1), 73–81.

Mann, G., & O'Neil, C. (2016). Hiring algorithms are not neutral. *Harvard Business Review, 9*, 2016.

Markham, A. N. (1998). *Life online: Researching real experience in virtual space* (Vol. 6). Rowman Altamira.

Markham, A., & Buchanan, E. (2017). Research ethics in context: Decision-making in digital research. In *The Datafied Society* (pp. 201–209). Amsterdam University Press.

Markham, A. N., & Buchanan, E. (2015). Ethical considerations in digital research contexts. *Encyclopedia for Social & Behavioral Sciences*, 606–613.

Marres, N. (2017). *Digital sociology: The reinvention of social research.* John Wiley & Sons.

Marres, N., & Weltevrede, E. (2013). Scraping the social? *Journal of Cultural Economy, 6*(3), 313–335.

Martey, R.M. and Shiflett, K. (2012). Reconsidering site and self: Methodological frameworks for virtual-world research. *International Journal of Communication,* 6, p.22.

Marvin, C. (1990). *When old technologies were new: Thinking about electric communication in the late nineteenth century.* Oxford University Press.

Marwick, A. E. (2012). The public domain: Surveillance in everyday life. *Surveillance & Society, 9*(4), 378–393.

Marwick, A. E. (2013). *Status update: Celebrity, publicity, and branding in the social media age.* Yale University Press.

Marwick, A. E. (2015). Instafame: Luxury selfies in the attention economy. *Public Culture, 27*(1 75), 137–160.

Martey, R.M. and Shiflett, K. (2012). Reconsidering site and self: Methodological frameworks for virtual-world research. *International Journal of Communication,* 6, p.22.

Marwick, A. E., & boyd, d. (2011). I tweet honestly, I tweet passionately: Twitter users, context collapse, and the imagined audience. *New Media and Society, 13*(1), 114–133.

Massanari, A. (2013). Playful participatory culture: Learning from Reddit. *AoIR Selected Papers of Internet Research.*

Matamoros-Fernández, A., & Farkas, J. (2021). Racism, hate speech, and social media: A systematic review and critique. *Television and New Media, 22*(2), 205–224.

Mathew, B., Dutt, R., Goyal, P., & Mukherjee, A. (2019, June). Spread of hate speech in online social media. In *Proceedings of the 10th ACM conference on web science* (pp. 173–182)

Mathrani, A., Sarvesh, T., & Umer, R. (2022). Digital divide framework: Online learning in developing countries during the COVID-19 lockdown. *Globalisation, Societies and Education, 20*(5), 625–640.

McCluskey, M. (2020). These TikTok creators say they're still being suppressed for posting Black Lives Matter content. *Time Magazine.*

McCrow-Young, A. (2021). Approaching Instagram data: reflections on accessing, archiving and anonymising visual social media. *Communication Research and Practice, 7*(1), 21–34.

McRoberts, S., Ma, H., Hall, A., & Yarosh, S. (2017). Share first, save later: Performance of self through Snapchat stories. *Proceedings of the 2017 CHI Conference on Human Factors in Computing Systems,* 6902–6911.

Mead, G. H. (1934). Mind, self, and society. University of Chicago Press.

Meier, J. V, Noel, J. A., & Kaspar, K. (2021). Alone together: Computer-mediated communication in leisure time during and after the COVID-19 pandemic. *Frontiers in Psychology, 12,* 2040.

Meikle, G. (2016). *Social media: Communication, sharing and visibility.* Routledge.

Meikle, G., & Young, S. (2011). *Media convergence: Networked digital media in everyday life.* Macmillan International Higher Education.

Mellor, P. A. (1993). Reflexive traditions: Anthony Giddens, high modernity, and the contours of contemporary religiosity. *Religious Studies, 29*(1), 111–127.

Micheli, M., Lutz, C., & Büchi, M. (2018). Digital footprints: an emerging dimension of digital inequality. *Journal of Information, Communication and Ethics in Society, 16*(3), 242–251.

Mickey, E. L. (2022). The organization of networking and gender inequality in the new economy: Evidence from the tech industry. *Work and Occupations, 49*(4), 383–420.

Miguel, C. (2016). Visual intimacy on social media: From selfies to the co-construction of intimacies through shared pictures. *Social Media+ Society, 2*(2), 2056305116641705.

Miguel, C. (2018). Personal relationships and intimacy in the age of social media. In *Personal relationships and intimacy in the age of social media.* Springer International Publishing. https://doi.org/10.1007/978-3-030-02062-0

Miller, A. G., Collins, B. E., & Brief, D. E. (1995). Perspectives on obedience to authority: The legacy of the Milgram experiments. In *Journal of Social Issues* (Vol. 51, Issue 3, pp. 1–19). Wiley Online Library.

Miller, V. (2008). New media, networking and phatic culture. *Convergence, 14*(4), 387–400.

Miller, V. (2011). *Understanding digital culture.* Sage.

Millington, B. (2014). Amusing ourselves to life: Fitness consumerism and the birth of bio-games. *Journal of Sport and Social Issues, 38*(6), 491–508.

Mills, C. W. (1959). The sociological imagination. *The Sociological Imagination,* 9–25.

Milner, R. M. (2018). The world made meme: Public conversations and participatory media. Information Society Series.

Mittelstadt, B. D., Allo, P., Taddeo, M., Wachter, S., & Floridi, L. (2016). The ethics of algorithms: Mapping the debate. *Big Data & Society*, *3*(2), 2053951716679679.

Mittmann, G., Woodcock, K., Dörfler, S., Krammer, I., Pollak, I., & Schrank, B. (2022). "TikTok is my life and snapchat is my ventricle": A mixed-methods study on the role of online communication tools for friendships in early adolescents. *The Journal of Early Adolescence*, *42*(2), 172–203.

Møller, K., & Robards, B. (2019). Walking through, going along and scrolling back. *Nordicom Review*, *40*, 95–109.

Monahan, T. (2010). Surveillance as governance: social inequality and the pursuit of democratic surveillance. Surveillance and democracy, (2010), 91–110.

Morris, J. (2021). Surveillance by Amazon: The warrant requirement, tech exceptionalism, & Ring scurity. *Boston University Journal of Science and Technology Law*, *27*.

Morris, N. J., & Orton-Johnson, K. (2022). Camping at home: Escapism, self-care, and social bonding during the COVID-19 pandemic. *Annals of Leisure Research*, 1–22.

Mortensen, T. E. (2018). Anger, fear, and games: The long event of# GamerGate. *Games and Culture*, *13*(8), 787–806.

Mount, H. (2015). Was Albert Einstein right about a generation of idiots? *Daily Mail Online*. https://www.dailymail.co.uk/news/article-2929268/Was-Einstein-right-Physicist-said-feared-technology-surpass-human-interaction-photos-time-not-far-off.html

Mullins, J. (2014). *9 Reasons Technology Has Ruined Relationships—E! Online*. E News. https://www.eonline.com/news/573361/9-reasons-technology-has-ruined-relationships-friendships-and-your-life

Murphy, M. (2013). Putting selfies under a feminist lens | Georgia Straight Vancouver's News & Entertainment Weekly. *The Georgia Straight*. https://www.straight.com/life/368086/putting-selfies-under-feminist-lens

Murray, D. C. (2015). Notes to self: The visual culture of selfies in the age of social media. *Consumption Markets and Culture*, *18*(6), 490–516.

Mustafaraj, E., Finn, S., Whitlock, C., & Metaxas, P. T. (2011, October). Vocal minority versus silent majority: Discovering the opionions of the long tail. In *2011 IEEE Third International Conference on Privacy, Security, Risk and Trust and 2011 IEEE Third International Conference on Social Computing* (pp. 103–110). IEEE.

Nakamura, L. (2002). Cybertypes. In *Race, ethnicity, and identity on the Internet*. https://doi.org/10.1016/j.biopsych.2005.02.001

Napoli, P. M., & Obar, J. A. (2014). The emerging mobile Internet underclass: A critique of mobile Internet access. *The Information Society*, *30*(5), 323–334.

Nayak, A. and Kehily, M. J. (2013). *Gender, youth and culture: Young masculinities and femininities*. Macmillan International Higher Education.

Neff, G., & Nafus, D. (2016). *Self-tracking*. MIT Press.

Negroponte, N. (1995). being digital *NY: Vintage Publishing*.

Neville, S. J. (2020). Eavesmining: A critical audit of the Amazon Echo and Alexa conditions of use. *Surveillance & Society*, *18*(3), 343–356.

Nichols, G., Tacon, R. and Muir, A. (2013). Sports clubs' volunteers: Bonding in or bridging out? *Sociology, 47*(2), 350–367.

Nie, N. H. (2001). Sociability, interpersonal relations, and the Internet: Reconciling conflicting findings. *American Behavioral Scientist, 3*, 420–435.

Nieva, R. (2019). At F8, Zuckerberg unveils Facebook's new mantra: 'The future is private'. *CNET*.

Nimrod, G., & Adoni, H. (2012). Conceptualizing e-leisure. *Loisir et Société/Society and Leisure, 35*(1), 31–56.

Nissenbaum, A., & Shifman, L. (2017). Internet memes as contested cultural capital: The case of 4chan's/b/board. *New Media & Society, 19*(4), 483–501.

Nissenbaum, H. (2010). *Privacy in context: Technology, policy, and the integrity of social life*. Stanford University Press.

Noble, S. U. (2018). *Algorithms of Oppression*. New York University Press.

Norberg, P. A., Horne, D. R., & Horne, D. A. (2007). The privacy paradox: Personal information disclosure intentions versus behaviors. *Journal of Consumer Affairs, 41*(1), 100–126.

Novick, G. (2008). Is there a bias against telephone interviews in qualitative research? *Research in Nursing & Health, 31*(4), 391–398.

Obar, J. A., & Oeldorf-Hirsch, A. (2020). The biggest lie on the internet: Ignoring the privacy policies and terms of service policies of social networking services. *Information, Communication & Society, 23*(1), 128–147.

Obermeyer, Z., Powers, B., Vogeli, C., & Mullainathan, S. (2019). Dissecting racial bias in an algorithm used to manage the health of populations. *Science, 366*(6464), 447–453.

O'Brien, J. (1999). Writing in the body. In *Communities in cyberspace*, (pp. 76–105). Smith, M. A., & Kollock, P. (Eds.). (1999). *Communities in cyberspace*. Psychology Press.

O'Connor, H., & Goodwin, J. (2012). Revisiting Norbert Elias's sociology of community: Learning from the Leicester re-studies. *Sociological Review, 60*(3), 476–497.

O'Connor, H., & Madge, C. (2017). Online interviewing. *The SAGE Handbook of Online Research Methods, 2*, 416–434.

O'Connor, K. W., & Schmidt, G. B. (2015). 'Facebook fired' legal standards for social media–based terminations of K-12 public school teachers. *Sage Open, 5*(1), 2158244015575636.

Ofcom. (2022). *Media use and attitudes report 2022* (Issue March).

Ogura, T. (2006). Electronic government and surveillance-oriented society. In *Theorizing surveillance* (pp. 270–295). Willan.

Oliffe, J. L., Kelly, M. T., Gonzalez Montaner, G., & Yu Ko, W. F. (2021). Zoom interviews: Benefits and concessions. *International Journal of Qualitative Methods, 20*, 16094069211053522.

O'Neil, C. (2017). *Weapons of math destruction: How big data increases inequality and threatens democracy*. Crown.

Opdenakker, R. (2006). Advantages and disadvantages of four interview techniques in qualitative research. *Forum Qualitative Sozialforschung/Forum: Qualitative Social Research, 7*(4).

O'Reilly, T. (2009). *What is web 2.0.* 'O'Reilly Media, Inc.'

Ortega, C., del Valle, R. S. S., & Peñafiel, R. (2011). Cultural (transformation) Observatories in Spain. *New challenges of cultural observatories.* (pp. 209–237). Servicio de Publicaciones= Argitalpen Zerbitzua.

Orton-Johnson, K. (2014). Knit, purl and upload: New technologies, digital mediations and the experience of leisure. *Leisure studies, 33*(3), 305–321.

Orton-Johnson, K. (2021). Digitally mediated motherhood during the COVID-19 pandemic. *Mothers, Mothering, and COVID-19: Dispatches from the Pandemic,* 291–302. Dementer Press

Ostrovsky, A.M. and Chen, J. R. (2020). TikTok and its role in COVID-19 information propagation. *Journal of Adolescent Health, 67*(5), 730.

Paasonen, S. (2017). Infrastructures of intimacy. In *Mediated intimacies* (pp. 103–116). Routledge.

Page, R. (2015). The narrative dimensions of social media storytelling. In *The Handbook of narrative analysis* (pp. 329–347). John Wiley & Sons.

Pahl, R. (2005). Are all communities communities in the mind?. *The Sociological Review, 53*(4), 621–640.

Palen, L., & Dourish, P. (2003, April). Unpacking" privacy" for a networked world. In *Proceedings of the SIGCHI conference on Human factors in computing systems* (pp. 129–136).

Palys, T., & Atchison, C. (2012). Qualitative research in the digital era: Obstacles and opportunities. *International Journal of Qualitative Methods, 11*(4), 352–367.

Papacharissi, Z. (Ed.). (2010). A networked self: Identity, community, and culture on social network sites. Routledge.

Papacharissi, Z. (2013). Audiences as media producers: Content analysis of 260 blogs. In *Self-Mediation* (pp. 77–92). Routledge.

Papacharissi, Z. (2018). *A networked self and love.* Routledge.

Papacharissi, Z., & Gibson, P. L. (2011). Fifteen minutes of privacy: Privacy, sociality, and publicity on social network sites. In *Privacy online: Perspectives on privacy and self-disclosure in the social web* (pp. 75–89). Berlin, Heidelberg: Springer Berlin Heidelberg.

Pappas, V., & Chikumbu, K. (2020). *A Message to Our Audience.* https://newsroom.tiktok.com/en-us/a-message-to-our-black-community

Pariser, E. (2011). *The filter bubble. What the internet is hiding from you.* London. Penguin

Parkins, W. (2004). Celebrity knitting and the temporality of postmodernity. *Fashion Theory, 8*(4), 425–441.

Parry, D. C., & Light, T. P. (2014). Fifty shades of complexity: Exploring technologically mediated leisure and women's sexuality. *Journal of Leisure Research, 46*(1), 38–57.

Pasquale, F. (2015). *The black box society: The secret algorithms that control money and information.* Harvard University Press.

Patterson, D. (2016). What the Finsta? The darker world of teenagers and Instagram. Huffingtonpost.Com. https://www.huffpost.com/entry/what-the-finsta-the-darker-world-of-teenagers-and_b_57eb9e03e4b07f20daa0fefb?guccounter=1

Patton, P. (1987). *Open road: A celebration of the American highway.* Touchstone.

Pearce, W., Özkula, S. M., Greene, A. K., Teeling, L., Bansard, J. S., Omena, J. J., & Rabello, E. T. (2020). Visual cross-platform analysis: Digital methods to research social media images. *Information, Communication & Society*, 23(2), 161–180.

Pearson, E. (2009). All the world wide web's a stage: The performance of identity in online social networks. *First Monday*, 14(3).

Pearson, M. (n.d.). *#BlackTwitter: LMCs Andre Brock Works to Unravel the Online Complexities of Race, Culture, and Technology*. Retrieved 4 May 2021, from https://iac.gatech.edu/research/features/black-twitter-andre-brock

Petrosyan, A. (2023). *Internet and social media users in the world 2023 | Statista*. https://www.Statista.Com/Statistics/617136/Digital-Population-Worldwide/#:~:Text=Worldwide%20digital%20population%202023&text=As%20of%20April%202023%2C%20there,Population%2C%20were%20social%20media%20users. https://www.statista.com/statistics/617136/digital-population-worldwide/

Pinckney, H. P., Mowatt, R. A., Outley, C., Brown, A., Floyd, M. F., & Black, K. L. (2018). Black Spaces/white Spaces: Black lives, leisure, and life politics. *Leisure Sciences*, 40(4), 267–287.

Pink, S. (2015). Going forward through the world: Thinking theoretically about first person perspective digital ethnography. *Integrative Psychological and Behavioral Science*, 49(2), 239–252.

Pink, S. (2016). Digital ethnography. *Innovative Methods in Media and Communication Research*, 161–165.

Pink, S. (2017). Technologies, possibilities, emergence and an ethics of responsibility: Refiguring techniques. In *Refiguring techniques in digital visual research* (pp. 1–12). Springer.

Piwek, L., & Joinson, A. (2016). 'What do they snapchat about?' Patterns of use in time-limited instant messaging service. *Computers in Human Behavior*. https://doi.org/10.1016/j.chb.2015.08.026

Plant, S. (2000). The effects of mobile telephones on social and individual life. *Report Commissioned by Motorola*.

Pollitt, A. (2015). Saying no to the tyranny of perfection on Instagram. *Stylist*. https://www.stylist.co.uk/beauty/instagram-instarealism-selfies-filters-facetune-mindy-kaling-adriana-lima-fearne-cotton/137183

Porlezza, C. (2019). From participatory culture to participatory fatigue: The problem with the public. *Social Media and Society*, 5(3). https://doi.org/10.1177/2056305119856684

Poser, S. (2011). *Leisure time and technology*. Institut für Europäische Geschichte.

Poushter, J. (2017). *Smartphones are common in advanced economies, but digital divides remain*. Pew Research Center. http://www.pewresearch.org/fact-tank/2017/04/21/smartphones-are-common-in-advanced-economies-but-digital-divides-remain/

Pridmore, J., & Mols, A. (2020). Personal choices and situated data: Privacy negotiations and the acceptance of household Intelligent Personal Assistants. *Big Data & Society*, 7(1), 2053951719891748.

Prinsloo, P., Khalil, M., & Slade, S. (2021). Learning analytics in a time of pandemics: Mapping the field. *EDEN Conference Proceedings*, 1, 59–70.

Prinsloo, P., & Slade, S. (2016). Student vulnerability, agency, and learning analytics: An exploration. *Journal of Learning Analytics, 3*(1), 159–182.

Procter, J. (2004). *Stuart Hall*. Routledge.

Przybylski, A. (2020). *Gaming may not be as bad as you think – Oxford research | University of Oxford*. https://www.ox.ac.uk/news/arts-blog/gaming-may-not-be-bad-you-think-oxford-research

Putnam, R. D. (1995). Bowling Alone: America's Declining Social Capital. *Journal of Democracy, 6*(1).

Putnam, Robert D. (2000). Bowling alone: America's declining social capital. In *Culture and politics: A reader*, pp. 223–234. Palgrave Macmillan

Raessens, J. (2006). Playful identities, or the ludification of culture. *Games and Culture, 1*(1), 52–57.

Raghavan, M., Barocas, S., Kleinberg, J., & Levy, K. (2020). Mitigating bias in algorithmic hiring: Evaluating claims and practices. *Proceedings of the 2020 Conference on Fairness, Accountability, and Transparency*, 469–481.

Raghunandan, K., Punch, S., Vanderbeck, R., & Skelton, T. (2018). Young people in the digital age: Metrics of friendship. *Families, intergenerationality, and peer group relations*, 415–434.

Rainie, L., & Wellman, B. (2012a). Networked relationships. In *Networked: The new social operating system* (pp. 117–146). https://doi.org/40020925681

Rainie, L., & Wellman, B. (2012b). Networked: The new social operating system. In *Communications of the ACM*. https://doi.org/10.1145/506218.506221

Rangaswamy, N., & Arora, P. (2016). The mobile internet in the wild and every day: Digital leisure in the slums of urban India. *International Journal of Cultural Studies, 19*(6), 611–626.

Raub, M. (2018). Bots, bias and big data: Artificial intelligence, algorithmic bias and disparate impact liability in hiring practices. *Ark. L. Rev., 71*, 529.

Rayaprolu, (2023). Creator Economy Statistics: Everything You Need To Know https://techjury.net/blog/creator-economy-statistics/

Raynes-Goldie, K. (2010). Aliases, creeping, and wall cleaning: Understanding privacy in the age of Facebook. *First Monday*.

Reade, J. (2021). Keeping it raw on the 'gram: Authenticity, relatability and digital intimacy in fitness cultures on Instagram. *New Media & Society, 23*(3), 535–553.

Reed, T. V. (2018). Digitized lives. In *Digitized Lives*. https://doi.org/10.4324/9781315143415

Reid, E. M. (1991). Electropolis: Communication and community on internet relay chat. *Communication*. Unpublished thesis University of Melbourne Department of History.

Rendell, J. (2021). Staying in, rocking out: Online live music portal shows during the coronavirus pandemic. *Convergence, 27*(4), 1092–1111.

Rettie, R (2004). Using Goffman's frameworks to explain presence and reality. *Presence 2004*, 117–124.

Reuter, M., & Köver, C. (2019). *TikTok: Cheerfulness and censorship*. Netzpolitik.Org. https://netzpolitik.org/2019/cheerfulness-and-censorship/

Rheingold, H. (1993). *"The virtual community"*. Addison-Wesley.

Rheingold, H. (1994). *The Virtual Community: Homesteading on the Electronic Frontier*. Addison-Wesley.

Rheingold, H. (2006). Social networks and the nature of communities. In *Networked Neighbourhoods: The Connected Community in Context* (pp. 47–75). London: Springer London.

Rheingold, H. (2012). What the WELL's rise and fall tell us about online community. *The Atlantic*. https://www.theatlantic.com/technology/archive/2012/07/what-the-wells-rise-and-fall-tell-us-about-online-community/259504/

Ribeiro-Navarrete, S., Saura, J. R., & Palacios-Marqués, D. (2021). Towards a new era of mass data collection: Assessing pandemic surveillance technologies to preserve user privacy. *Technological Forecasting and Social Change, 167*. https://doi.org/10.1016/J.TECHFORE.2021.120681

Rick, O. J. C., & Bustad, J. J. (2021). Cycling in the flattened city: Urban assemblages and digital visual research. *Somatechnics, 11*(2), 246–264.

Rieder, B., & Röhle, T. (2017). *Digital methods: From challenges to Bildung*. In Van Es, K., & Schäfer, M. T. (eds) (2017). *The datafied society. Studying culture through data*. Amsterdam University Press.

Roberts, J. A., & David, M. E. (2016). My life has become a major distraction from my cell phone: Partner phubbing and relationship satisfaction among romantic partners. *Computers in Human Behavior, 54*, 134–141.

Roberts, K. (2020). Locked down leisure in Britain. *Leisure Studies, 39*(5), 617–628.

Robinson, L. (2007). The cyberself: The self-ing project goes online, symbolic interaction in the digital age. *New Media and Society, 9*(1), 93–110.

Rocamora, A. (2011). Personal fashion blogs: Screens and mirrors in digital self-portraits. *Fashion Theory – Journal of Dress Body and Culture, 15*(4), 407–424.

Rogers, R. (2013). *Digital methods*. MIT press.

Rogers, R. (2017). Digital methods for cross-platform analysis. In T. E. Burgess, J., Marwick, A. and Poell (Eds.), *The SAGE handbook of social media* (pp. 91–110).

Rogers, R. (2019). *Doing digital methods*. Sage.

Rogers, R. (2021). Visual media analysis for Instagram and other online platforms. *Big Data & Society, 8*(1), 20539517211022370.

Rogerson, M., Gibbs, M., & Smith, M. (2015). *Digitising boardgames: Issues and tensions*. Proceedings of DiGRA 2015: Diversity of play: Games – Cultures – Identities

Rojas de Francisco, L., López-Sintas, J., & García-Álvarez, E. (2016). Social leisure in the digital age. *Loisir et Société/Society and Leisure, 39*(2), 258–273.

Rojek, C. (1985). Capitalism and Leisure Theory, London.

Rojek, C. (1999). *Leisure and culture*. Springer.

Ronson, J. (2016). *So you've been publicly shamed*. Riverhead Books.

Rose, G. (2016). *Visual methodologies: An introduction to researching with visual materials*. Sage.

Rosenfeld, M. J., & Thomas, R. J. (2012). Searching for a mate: The rise of the Internet as a social intermediary. *American Sociological Review, 77*(4), 523–547

Rosner, D. K., & Ryokai, K. (2009). Reflections on craft: Probing the creative process of everyday knitters. *Proceedings of the Seventh ACM Conference on Creativity and Cognition*, 195–204.

Rottinghaus, A. R. (2021). Smart homes and the new white futurism. *Journal of Futures Studies*, 25(4), 45–56.

Routh, P. (2015). A poststructuralist review of selfies: Moving beyond heteronormative visual rhetoric. *(E) Dialogue*, 1(1), 4–14.

Rutter, J. and Smith, G.W.H. (2005). Ethnographic presence in nebulous settings. In *Virtual Methods: Issues in Social Research on the Internet* (pp. 81–92). Berg.

Sadler, N. (2021). *Fragmented narrative: Telling and interpreting stories in the Twitter age*. Routledge.

Saker, M. (2017). Foursquare and identity: Checking-in and presenting the self through location. *New Media and Society*, 19(6), 934–949.

Salehan, M. and Negahban, A. (2013). Social networking on smartphones: When mobile phones become addictive. *Computers in Human Behavior*, 29(6), 2632–2639.

Saltz, J. (2014). Art at arm's length: A history of the selfie. *New York Magazine*, 71–75.

Samorani, M., & Blount, L. G. (2020). Machine learning and medical appointment scheduling: Creating and perpetuating inequalities in access to health care. *American Journal of Public Health*, 110(4), 440–441). American Public Health Association.

Sander, T. H., & Putnam, R. D. (2010). Still bowling alone? The post-9/11 split. *Journal of Democracy*, 21, 9.

Savage, M., & Burrows, R. (2007). The coming crisis of empirical sociology. *British Sociological Association*, 41(5), 885–899.

Savolainen, L., Uitermark, J., & Boy, J. D. (2022). Filtering feminisms: Emergent feminist visibilities on Instagram. *New Media and Society*, 24(3), 557–579.

Schellewald, A. (2021). Communicative forms on TikTok: Perspectives from digital ethnography. *International Journal of Communication*, 15, 1437–1457.

Schiano, D., Chen, C. P., & Isaacs, E. (2002). How teens take, view, share and store photos. *Conference on Computer Supported Cooperative Work CSCW 2002, September*, 667–676.

Schmidt, J. (2007). Blogging practices: An analytical framework. *Journal of Computer-Mediated Communication*, 12(4), 1409–1427.

Schultz, C. S., & McKeown, J. K. L. (2018). Introduction to the special issue: Toward 'digital leisure studies'. *Leisure Sciences*, 40(4), 223–238.

Schwarz, O. (2010). On friendship, boobs and the logic of the catalogue: Online self-portraits as a means for the exchange of capital. *Convergence*, 16(2) 163–183.

Sclater, N., Peasgood, A., & Mullan, J. (2016). Learning analytics in higher education. *London: Jisc. Accessed February*, 8(2017), 176.

Seeler, S., Lück, M., & Schänzel, H. A. (2019). Exploring the drivers behind experience accumulation – The role of secondary experiences consumed through the eyes of social media influencers. *Journal of Hospitality and Tourism Management,* *41,* 80–89.

Seko, Y. (2013, May). Picturesque wounds: A multimodal analysis of self-injury photographs on Flickr. In *Forum Qualitative Sozialforschung/Forum: Qualitative Social Research* (Vol. 14, No. 2).

Selinger, E., & Hartzog, W. (2016). Facebook's emotional contagion study and the ethical problem of co-opted identity in mediated environments where users lack control. *Research Ethics, 12*(1), 35–43.

Selwyn, N. (2004). Reconsidering political and popular understandings of the digital divide. *New Media & Society, 6*(3), 341–362.

Selwyn, N. (2019). *What is digital sociology?* John Wiley & Sons.

Selwyn, N., O'Neill, C., Smith, G., Andrejevic, M., & Gu, X. (2023). A necessary evil? The rise of online exam proctoring in Australian universities. *Media International Australia, 186*(1), 149–164.

Senft, T. M., & Baym, N. K. (2015). What does the selfie say? Investigating a global phenomenon. *International Journal of Communication, 9*(1), 1588–1606.

Sessions, L. F. (2009). 'You looked better on MySpace' Deception and authenticity on Web 2.0. *First Monday, 14*(7).

Shah, S. G. S., Nogueras, D., van Woerden, H. C., & Kiparoglou, V. (2020). The COVID-19 Pandemic: A pandemic of lockdown loneliness and the role of digital technology. *J Med Internet Res, 22*(11).

Shaul, B. (2020). App Annie: TikTok Was the Most-Downloaded App in Q1 2020. *Adweek.* https://www.adweek.com/performance-marketing/app-annie-tiktok-was-the-most-downloaded-app-in-q1-2020/

Shaw, S. M. (1985). Gender and leisure: Inequality in the distribution of leisure time. *Journal of Leisure Research, 17*(4), 266–282.

Shead, S. (2020). *TikTok apologizes after being accused of censoring #BlackLivesMatter posts.* CNBC. https://www.cnbc.com/2020/06/02/tiktok-blacklivesmatter-censorship.html

Shifman, L. (2013). *Memes in digital culture.* MIT Press.

Shirky, C. (2009). *Here comes everybody: How change happens when people come together.* Penguin.

Shirky, C. (2012). How the Internet will (one day) transform government. TED Global.

Šikić-Mićanović, L., Zdravković, Ž., & Anić, J. R. (2021). Leisure time: Gender and regional inequalities in Croatia. *World Leisure Journal, 63*(4), 355–373.

Silk, M., Millington, B., Rich, E., & Bush, A. (2016). (Re-)thinking digital leisure. *Leisure Studies, 35*(6), 712–723. Routledge.

Silva, P. D. da, & Garcia, J. L. (2012). YouTubers as satirists: Humour and remix in online video. *JeDEM-Ejournal of EDemocracy and Open Government, 4.*

Silverstone, R., & Haddon, L. (2016). *Design and the domestication of information and communication technologies: Technical change and everyday life Book section.*

Sintas, J. L., Belbeze, M. P. L., & Lamberti, G. (2023). Socially patterned strategic complementarity between offline leisure activities and internet practices among young people. *Leisure Sciences*, *45*(1), 24–45.

Sintas, J. L., De Francisco, L. R., & Álvarez, E. G. (2015). The nature of leisure revisited: An interpretation of digital leisure. *Journal of Leisure Research*, *47*(1), 79–101.

Sivan, A., Tam, V., Siu, G., & Stebbins, R. (2019). Adolescents' choice and pursuit of their most important and interesting leisure activities. *Leisure Studies*, *38*(1), 98–113.

Slater, D. (1998). Trading sexpics on IRC: Embodiment and authenticity on the internet. *Body and Society*, *4*(4), 91–117.

Smets, K. (2019). Media and immobility: The affective and symbolic immobility of forced migrants. *European Journal of Communication*, *34*(6), 650–660.

Smith, M.A. and Kollock, P. eds. (1999). *Communities in cyberspace*. Psychology Press.

Smith, S. P. (2021). Landscapes for 'likes': Capitalizing on travel with Instagram. *Social Semiotics*, *31*(4), 604–624.

Snow, D. A., & Anderson, L. (1987). Identity work among the homeless: The verbal construction and avowal of personal identities. *American Journal of Sociology*, *92*(6), 1336.

Snyder, L. (2002). Confidentiality and anonymity. *Walking the Tightrope: Ethical Issues for Qualitative Researchers*, 70.

Social Films (2021). *TikTok UK Statistics (2021) | Everything you need to know | Social Films*. Social Films. https://www.socialfilms.co.uk/blog/tiktok-uk-statistics

Solove, D. J. (2008). *Understanding privacy. GWU Legal Studies Research Paper No. 420*.

Solove, D. J. (2010). *Understanding privacy*. Harvard university press.

Son, J. S., & Chen, C.-C. (2018). Does using a smartphone for work purposes 'ruin' your leisure? Examining the role of smartphone use in work–leisure conflict and life satisfaction. *Journal of Leisure Research*, *49*(3–5), 236–257.

Sontag, S. (1977). On Photography. In *Vasa*.

Spanakis, P., Peckham, E., Mathers, A., Shiers, D., & Gilbody, S. (2021). The digital divide: Amplifying health inequalities for people with severe mental illness in the time of COVID-19. *The British Journal of Psychiatry*, *219*(4), 529–531.

Speed, C. (2010). Developing a sense of place with locative media: An 'underview effect'. *Leonardo*, *43*(2), 169–174.

Spencer, L. and Pahl, R. (2006). *Rethinking friendship: Hidden solidarities today*. Princeton University Press.

Standage, T. (1998). *The Victorian Internet: The remarkable story of the telegraph and the nineteenth century's online pioneers*. IEEE Annals of the History of Computing, *23*(1), 63–64.

Stebbins, R. A. (2017). *Serious leisure*. Routledge.

Steinkuehler, C. A., & Williams, D. (2006). Where everybody knows your (screen) name: Online games as 'third places'. *Journal of Computer-Mediated Communication*, *11*(4), 885–909.

Stern, J. (2022). Five chats to help you understand ChatGPT. *The Atlantic*. https://www.theatlantic.com/technology/archive/2022/12/openai-chatgpt-chatbot-messages/672411/

Stets, J. E., & Burke, P. J. (2000). Identity theory and social identity theory. *Social Psychology Quarterly*, *63*(3), 224.

Stewart, B. (2020). Online exam monitoring can invade privacy and erode trust at universities. *The Conversation.* Https://Theconversation. Com/Online-Exam-Monitoring-Can-Invade-Privacy-and-Erode-Trust-at-Universities-149335.

Stinson, C. (2022). Algorithms are not neutral. *AI and Ethics, 2*(4), 763–770.

Stoecklin, D., Gervais, C., Kutsar, D., & Heite, C. (2021). Lockdown and children's well-being: Experiences of children in Switzerland, Canada and Estonia. *Childhood Vulnerability Journal, 3*(1), 41–59.

Stone, A. R. (1996). *The war of desire and technology at the close of the mechanical age.* MIT Press.

Sujon, Z. (2018). The triumph of social privacy: Understanding the privacy logics of sharing behaviors across social media. *International Journal of Communication, 12,* 21.

Sujon, Z. (2021). *The social media age.* Sage.

Sumartojo, S., & Pink, S. (2017). Empathetic visuality: GoPros and the video trace. In *Refiguring techniques in digital visual research* (pp. 39–50). Springer.

Sundén, J. (2003). Material virtualities: Approaching online textual embodiment. *Order A Journal On The Theory Of Ordered Sets And Its Applications, 13*(13).

Surianshah, S. (2021). Digital divide in education during covid-19 pandemic. *Jurnal Ekonomi Malaysia, 55*(3), 103–112.

Swisher, K. (2020). Opinion | Amazon wants to get even closer. skintight. *The New York Times.* https://www.nytimes.com/2020/11/27/opinion/amazon-halo-surveillance.html

Sysling, F. (2020). Measurement, self-tracking and the history of science: An introduction. *History of Science, 58*(2), 103–116.

Taber, L. and Whittaker, S. (2020, April). "On Finsta, I can say' Hail Satan'": Being Authentic but Disagreeable on Instagram. In Proceedings of the 2020 CHI conference on human factors in computing systems (pp. 1–14).

Tao, M. and Ellison, N.B. (2023). "It's Your Finsta at the End of the Day... Kind of": Understanding Emerging Adults' Self-Presentational Changes on Secondary Accounts. *Social Media+ Society. 9*(1). https://doi.org/10.1177/20563051231152812.

Tavani, H. T. (2008). Informational privacy: Concepts, theories, and controversies. *The Handbook of Information and Computer Ethics,* 131–164.

Tembeck, T. (2016). Selfies of ill health: Online autopathographic photography and the dramaturgy of the everyday. *Social Media and Society, 2*(1).

Tene, O., & Polonetsky, J. (2013). Issue 5 Article 1 2013 Data for all: Privacy and user control in the age of analytics, 11 Nw. In *Northwestern Journal of Technology and Intellectual Property* (Vol. 11).

Terranova, T. (2012). Free labor. In *Digital Labor* (pp. 41–65). Routledge.

The Feminist Griote. (2013). *The Radical Politics of #selfies.* http://thefeministgriote.com/the-radical-politics-of-selfies/

Thomas, J. (1996). Introduction: A debate about the ethics of fair practices for collecting social science data in cyberspace. *The Information Society, 12*(2), 107–118.

Thomee, S., Harenstam, A., & Hagberg, M. (2011). Mobile phone use and stress, sleep disturbances, and symptoms of depression among young adults—A prospective cohort study. *BMC Public Health, 11*(1), 66.

Thompson, C. (2008). Brave new world of digital intimacy. *The New York Times.*

Thorpe, H. (2017). Action sports, social media, and new technologies: Towards a research agenda. *Communication & Sport, 5*(5), 554–578.

Thunberg, S., & Arnell, L. (2022). Pioneering the use of technologies in qualitative research–A research review of the use of digital interviews. *International Journal of Social Research Methodology, 25*(6), 757–768.

Thurlow, C., Lengel, L., Lengel, L.B. and Tomic, A. (2004). *Computer mediated communication.* Sage.

Tifentale, A., & Manovich, L. (2015). Selfiecity: Exploring photography and self-fashioning in social media. In *Postdigital aesthetics* (pp. 109–122). Springer.

Tiggemann, M., & Zaccardo, M. (2015). 'Exercise to be fit, not skinny': The effect of fitspiration imagery on women's body image. *Body Image, 15*, 61–67.

Tiggemann, M., & Zaccardo, M. (2018). 'Strong is the new skinny': A content analysis of #fitspiration images on Instagram. *Journal of Health Psychology, 23*(8), 1003–1011.

Tiidenberg, K. (2018). Ethics in digital research. *The SAGE Handbook of Qualitative Data Collection*, pp. 466–479.

Tiidenberg, K., & Gómez Cruz, E. (2015). Selfies, image and the re-making of the body. *Body and Society, 21*(4), 77–102.

Till, C. (2014). Exercise as labour: Quantified self and the transformation of exercise into labour. *Societies, 4*, 446–462.

Todd, C. (2015). Commentary: GamerGate and resistance to the diversification of gaming culture. *Women's Studies Journal, 29*(1), 64.

Toffler, A., & Alvin, T. (1980). *The third wave* (Vol. 484). Bantam Books.

Tönnies, F. (1963). Community & society: (Gemeinschaft und Gesellschaft). In *Harper torchbooks. Academy library.*

Tsikata, P. Y. (2015). The subaltern speaks back into the image factory: Justine Sacco's AIDS tweet cross-pollinates social and mass media. *Communication, 41*(1), 90–107.

Tufekci, Z. (2012). Facebook, youth and privacy in networked publics. *Sixth International AAAI Conference on Weblogs and Social Media.*

Tufekci, Z. (2017). With this data, Amazon won't be able to just sell you clothes or judge you. it could analyze if you're depressed or pregnant and much else. Twitter. https://twitter.com/zeynep/status/857269154822443009?lang=en.

Turkle, S. (1995). Life on the Screen: Identity in the age of the Internet. Simon and Schuster.

Turkle, S. (2007). Authenticity in the age of digital companions. Interaction studies, 8(3), 501–517.

Turkle, S. (2011). *Alone Together Why we expect more from technology and less from each other.* Basic Books.

Turkle, S. (2016). *Reclaiming conversation: The power of talk in a digital age.* Penguin.

Turner, A. (2022). *How many people have smartphones worldwide.* BankMyCell. https://www.bankmycell.com/blog/how-many-phones-are-in-the-world

Turney, J. (2009). *The culture of knitting.* Berg.

Twitch Stream Aid: Go live to save lives on 3/28 | Twitch Blog. (2020). Twitch. https://blog.twitch.tv/en/2020/03/26/twitch-stream-aid-go-live-to-save-lives-on-328/

Urry, J. (2000). *Sociology beyond societies: Mobilities for the twenty-first century.* Psychology Press.

Urry, J., & Larsen, J. (2011). *The tourist gaze 3.0.* Sage.

Utz, S., Muscanell, N., & Khalid, C. (2015). Snapchat elicits more jealousy than Facebook: A comparison of Snapchat and Facebook use. *Cyberpsychology, Behaviour, and Social Networking , 18*(3), 141–146.

Valtchanov, B. L., & Parry, D. C. (2017). 'I like my peeps': Diversifying the net generation's digital leisure. *Leisure Sciences, 39*(4), 336–354.

van Deursen, A. J. A. M., & Helsper, E. J. (2015). The third-level digital divide: Who benefits most from being online? In *Communication and information technologies annual.* Emerald Group Publishing Limited.

van Deursen, A. J. A. M., & Helsper, E. J. (2018). Collateral benefits of Internet use: Explaining the diverse outcomes of engaging with the Internet. *New Media & Society, 20*(7), 2333–2351.

van Deursen, A. J. A. M., Helsper, E., Eynon, R., & van Dijk, J. A. G. M. (2017). The compoundness and sequentiality of digital inequality. *International Journal of Communication, 11*, 452–473.

van Dijck, J. (2008). Digital photography: Communication, identity, memory. *Visual Communication, 7*(1), 57–76.

van Dijk, J. (2012). The network society. In *Network Society.*

van Dijck, J. (2013a). Facebook and the imperative of sharing. In *The Culture of Connectivity* (pp. 45–67). https://doi.org/10.1093/acprof:oso/9780199970773.003.0003

van Dijck, J. (2013b). 'You have one identity': Performing the self on Facebook and LinkedIn. *Media, Culture and Society, 35*(2), 199–215.

van Dijck, J. (2014). Datafication, dataism and dataveillance: Big Data between scientific paradigm and ideology. *Surveillance & Society, 12*(2), 197–208.

van Dijk, J. (2020). *The digital divide.* John Wiley & Sons.

Van Dijck, J., & Nieborg, D. (2009). Wikinomics and its discontents: a critical analysis of Web 2.0 business manifestos. *New media & society, 11*(5), 855–874.

van House, N. A. (2009). Collocated photo sharing, story-telling, and the performance of self. *International Journal of Human Computer Studies, 67*(12), 1073–1086.

Vannini, P., & Stewart, L. M. (2017). The GoPro gaze. *Cultural Geographies, 24*(1), 149–155.

Varnelis, K. (2012). *Networked publics.* MIT Press.

Vaterlaus, J. M., Barnett, K., Roche, C., & Young, J. A. (2016). "Snapchat is more personal": An exploratory study on Snapchat behaviors and young adult interpersonal relationships. *Computers in Human Behavior, 62*, 594–601.

Vivienne, S. (2017). 'I will not hate myself because you cannot accept me': Problematizing empowerment and gender-diverse selfies. *Popular Communication, 15*(2), 126–140.

Vlasceanu, M., & Amodio, D. M. (2022). Propagation of societal gender inequality by internet search algorithms. *Proceedings of the National Academy of Sciences, 119*(29), e2204529119.

Vogels, E. et al. (2020). (2020). *"53% of Americans Say the Internet Has Been Essential During the COVID-19 Outbreak"*. Pew Research Center. https://www.pewresearch.org/internet/2020/04/30/53-of-americans-say-the-internet-has-been-essential-during-the-covid-19-outbreak/

Vooris, R., Blaszka, M., & Purrington, S. (2019). Understanding the wearable fitness tracker revolution. *International Journal of the Sociology of Leisure, 2*(4), 421–437.

Wajcman, J. (2008). Life in the fast lane? Towards a sociology of technology and time. *The British Journal of Sociology, 59*(1), 59–77.

Wajcman, J. (2014). *Pressed for time*. University of Chicago Press.

Wajcman, J., Bittman, M., & Brown, J. E. (2008). Families without borders: Mobile phones, connectedness and work-home divisions. *Sociology, 42*(4), 635–652.

Walker Rettberg, J. (2014). *Seeing ourselves through technology: How we use selfies, blogs and wearable devices to see and shape ourselves*. Springer Nature.

Walther, J. B. (2002). Research ethics in Internet-enabled research: Human subjects issues and methodological myopia. *Ethics and Information Technology, 4*(3), 205–216.

Warfield, K., Cambre, C., & Abidin, C. (2016). Introduction to the Social Media+ Society special issue on selfies: Me-diated inter-faces. *Social Media+ Society, 2*(2), 2056305116641344.

Warren, S. D., & Brandeis, L. D. (1890). Right to privacy. *Harv. L. Rev., 4*, 193.

Watts, G. (2020). COVID-19 and the digital divide in the UK. *The Lancet Digital Health, 2*(8), e395–e396.

Weimann, G., & Masri, N. (2023). Research note: Spreading hate on TikTok. *Studies in conflict & terrorism, 46*(5), 752–765.

Wellman, B. (1979). The community question: The intimate networks of East Yorkers. *American Journal of Sociology, 84*(5), 1201–1231.

Wellman, B. (1997). Review: The road to utopia and dystopia on the information highway. *Contemporary Sociology, 26*(4), 445–449.

Wellman, B., Boase, J., & Chen, W. (2002). The networked nature of community: Online and offline. *IT & Society, 1*(1), 151–165.

Wellman, B., & Gulia, M. (1999). Net-surfers don't ride alone: Virtual communities as communities. In *Networks in the global village: Life in contemporary communities* (Issue 7, pp. 331–366).

West, E. (2019). Amazon: Surveillance as a service. *Surveillance and Society, 17*(1–2), 27–33.

Westcott, H., & Owen, S. (2013). Friendship and trust in the social surveillance network. *Surveillance & Society, 11*(3), 311–323.

White, A. E., Weinstein, E., & Selman, R. L. (2018). Adolescent friendship challenges in a digital context: Are new technologies game changers, amplifiers, or just a new medium?. *Convergence, 24*(3), 269–288.

Widn-Wulff, G., Ek, S., Ginman, M., Perttil, R., Sdergrd, P., & Ttterman, A. K. (2008). Information behaviour meets social capital: A conceptual model. *Journal of Information Science, 34*(3), 346–355.

Wiles, R., Crow, G., Heath, S., & Charles, V. (2008). The management of confidentiality and anonymity in social research. *International journal of social research methodology, 11*(5), 417–428.

Wiles, R., Crow, G., Heath, S., & Charles, V. (2008). The management of confidentiality and anonymity in social research. *International journal of social research methodology, 11*(5), 417–428.

Wilken, R., & Goggin, G. (2013). Mobile technology and place. In Wilken, R., & Goggin, G. (Eds.). (2013). *Mobile technology and place.* Routledge. *Mobile Technology and Place.* https://doi.org/10.4324/9780203127551

Wilken, R., & Humphreys, L. (2021). Placemaking through mobile social media platform Snapchat. *Convergence: The International Journal of Research into New Media Technologies, 27*(3), 579–593. https://doi.org/10.1177/1354856521989518

Williams, L. (2015). *6 ways social media ruining our friendships.* https://relevantmagazine.com/culture/6-ways-social-media-ruining-our-friendships/

Williams, L. (2016). Rinstagram or Finstagram? The curious duality of the modern Instagram user. *The Guardian.* https://www.theguardian.com/technology/2016/sep/26/rinstagram-finstagram-instagram-accounts

Williams, L. (2022). I Need a Distinction Between the Good in Me and the Not as Good in Me: Black Adolescent Girls' Binary Use of Instagram and Its Impact on Identity Expression. *Journal of African American Studies, 26*(1), pp.81–99.

Willis, J. E., Slade, S., & Prinsloo, P. (2016). Ethical oversight of student data in learning analytics: A typology derived from a cross-continental, cross-institutional perspective. *Educational Technology Research and Development, 64*(5), 881–901.

Willson, M. (2017). Algorithms (and the) everyday. *Information, Communication & Society, 20*(1), 137–150.

Wilson, J. (1980). Sociology of leisure. *Annual Review of Sociology, 6*(1), 21–40.

Windasari, N. A., & Lin, F. R. (2021). Why do people continue using fitness wearables? The effect of interactivity and gamification. *Sage Open, 11*(4), 21582440211056606.

Wittenborn, S. (2020). Digital place-making practices and daily struggles of Venezuelan (forced) migrants in Brazil. In K. Smets, M. Georgiou, & K. Leurs (Eds.), Alencar, A. (2020). Digital place-making practices and daily struggles of Venezuelan (forced) migrants in Brazil. *The SAGE handbook of migration and media,* 503–514.

Wong, M. (2020). Hidden youth? A new perspective on the sociality of young people 'withdrawn' in the bedroom in a digital age. *New Media & Society, 22*(7), 1227–1244.

Woodhouse, T. (2020, August). *Mobile devices are too expensive for billions of people—And it's keeping them offline—Alliance for Affordable Internet.* Https://A4ai.Org/News/Mobile-Devices-Are-Too-Expensive-for-Billions-of-People-and-Its-Keeping-Them-Offline/. https://a4ai.org/news/mobile-devices-are-too-expensive-for-billions-of-people-and-its-keeping-them-offline/

Woodward, K. (1997). Concepts of identity and difference. In *Identity and difference* (pp. 7–50).

Woodward, K. (2005). *Questioning identity: gender, class, nation.* Routledge.

Xiao, S., Metaxa, D., Park, J.S., Karahalios, K. and Salehi, N. (2020, April). Random, messy, funny, raw: Finstas as intimate reconfigurations of social media. In Proceedings of the 2020 CHI conference on human factors in computing systems (pp. 1–13).

Yarger, L., Payton, F. C., & Neupane, B. (2019). Algorithmic equity in the hiring of underrepresented IT job candidates. *Online Information Review, 44*(2), 383–395.

Yerkes, M. A., Roeters, A., & Baxter, J. (2020). Gender differences in the quality of leisure: A cross-national comparison. *Community, Work & Family, 23*(4), 367–384.

Young, A. L., & Quan-Haase, A. (2013). Privacy protection strategies on Facebook: The Internet privacy paradox revisited. *Information, Communication & Society, 16*(4), 479–500.

Young, M., & Willmott, P. (1957). *Family and kinship in East London.* Penguin.

Zheng, Y., & Walsham, G. (2021). Inequality of what? An intersectional approach to digital inequality under Covid-19. *Information and Organization, 31*(1), 100341.

Zijlstra, J., & Liempt, I. V. (2017). Smart(phone) travelling: Understanding the use and impact of mobile technology on irregular migration journeys. *International Journal of Migration and Border Studies, 3*(2–3), 174–191.

Zimmer, M. (2020). 'But the data is already public': On the ethics of research in Facebook. In *The Ethics of Information Technologies* (pp. 229–241). Routledge.

Zuboff, S. (2015). Big other: Surveillance capitalism and the prospects of an information civilization. *Journal of Information Technology, 30*(1), 75–89.

Zuboff, S. (2019). *The age of surveillance capitalism: The fight for a human future at the new frontier of power: Barack Obama's books of 2019.* Profile books.

Index